# SWEDISH:
# AN ESSENTIAL GRAMMAR

Titles of related interest published by Routledge:

Colloquial Swedish: The Complete Course for Beginners
Swedish Dictionary
Swedish: An Essential Grammar

Colloquial Danish: A Complete Language Course
Danish Dictionary
Danish: A Comprehensive Grammar

Colloquial Norwegian: A Complete Language Course
Norwegian Dictionary
Norwegian: An Essential Grammar

# SWEDISH: AN ESSENTIAL GRAMMAR

Philip Holmes and Ian Hinchliffe

Routledge
Taylor & Francis Group

LONDON AND NEW YORK

First published 1997
by Routledge
2 Park Square, Milton Park, Abingdon, Oxon, OX14 4RN

Simultaneously published in the USA and Canada
by Routledge
270 Madison Ave, New York, NY 10016

Reprinted 2000, 2001, 2003, 2005, 2006

*Routledge is an imprint of the Taylor & Francis Group, an informa business*

© 1997 Philip Holmes and Ian Hinchliffe

Typeset in Times by
Florence Production Ltd, Stoodleigh, Devon

Printed and bound in Great Britain by
TJ International Ltd, Padstow, Cornwall

*British Library Cataloguing in Publication Data*
A catalogue record for this book is available from the British Library

*Library of Congress Cataloguing in Publication Data*
A catalogue record for this book has been requested

Holmes, Philip
    Swedish : An Essential Grammar / Philip Holmes and Ian Hinchliffe.
       p. cm. – (Routledge Grammars)
    Includes bibliographical references and index.
    1. Swedish language–Grammar. I. Hinchliffe, Ian. II. Title. III. Series.
PD5112.H67 1996
439.782'421–dc20        96–41334

ISBN:10 0–415–16160–6 (hbk)
ISBN:10 0–415–16048–0 (pbk)

ISBN:13 978–0–415–16160–2 (hbk)
ISBN:13 978–0–415–16048–3 (pbk)

# CONTENTS

# PREFACE

In this book we hope to do two things: firstly, to provide learners of Swedish with a concise description of the structure of the language, as well as some account of spelling, punctuation, word formation and the differences between spoken and written Swedish; and secondly, to describe in greater detail those areas of Swedish that in our experience may pose a challenge for English-language learners.

The book is largely traditional in its approach and terminology. Most of the linguistic and grammatical terms used are explained in a separate glossary at the end of the book.

With its many tables and charts the book is intended to be easy to use; it will often be possible for the learner to predict patterns in many new words from just a few simple rules. The index contains paragraph references both to linguistic concepts and to some key Swedish and English words and their uses. In many cases the index should serve as a starting point for a search.

Translations of many of the examples are provided. These translations have been kept fairly literal in order to help the learner see contrasts and correlations between Swedish and English.

We would like to thank Olle Kjellin for his invaluable help in preparing the sections on pronunciation, stress and accent, and Claes Christian Elert for permission to use ideas and examples from his *Ljud och ord i svenskan 2*, Stockholm (1981). Many other students and colleagues, including Brita Green, Jyrki Pietarinen and Vera Croghan, have provided valuable suggestions.

Learners who have progressed to an intermediate level or simply want more thorough explanations of points of grammar and usage may wish to refer to our much more detailed *Swedish: A Comprehensive Grammar*, Routledge 1992, reprinted with changes in 1998.

Readers may wish to know that a set of 114 grammar exercises is available to accompany this book, either in book form (with a Key to answers), or on disk as computer-aided exercises for the PC. Both are available from Hull Swedish Press, Department of Scandinavian Studies, The University of Hull, Hull, HU16 5RX, UK or please e-mail: P.A.Holmes@scand.hull.ac.uk.

# SYMBOLS AND ABBREVIATIONS USED IN THE TEXT

| | |
|---|---|
| [iː] | phonetic script. The phonetic symbols used are those of the International Phonetic Alphabet |
| r**o**lig | long stressed vowel, long consonant |
| r**o**ll | short stressed vowel |
| köp**a** | unstressed vowel |
| 'kall**a**, stu'd**e**ra | stressed syllable |
| 2+ syllables | two or more syllables |
| lite/t/, /att/ | letter, syllable or word may be omitted |
| ring**er** | stem **ring** plus ending -**er** |
| förr/förut | alternatives |
| hann (<hinna) | **hann** derives from **hinna** |
| **x** > **y** | **x** becomes **y**, e.g. when an ending is added |
| ⊗ | 'plus zero', i.e. no ending is added, to distinguish a word or form from one to which an ending is added |
| * | irregular forms |
| C | consonant |
| CA | clausal adverbial |
| conj. | conjunction |
| cons. | consonant |
| FE | first element |
| FV | finite verb |
| IP | infinitive phrase |
| itr | intransitive |
| L | link |
| lit. | literally |
| MC | main clause |
| NFV | non-finite verb |
| NP | indefinite noun phrase |
| OA | other adverbial |
| Obj/comp, O/C | object/complement |
| Part | verb particle |
| S | subject |
| SC, subcl | subordinate clause |
| T | topic |
| tr | transitive |
| V | vowel |
| **V**-question | question introduced by an interrogative pronoun (**V**-word) |
| W | words brought forward, as being more important |
| $X^1$, $X^2$ | extra position |

# INTRODUCTION

## SOME ADVICE FOR THE BEGINNER

In our opinion the secret to learning good Swedish lies in three main areas: pronunciation, stress and word order.

Pronunciation is aided by the fact that Swedish is a phonetic language – that is to say, a particular group of letters nearly always corresponds to a particular sound (unlike English which is notorious in its lack of this correspondence, e.g. 'rough, through, bough, cough', etc.). It is possible to learn a few simple rules for Swedish pronunciation which are outlined at the beginning of this book, and which are accurate predictors in nearly all cases, the only exceptions being foreign loanwords.

Stress is important too, both as regards which words in the sentence have stress and where within a particular word the stress comes. This is explained in **16f**.

Swedish also has two word accents, which is why Swedes seem to 'sing' when they pronounce some words. The rules for the occurrence of these accents are detailed in **18ff**.

Word order and sentence structure are the basic building blocks of the language, a sure foundation that cannot be ignored if the learner wishes to speak and write understandable Swedish beyond a very basic level. Swedish main clause word order, for example, is much more flexible than English order, e.g. the sentence more often begins with a word (or words) other than the subject and sentence elements may appear in several different positions in main and subordinate clauses. A large section of this book is devoted to a systematic account of word order.

## SIMILARITIES BETWEEN SWEDISH AND ENGLISH

This is a comparative grammar, deliberately concentrating on the differences between Swedish and English, some of which we have just outlined, and thereby addressing specifically the needs of English-speaking learners. But it is also necessary to bear in mind just how *similar* these two languages are. A few of the major similarities which will help the learner acquire a knowledge of Swedish are outlined below.

*Vocabulary*

1 Both Swedish and English are Germanic languages and they possess a large core vocabulary of words that are identical or almost identical:

**arm, fot, finger, gräs, hus, knä, lamm, oss, skarp, son, två, tre, vi**
arm, foot, finger, grass, house, knee, lamb, us, sharp, son, two, three, we

2 Many English and American-English words have been borrowed into Swedish:

**baby, bestseller, check, cykel, deodorant, jeans, jobb, match, potatis, reporter, service**

*Grammar*

1 In both languages only nominative and genitive cases are found for nouns:

| | |
|---|---|
| **skepparen i båten** | the skipper in the boat |
| **skepparens katt** | the skipper's cat |

Both languages have subject and object forms of pronouns:

| | |
|---|---|
| **vi** | we |
| **oss** | us |

2 A similar distinction is found between adjectives and adverbs:

| | |
|---|---|
| **dyr** | dear |
| **dyrt** | dearly |

3 The languages have similar methods for comparing adjectives:

– with inflexional endings:

| | |
|---|---|
| **fet** | fat |
| **fetare** | fatter |
| **fetast** | fattest |

– without inflexional endings:

| | |
|---|---|
| **typisk** | typical |
| **mer typisk** | more typical |
| **mest typisk** | most typical |

4 Both languages have weak verbs with a dental ending (incorporating **-d/-t**) in the past tense:

| | |
|---|---|
| **Vi cyklade.** | We cycled. |
| **De kysste mig.** | They kissed me. |

5 Both languages have strong verbs with a vowel change in the past tense:

| | |
|---|---|
| **Vi sitter.** | We sit. |
| **Vi satt.** | We sat. |

6 The languages have similar modal auxiliary verbs:

| | |
|---|---|
| **kan, ska, måste** | can, shall, must |
| **De kan komma.** | They can come. |

7 The languages have a similar use of tenses:

| | |
|---|---|
| **Vi är här nu.** | We are here now. |
| **Han kom i april men han ska åka hem nästa vecka.** | He came in April but he will go home next week. |
| **Han har redan kommit.** | He has already arrived. |

8 The languages have a similar use of the formal subject (Sw. **det** = 'it/there'):

| | |
|---|---|
| **Det är kallt här.** | It is cold here. |
| **Det finns ett museum där.** | There is a museum there. |

9 Both languages have inverted (verb-subject) word order for questions:

| | |
|---|---|
| **Var är vi?** | Where are we? |
| **Är du sjuk?** | Are you sick? |

10 Both languages have only pre-positioned adjectives:

| | |
|---|---|
| **en varm sommar** | a warm summer |
| **den varma sommaren** | the warm summer |

# 1  PRONUNCIATION

## VOWELS

The contrast between stressed and unstressed vowels is important in Swedish:

Stressed vowels may be either long or short:

**m<u>a</u>t**  [mɑ:t]  **m<u>a</u>tt**  [mat]

Unstressed vowels are always short:

**ställ<u>e</u>**  [stelə]  **köp<u>e</u>r**  [çø:pər]

Short vowels are very short, shorter than in English. Long vowels are very long, longer than in English.

### 1  STRESSED VOWELS AND THEIR PRONUNCIATION

Nine different letters represent 21 different vowel sounds:

*Back vowels*

|  | A |  | Å |  |  | O |  |
|---|---|---|---|---|---|---|---|
| [ɑ:] | [a] | [o:] | [ɔ] | [ω:] | [ω] | [o:] | [ɔ] |
| glas | glass | hål | håll | rot | rott | ordna | kopp |
| dam | damm | gråt | grått | mor | moster | kol | boll |
| tak | tack | mås | måste | tro | trodde | son | folk |

*Front vowels*

|  | U |  | E |  |  |  | Ä |  |  |
|---|---|---|---|---|---|---|---|---|---|
| [ʉ:] | [u] | [e:] | [e] | [æ:] | [æ] | [ɛ:] | [e] | [æ:] | [æ] |
| brun | brunn | fet | fett | Per | herr | väg | vägg | bära | märka |
| bus | buss | vek | veck | erfaren | verk | räka | räcka | kära | kärra |
| ful | full | heta | hetta | Erling | Sverige | släpa | släppa | järn | värk |

| I | | Y | | Ö | | | |
|---|---|---|---|---|---|---|---|
| [i:] | [i] | [y:] | [y] | [ø:] | [ø] | [œ:] | [œ] |
| **fin** | **finns** | **byt** | **bytt** | **hög** | **högg** | **höra** | **förra** |
| **sil** | **sill** | **nys** | **nyss** | **mjöl** | **mjölk** | **gör** | **större** |
| **piga** | **pigga** | **flyta** | **flytta** | **blöta** | **blötta** | **för** | **först** |

*Notes:*

1 Pronunciation of letter O: When long the pronunciation [ɷ:] is more common than [o:], e.g. **stor** [stɷ:r] is more usual than **ordna** [o:dna]. When short the pronunciation [ɔ] is more common than [ɷ] e.g. **kosta** [kɔsta] is more usual than **ost** [ɷst].

2 In the pronunciation of some vowels, especially A, Å, O, U there is a marked difference in quality (position of tongue and lips) between long and short.

3 Pronunciation of E, Ä, Ö before R is more open than in other positions.

4 Some long vowels in Swedish are diphthongs ending in a fricative end-phase:

i   [iʲ]       y   [yʲ]       u   [ʉʷ]       o   [ɷʷ]

5 U is occasionally pronounced as V in the combination **eu** in loanwords:

**neuros** [nevro:s], **terapeut** [terapeft]

But notice also: **Europa** [erɷ:pa]

## *Approximate equivalent to pronunciation (Here 'English' = British English):*

Long **a**   [ɑ:]   'a' in English 'father, dark'
Short **a**   [a]   'a' in English 'hat, hand'
Long **å**   [o:]   'a' in English 'all', but with lip-rounding
Short **å**   [ɔ]   'o' in English 'hot'
Long **o**   [ɷʷ]   'oo' in English 'doom, moon', with extreme lip-rounding and w-like fricative end-phase
Short **o**   [ɷ]   'oo' in English 'book' with less extreme lip-rounding
Long **u**   [ʉʷ]   Long **u** has no equivalent but is similar to 'u' in English 'futile', 'putrid'. With extreme lip-rounding and w-like fricative end-phase
Short **u**   [u]   'u' in English 'full', lax lip-rounding
Long **e**   [e:]   No equivalent in English, cf. French 'été'
Short **e**   [e]   'e' in English 'pen', 'best'
Long **ä**   [ɛ:]   'ea' in English 'bear', but longer
Short **ä**   [e]   'e' in English 'pen', 'best'
Long **i**   [i:ʲ]   'ee' in English 'bee' but more closed and j-like fricative end-phase
Short **i**   [i]   'i' in English 'hit', 'miss'

| | | |
|---|---|---|
| Long **y** | [y:ʲ] | No equivalent in English, cf. German 'ü' in 'Tür'. Open lip-rounding with j-like fricative end-phase |
| Short **y** | [y] | No equivalent in English, cf. German 'ü' in 'dünn' |
| Long **ö** | [ø:] | No equivalent in English, cf. French 'eu' in 'peu' but much longer with lip-rounding |
| Short **ö** | [ø] | 'u' in English 'hurt', though much shorter |
| NB **i/y** | | The only difference is that **y** has lip-rounding |
| **y/u** | | The difference is the quality of the fricative end-phase |

## 2  PRONUNCIATION OF UNSTRESSED VOWELS

Unstressed vowels (marked ˳) occur in unstressed syllables before or after a stressed syllable:

**för'stå̠**          **po̠'tati̠s**          **'skri̠ve̠r**          **'pojke̠**

1 Unstressed **i** in suffixes **-ig, -lig, -isk, -ing, -is, -it**:

**sandi̠g, böjli̠g, typi̠sk, parkeri̠ng, godi̠s, sprungi̠t**

2 Unstressed **a** in many inflexional endings and suffixes:

| | |
|---|---|
| **bilar** (noun plural) | **bilarna** (noun plural definite) |
| **dåliga** (adjective plural) | **roligast** (adjective superlative) |
| **tala** (verb infinitive) | **talar** (verb present) |
| **talade** (verb past) | **talat** (verb supine) |
| **arbetare** (noun denoting person, occupation) | |
| **hemma, borta** (adverbs of location) | |

3 Unstressed **o**

**flickor** (noun plural) Sometimes pronounced [flikɷr], [flikɛr] or [flikər]

**nio, tio** (numerals) Often pronounced [ni:ə], [ti:ə]

**tjugo** (numeral) Pronounced [çʉ:gu] or [çʉ:gə]

Before **r** [ɷ] alternates with [ɔ]: **motor** [mɷ:tɷr] or [mɷ:tɔr]

4 Unstressed **e**

Usually [ə]: **gubbe, pojke, cykel, vacker, damer, köper, skriven**

Notice that **e** is never silent:

| | |
|---|---|
| cf. English 'spade' [speid] | Swedish **spade** [spɑ:də] |
| English 'rune' [ru:n] | Swedish **Rune** [rʉ:nə] |

## 3   VOWEL LENGTH

1 Rules for predicting vowel length from written form: (V = Vowel, C = Consonant)

| | | |
|---|---|---|
| Rule 1 Stressed vowels in open syllables are long: | **få** | V |
| Rule 2 Stressed vowels followed by one consonant are long | **får** | VC |
| Rule 3 Stressed vowels followed by two or more consonants are short: | **fått** | VCC |
| (long consonant or consonant group) | **fångna** | VCC |
| | **fångst** | VCCCC |
| Rule 4 Unstressed vowels are always short: | **tala, köper** | |

In accordance with Rule 1:
Stressed vowels before other vowels are long:   **trio, Dorotea**

In accordance with Rule 3:
Stressed vowels before **-sj**, **-ng** (and equivalents) are short:   **usch, lång, restaurang**
Stressed vowels before **-rm**, **-rb** are short (cf. English):   **arm, charm, arbete**

An exception to Rule 2:
Stressed vowels before **-x** [ks] are short:   **sax, flaxa, maximum**

An exception to Rule 3:
Stressed vowels before **-rn**, **-ln**, **-rl**, **-rd** are long:   **barn, aln, härlig, gård**

2 Vowel length and inflexional endings

Despite Rule 3 above, vowel length is not normally affected by the addition of inflexional endings or word formation suffixes:

| | |
|---|---|
| **fin** | **fint** (neuter ending on adjective) |
| **söka** | **sökte** (past tense ending on verb) |
| **sjuk** | **sjuklig** (adjectival suffix) |

However, if the stem ends in, or the inflexional ending begins in, a **d/t**, then the vowel is shortened according to Rule 3:

| | |
|---|---|
| **betyda** | **betydde** (past tense ending on verb) |
| **möta** | **mötte** (past tense ending on verb) |
| **vit** | **vitt** (neuter ending on adjective) |

Similarly, if the stem ends in a long stressed vowel and the inflexional ending begins in a **d/t**, then the vowel is shortened according to Rule 3:

| | |
|---|---|
| **blå** | **blått** (neuter ending on adjective) |
| **klä** | **klädd** (past participle ending on verb) |
| **tre** | **trettio** ('-ty' ending on numeral) |
| **sju** | **sjutton** ('-teen' ending on numeral) |

## 4  SYLLABLE LENGTH

1 A syllable consists of a vowel on its own or accompanied by one or more consonants before or after the vowel. There are the same number of syllables in a word as there are vowels. The following are all syllables:

| **ö** | **på** | **två** | **att** | **alm** | **halm** | **hos** | **hemskt** |
|---|---|---|---|---|---|---|---|
| V | CV | CCV | VCC | VCC | CVCC | CVC | CVCCCC |

Many words have two syllables:

| **poj-ke** | **å-ker** | **kal-la** |
|---|---|---|
| CVC-CV | V-CVC | CVC-CV |

Some words have many syllables:

| **parkera:** | | | **industriarbetare:** | | | | | | |
|---|---|---|---|---|---|---|---|---|---|
| **par** | **-ke** | **-ra** | **in** | **-du** | **-stri** | **-ar** | **-be** | **-ta** | **-re** |
| CVC | -CV | -CV | VC | -CV | -CCCV | -VC | -CV | -CV | -CV |

2 All stressed syllables in Swedish are long, and contain:

a long vowel:                               **al**     **is**

OR

a short vowel + a long consonant:    **all**   **alm**   **arm**   **arg**
(double consonant or consonant group)   **all-tid**  **al-mar**  **ar-mar**  **ar-ga**
                                        **hiss**  **lis-ta**

See also **1f** above.

# CONSONANTS AND CONSONANT GROUPS

There are 20 different letters representing 23 different sounds.

Consonants **b, d, f, g, l, m, n, p, r, s, t, z** may be doubled:

**mamma, falla, hatt, jazz**

When they either precede or follow a vowel the letters **b**, **d**, **f**, **h**, **m**, **n**, **v** are usually pronounced as in English. But notice also the pronunciation of **d** in the group **rd** in **10**.

Consonants **p**, **t** and **k** are usually pronounced [p], [t], [k] (but see also **8** below), though they may also be strongly aspirated: **pappa** [pʰapa], **ta** [tʰa:], **kasta** [kʰasta].

Remember: Vowels are short before a long consonant (double consonant or consonant group):

**hal** – **hall**

## 5  s, z, c, sc

s  [s]  is always voiceless in Swedish like 's' in English 'sit', *not* as in English 'please':

**Lisa, läsa, stycke, ros, musik, stum**

z  [s]  is pronounced exactly as Swedish **s**:

**zon, zoologi**

[ts]  in some German names:

**Schweiz**

c  [s]  as in English 'centre' before **e**, **i**, **y**:

**centrum, cirka, cykel**

[k]  as in English 'cotton' before **a**, **o**, **u**:

**camping, cocktail, curry**

sc  [s]  as in English 'scene'

**scen, fosforescent**

[ʃ]  as in English 'fascist'

**fascist, crescendo, fascinerande**

## 6  j, gj, dj, hj, lj

j  [j]  is pronounced as consonant 'y' in English 'young' before all vowels and at the end of a word:

**ja, jul, jobb, jeans, Jimmy, Jenny, järn**

**haj, hej, detalj, familj, kampanj**

[ʃ]  in a few loanwords:

**à jour, journal, journalist, jalusi, just, projekt**

**gj-, dj-, hj-, lj-** the first letter is silent and these groups are pronounced as Swedish **j**:

> **gjorde, djup, hjälp, ljus**

## 7　r, t, l, x, w

r　[r]　in Central and Northern Sweden is a tongue-tip trilled 'r' as in Scottish. This sound is found at the beginning and end of syllables:

> **rum, dörr, norr**

　[ɹ]　in Southern Sweden there is a tongue root 'r', not unlike German and French 'r'.

t　[t]　is pronounced with the tip of the tongue on the back of the upper teeth and is thus slightly 'sharper' than in English:

> **titta, tratt**

*Note:* In loanwords **t** may be pronounced variously:

1 As [ʃ] in some words in **-tion**　　　**station**

2 As [tʃ] in some words in **-tion**　　　**motion**

3 As [ts] in words in **-ti**　　　**initiativ, aktie**

l　[l]　is pronounced as 'l' in English 'like', *not* as in 'elk':

> **lilla, till, Ulla**

x　[ks]　is voiceless and pronounced as 'x' in English 'excited' *not* as in 'exist':

> **växa, exempel, strax**

*Note:* In loanwords **x** in an initial position is pronounced as **s: xenofobi**

w　[v]　is pronounced as 'v' and is nowadays found only in names and loanwords:

> **Wasa, Wahlström och Widstrand, whisky, wellpapp, WC** [ve:se:]

## 8　g, k, sk

The pronunciation of initial **g-, k-, sk-** varies according to the vowel following:

1 'Soft' *g-*, *k-*, *sk-*

Before the vowels **e**, **i**, **y**, **ä**, **ö** these consonants are palatalized:

**g-**  [j]      is pronounced as Swedish **j** or English consonant 'y' in 'young':

**Gösta, gymnasium, gärna**

**k-**  [ç]      is pronounced something like German 'ch' in 'ich':

**köpa, källare, kyrka**

**sk-**  [ʃ]      is pronounced something like 'sh' in English 'shirt', but further
         back and always with lip-rounding:

**skinka, skön, skära**

Like soft **g** [j] go syllables ending in **-lg** [lj], **-rg** [rj]:

**helg, älg, Borg, Berg**

Note also: **galge, Norge, Sverige** [sverja], **orgel**

Like soft **k** [ç] go words beginning with the letters **kj-**, **tj-**, **ch-**:

**kjol, kjortel, tjugo, check**

(This occurs before all vowels, cf. **k-**)

2 **'Sje-ljud'** (soft *sk* sound or *sj* sound)

There are two variants of the Swedish sound:

[ɧ] 'Back **sj**-sound', formed by raising the back of the tongue:

**skina, skytte**

[ʂ] 'Front **sj**-sound', formed by raising the middle or front of the tongue:

**sköterska, Askim**. (Pronunciation varies in dialect and idiolect.)

Like back **sj** go words beginning with the letters **sj-**, **skj-**, **stj-**, some loans
with **ch-**, **sch-**:

**sju, skjorta, stjärna, choklad, schack**

Like front **sj** go most words ending in **-sion**, **-tion**, **-rs**, **-sch** and their derivatives:

**vision, station, kors, Anders, dusch, missionera**

*Note:* Some loanwords in **-tion** are pronounced with [tʃ]:

**nation, portion, motion**

Like either front or back **sj** go some loanwords in **g**, **j**:

**generell, religiös, energi, journalist**

3 'Hard' **g-**, **k-**, **sk-**

Before the vowels **o**, **u**, **a**, **å** these are pronounced as in English:

**g-** [g]     is pronounced as 'g' in English 'gate':

>   **gata, gå, god**

**k-** [k]     is pronounced as 'k' in English 'keep':

>   **kaka, kål, kul**

**sk-** [sk]   is pronounced as 'sk' in English 'skill':

>   **ska, skor, skugga**

They are also usually 'hard' after all vowels:

>   **Stig, lägga, Sveg      Erik, doktor, lök      ask, besk, diska**

*Note:* Exceptions to the rules found for pronunciation given in (1) – (3) above are found in the following loan or foreign words:

| k | [k] | before a soft vowel | **arkiv, kille, fakir, monarki, Kiruna, bukett, keps, kö, prekär** |
|---|-----|---------------------|---|
| sk | [sk] | before a soft vowel | **skippa, skiss, skepsis, sketch, skelett** |
| sk | [ʃ] | before a hard vowel | **människa, marskalk** |

## 9   ng, gn, kn, mn

**-ng** [ŋ]    is pronounced as one sound, as in southern English 'singer':

>   **Inga, pengar, gånger**

**-gn** [ŋn]   is pronounced as Swedish **ng** + **n** (as in English 'ring-necked'):

>   **vagn, Ragnar, regn**

**gn-** [gn]   unlike English 'gnaw' the **g** is pronounced (as in English 'pregnant'):

>   **gnaga, Gnosjö**

**kn-** [kn]   unlike English 'knife' the **k** is pronounced (as in 'locknut'):

>   **kniv, knä, Knut**

**-mn**[u] [mn]   unlike English 'autumn' the **n** is pronounced (as in 'remnant'):

>   **hamn, namn**

## 10   rs, rd, rt, rn, rl

In Central and Northern Swedish these groups produce 'alveolar retroflex' sounds:

**rs**  [ş]  **rd**  [ɖ]  **rt**  [ţ]  **rn**  [ɳ]  **rl**  [ļ]

These are so called because the tongue tip is bent backwards against the alveolar ridge behind the upper teeth rather than (in the case of **d**, **t**, **n**, **l** alone) behind the teeth themselves. In the case of **rd**, **rt**, **rn**, **rl** these sounds may be difficult for the non-Swede to distinguish from normal **d**, **t**, **n**, **l**:

|      | **bord** | **bort** | **barn** | **Karl** |
|------|----------|----------|----------|----------|
| cf.  | **bod**  | **bot**  | **ban**  | **kal**  |

But **rs** [ş] is much easier to hear. It is the 'front **sj**-sound', pronounced as 'sh' in English 'sheep':

**fors, Lars, varsågod, störst, mars, person**

See also **15**.

## 11 OMITTING -d, -g, -t, -k, -l

1 The final **-g** of adjectives ending in **-ig** or **-lig** is nearly always omitted in the spoken language:

| | |
|---|---|
| **färdig, rolig** | [fɛːɖi], [rɷːli] |
| **färdigt, roligt** | [fɛːɖit], [rɷːlit] |
| **färdiga, roliga** | [fɛːɖia], [rɷːlia] |

2 In many commonly used words a final **-d**, **-g** or **-t** is often dropped in pronunciation. The final **-d**, **-g** or **-t** of many common monosyllabic nouns is unpronounced even in the plural and definite forms of the noun.

| | |
|---|---|
| **god, goda** | [gɷː], [gɷːa] |
| **röd, röda** | [røː], [røːa] |
| **med** | [meː] |
| **ved** | [ve] |
| **vid** | [vi] |
| **vad** | [va] |
| **det** | [deː] |
| **mycket, litet** | [mykə], [liːtə] |
| **alltid, aldrig** | [alti], [aldri] |
| **något, inget** | [noːgə], [nɔt], [iŋə] |
| **måndag, tisdag ...** | [mɔnda], [tista] (NB short unstressed a) |
| **bröd, brödet, bröden** | [brøː], [brøːt], [brøːn] |
| **träd, trädet, träden** | [trɛː], [trɛːt], [trɛːn] |
| **jag** | [jɑː] |
| **dag, dagen, dagar** | [dɑː], [dɑːn], [dɑːr] (NB long a) |

*Notes:*

1 The **-t** ending of some first conjugation verbs in their supine forms is frequently omitted in spoken Swedish.

2 For the pronunciation of pronominal forms **mig, dig, sig, det, de, dem** see **14**.

3 The spoken forms of **huvud**, 'head', an irregular 4th declension noun, are:

    sg. [huve] **huvud** pl. [huven] **huvuden**
    def.sg. [huvet] **huvudet** def.pl. [huvena] **huvudena**

4 The omission of a final **-t** in some French loanwords in spoken Swedish is a matter of personal preference:

    **konsert**, 'concert' is pronounced [kɔnsert] or [kɔnser]; **kuvert**, 'envelope' is pronounced [kuvert] or [kuver]

3 In some instances the **-d, -g** omitted is not at the end of the word. Some omissions are so common that the spoken form has become frequent even in the written language (see (2) below).

(a) omitted in pronunciation but not in spelling:

| | |
|---|---|
| **bredvid** | [breviːd] or [brevi] or [breːve] |
| **morgon** | [mɔrɔn] |
| **midsommar** | [misɔmar] |
| **förkläde, förklädet** | [førklɛː], [førklɛːt] |
| **trädgård, trädgården** | [trɛːgoːd], [trɛːgoːɳ] |

*Notes:*

1 Sometimes a truncated form of a noun ending in **-ad, -ag** may be used, but only in the definite singular form:

| | |
|---|---|
| **stad, staden** | [stɑːd], [stɑːn] |
| **månad, månaden** | [moːnad], [moːnan] |
| **skillnad, skillnaden** | [ʃilnad], [ʃilnan] |
| **da(g), dagen** | [dɑː], [dɑːn] NB. Indefinite singular form |

2 Note the change of vowel length in expressions ending in **-s** such as:

| | |
|---|---|
| **i måndags** | [i mɔndas] (short final vowel) |
| **i tisdags** | [i tiːstas] (short final vowel) |

3 **-d-** between **r** and **s** is often not pronounced in spoken Swedish:

| | |
|---|---|
| **vårdslös** | [voːʃløːs] |

(b) omitted in pronunciation and sometimes in spelling:

In many instances where **-d** + vowel or **-g** + vowel is omitted in spoken Swedish such omissions have become frequent in casual written Swedish.

Eight common examples of this phenomenon follow. Note how the preceding vowel is shortened!

|  | någon, något, (nån, nåt) | [nɔn], [nɔt] (short vowel) |
| (BUT: | några) | [noːra] (long vowel!) |
|  | sådan sådant sådana | [sɔn], [sɔnt], [sɔna] (short vowel) |
|  | (sån, sånt, såna) | |
|  | sedan (sen) | [sen] |
|  | någonsin, någonstans | [nɔnsin], [nɔnstans] (short vowel) |
|  | (nånsin, nånstans) | |

The omission of **-d** + vowel has been accepted in the singular indefinite form of three very common nouns and a number of less common ones:

**fader** pronounced and often written **far**
(BUT: definite form **fadern** in written and spoken Swedish!)
**moder** pronounced and often written **mor**
(BUT: definite form **modern** in written and spoken Swedish!)

**broder** pronounced and often written **bror**
(BUT: definite form **brodern** in written and spoken Swedish!)
*Note:* **farbrorn**, **farmorn** are sometimes encountered in written Swedish.

Cf. also **ladugård**        pronounced [lɑːgoːɖ].

Second conjugation verbs with stems in long **e** or long **ä** sounds followed by **-d** frequently omit the **-d** in the present tense:

| (**kläda**) – **kläder** | pronounced and written **klär** |
| (**breda**) – **breder** | pronounced and written **brer** |

(c) omitted in pronunciation and usually omitted in spelling:

Several words with original forms containing **-d**, **-g** have now dropped these unpronounced letters even in written Swedish:

| **aderton** | is now pronounced and spelt **arton** |
| **badstuga** | is now pronounced and spelt **bastu** |
| **förstuga** | is now pronounced and spelt **farstu** |
| **Södermanland** | is now pronounced and spelt **Sörmland** |

The longer forms of these words are seen only rarely or in formal written Swedish.

4 The final syllable **-de** in the past (preterite) tense of first conjugation verbs is usually dropped in spoken Swedish, such verbs thus ending in a short **-a** vowel sound.

| **han kallade** | is pronounced [han kala] |
| **vi ropade** | is pronounced [viː rɷːpa] |

*Note:* The final **-de** ending in the preterite tense of the verbs **lägga** and **säga** is usually omitted in spoken Swedish. The shorter forms thus created are **la** and **sa** (both with long vowel sounds). **Sa** is now the normal written form.

5 The final **-t** is often omitted in the spoken form of the first conjugation supine:

**Vi har jobbat.**                             is pronounced [vi: ha: jɔba]

6 The **-k** of adjectives whose basic form ends in **-k** is not usually pronounced when followed by **-t**:

**hemskt, kritiskt**                           [hemst], [kri:tist]

7 In a few well-defined words **-l** or **-ll** in spoken Swedish is generally omitted:

**värld** (and compounds)              [vɛ:ɖ]
**karl, karln, karlar**, chap          [kɑ:r], [kɑ:ɳ], [kɑ:rar]
(But: **Karl** as a boy's name         [kɑ:rl])
**till**                               [ti]
**skall** in older written Swedish     [ska] now usually written **ska**

## 12   OMITTING -e

The **-e** of the non-neuter definite (end) article **-en** is often omitted in spoken Swedish after **-r** or **-l**:

**konduktören**                        [kɔnduktø:ɳ]
**salen**                              [sɑ:ln]
**dörren**                             [dørɳ]
**kvällen**                            [kveln]

The final unstressed **-e** of many non-neuter nouns ending in **-are** which signify a trade or profession is dropped in spoken Swedish before the definite singular (end) article **-n**:

**bagaren, läraren, verkmästaren**, become: **bagarn, lärarn, verkmästarn** etc.

*Note:* The final **-e** in such words is usually dropped in both written and spoken Swedish when the words are used as a title before a name: **bagar Olsson, verkmästar Törnquist** etc.

## 13   VOICED CONSONANTS PRONOUNCED UNVOICED BEFORE -s, -t

The final voiced consonants **-d, -g, -v** of some common monosyllabic words are retained in written Swedish but become unvoiced **-t, -k, -f** in spoken Swedish when suffixed with **-s**. Note also that the preceding vowel is shortened before the suffixed **-s**.

**hur dags**, what time?               [hʉdaks]
**i Guds namn**, in Heaven's name      [i Guts namn]

**till havs**, at sea                    [ti hafs]

**högst**, at most                       [høkst]

*Note:* For **i måndas, i tisdags** etc, see **11** 3(a) Note 2.

A voiced **-g** (or **-gg**) is pronounced unvoiced as **-k** before a suffixed **-t**:

**styggt**, wicked                       [stykt]

**sagt**, said                           [sakt]

**lagt**, laid                           [lakt]

**högt**, high                           [høkt] NB short vowel

A voiced **-b** (or **-bb**) is pronounced unvoiced as **-p** before a suffixed **-s** or **-t**:

**Obs!**, Note                           [ɔps]

**snabbt**, quickly                      [snapt]

A similar phenomenon occurs in compound words when an element of the compound ending in **-d**, **-g**, **-v** is followed by **-s**. The voiced consonant becomes unvoiced, the preceding vowel is frequently shortened:

**dödstrött**, dog tired                 [døtstrøt]

**stadsbo**, town-dweller                [statsbɷ]

**dagstidning**, daily newspaper         [daksti:dniŋ]

**skogsbryn**, edge of the forest        [skɷksbry:n]

**havsbad**, beach                       [hafsbɑ:d]

*Notes:*

1 The addition˙of a genitive **-s** does not normally affect vowel length.

Compare: **en dags vandring** [dɑ:gs] and **en dagstur** [dakstʉ:r]

2 In the following cases complete assimilation has taken place of **t** to **s**:

**matsäck**                              [masek]

**statsråd**                             [stasro:d]

**skjuts**                               [ʃus]


## 14   WRITTEN AND SPOKEN FORMS OF SOME COMMON WORDS

1 Many of the Swedish personal pronouns are pronounced in a way that is not in accord with the standard written form.

| | | | |
|---|---|---|---|
| **jag** | pronounced [jɑ] | **mig** | pronounced [mɛj] |
| **du** | (cf. note 1) | **dig** | pronounced [dɛj] |
| | | **honom** | (cf. note 2) |
| | | **henne** | (cf. note 2) |
| | | **sig** | pronounced [sɛj] |

2 **Mej**, **dej**, **sej** are now accepted in most informal writing as alternatives to **mig**, **dig**, **sig** (see **68**).

*Notes:*

1 In very colloquial Swedish the **d-** of **du**, **dig** is frequently omitted following a verbal **-r** ending:

> **Ser 'u nåt? (Ser du något?)**      Can you see anything?

2 In the past **honom** and **henne** had spoken forms but except in certain dialects, these are no longer common:

> **honom** was pronounced **'en** or **'n** after a vowel    **Jag har aldrig sett 'n.**
> **henne** was pronounced **'na**                         **Jag gav 'na pengarna.**

3 **Dom** for both subject (**de**) and object (**dem**) form is accepted in most informal writing. **Dom** is also used in expressions like **dom här** and as the front article in, for example **dom nya bilarna**, in written Swedish, though this is regarded as slovenly.

4 **Det** is pronounced [de] (short vowel) when used as a pronoun and in expressions such as [de hɛ: hʉ:sət] (written **det här huset**) and [de ny:a hu:sət] (written **det nya huset**). In the past **den**, **det** used as object had the spoken forms **'en** (**'n** after a vowel) and **'et** (**'t** after vowel) but, except in certain dialects, these are no longer common.

> **Här har du geväret. Ta 't.**      Here's your rifle. Take it!

5 In spoken Swedish the possessive pronouns for 1st and 2nd persons plural **vår**, **er** etc. have colloquial forms which exist alongside the standard written forms:

> **Det är våran skola.**      It's our school.
> **Är det eran skola?**      Is it your school?
> **Det är vårat hus.**      It's our house.
> **Är det erat hus?**      Is it your house?

6 In addition to the examples in **11ff** there are other cases in which common written Swedish words are pronounced in a way that might not be expected:

| *Written Swedish* | *Spoken Swedish* |
| --- | --- |
| **förstås** | [føʃtɔs] |
| **och** (unstressed position) | [ɔ] |
| **och** (stressed position) | [ɔk] |
| **att**, to (before infinitive) | [ɔ] |
| **säga, säger, sa(de), sagt** | [sɛ:ja] [sɛ:jer] [sɑ:] [sakt] |
| **lade, lagt** | [lɑ:] [lakt] |
| **stod** | [stʊ:g] |
| **förstod** | [føʃtʊ:g] |

**vara, är, var, varit**          [vɑ:] (long vowel) [ɛ:] [vɑ:] [vat]
**ett ögonblick**                 [et ø:gɔmlik]

Some common Fourth and Fifth Declension nouns have colloquial forms existing alongside standard written and spoken forms. Many common verbs have colloquial forms existing alongside standard written and spoken forms.

## 15   ASSIMILATION

Where the final sound of one word and the initial sound of the next are difficult to pronounce together, some form of assimilation usually takes place in Swedish.

In fluent spoken Swedish **-r** as the last sound in a word before a word beginning with **s-** is assimilated with the **s-** to an 'sh-' sound (see **10**):

**Hur sa?**                        is pronounced [huʃa]
**Tack för senast**               is pronounced [takføʃe:nast]
**för stor**                      is pronounced [føʃtɷ:r]

*Note:* This kind of assimilation is less common in southern Sweden than in the rest of the country.

In fluent spoken Swedish, assimilation of **r** occurs with **d, t, n, l**:

**Kommer du?**                    is pronounced [kɔmədu]

In fluent spoken Swedish, a final **-n** after a short vowel in a word which is not heavily stressed is pronounced **-m** before a following **b-**:

**min bror, en boll**    become     [mimbrɷ:r], [embɔll]

# 2 STRESS AND ACCENT

The music of Swedish (prosody) is produced by three features:

| | |
|---|---|
| Sentence stress | Which words in the sentence receive stress? |
| Word stress | Which parts of the word are stressed? |
| Accent | Which tone, single peak (Accent 1) or double peak (Accent 2), does the word possess? |

## 16 SENTENCE STRESS

In principle all the semantically significant words in the sentence are stressed. In practice this may vary somewhat. In this paragraph different sentence elements (see **146**ff) are listed and the stress shown for different circumstances.

*KEY:*    e̱ = long stressed vowel, ẹ = short stressed vowel
e̥ = unstressed vowel

*Rules:*    *Examples:*

SUBJECT
Nouns are stressed

A̱nna har köpt ett hu̱s.
Hu̱set ligger va̱ckert.

Pronouns are unstressed

De̥t kostade mycket pe̱ngar.
Ho̥n hade inte rå̱d.

OBJECT
Nouns are stressed.

Hon äter mi̱ddag. Ka̱lle möter A̱nna.

Pronouns are unstressed
Object pronouns beginning the sentence are stressed

Han mö̱ter he̥nne. Han gör de̥t.
Ho̱nom har jag inte sett på lä̱nge.

For contrast objects are stressed.

Jag tycker inte o̱m ho̱nom, men jag gillar he̱nne.

VERB
No object, then verb stressed
Object, then verb unstressed

E̱va ä̱ter och dri̱cker.
E̱va dri̥cker ka̱ffe. Hon dri̥cker inte te̱.

Complement, then verb unstressed
Formal subject, then verb unstressed
Auxiliary verbs are unstressed

Hon ble̥v poli̱s. Han är sju̱k.
Det li̥gger en bo̱k på bo̱rdet.
Hon skḁ dri̥cka. Jag må̱ste gå nu.

NB also:

| | |
|---|---|
| For contrast verbs are stressed | **Han målar inte väggarna utan tapetserar dem.** |
| Particle verbs: the particles are stressed, the verbs unstressed | **Han satte på sig hatten. Föraren körde ombilen.** |

ADVERBIAL

| | |
|---|---|
| **Inte** is unstressed | **Hon vill inte. De är inte hemma.** |
| Other adverbials are usually stressed whether first or last in the sentence | **Här är han nu. Därför vill vi inte vänta längre. Stänger den inte tidigt idag?** |

## 17   WORD STRESS

Word stress is found only in words that have sentence stress.

1 Non-compounds:
Of these words, some 35% are monosyllables, 40% have stress on the first syllable (initial stress) and 25% stress on a different syllable (non-initial stress):

| | | | |
|---|---|---|---|
| Words with initial stress: | **'nyckel** | **'vinter** | **'koper** |
| | **'hallon** | **'gata** | |

Words with non-initial stress:

| | | | |
|---|---|---|---|
| words with the prefixes **be-, för-**: | **be'strida** | **be'tala** | **för'sök** |
| words with the suffix **-era**: | **par'kera** | **ser'vera** | |
| many foreign loans: | **restau'rang** | **re'vy** | **inka'pabel** |
| | **etymo'log** | **re'gister** | |
| words with foreign suffixes: | **regi'ssör** | **gym'nast** | **musi'kant** |

2 Compounds:
Compound words have a stress on each of the parts of the compound, but the melody of each part is different. This also varies from region to region.

| | |
|---|---|
| In central Swedish: | the first stress has a falling pitch ↘ the last stress has a rising pitch ↗ |

**husnyckel**

**järnvägsräls**

**SJ (Statens järnvägar)**

**centrallasarett**

**lastbilsförare**

**SKF (Svenska kullagerfabriken)**

## 18   ACCENT

There are two distinct accents (tones) for Swedish words of two or more syllables with sentence stress (and therefore also word stress). Compare the words **skriver** and **gammal**:

| | | |
|---|---|---|
| **skri̱-ver** | **gam̱-mal** | Both have stress on the first syllable, but the balance differs. |
| **s k r i v e r** | **g a m m a l** | They also have different tone patterns or melodies. |

**Gammal** has accent 2 (tonal accent) with two tone peaks, falling-rising in central Swedish.

**Skriver** has accent 1 with one tone peak (rising), the same as in stressed monosyllabic words:

    **en bil**            **en buss**            **en man**

(Notice that the second peak in accent 2 is identical with accent 1.)

## 19   FUNCTIONS OF ACCENT 1/ACCENT 2

Accent 2 is only found in polysyllabic words. The main function of accent 2 is to show that two syllables belong together – it is a 'connective function':

| Accent 1 | Accent 2 |
|---|---|
| **fem ton**<br>= five tons | **femton**<br>= fifteen |
| **Vi äter inte rått kött.**<br>= We don't eat raw meat. | **Vi äter inte råttkött.**<br>= We don't eat rat meat. |
| **Det var en vits i predikan.**<br>= There was a joke in the sermon. | **Det var en vitsig predikan.**<br>= It was a witty sermon. |
| **en stor mans dräkt**<br>= a great man's suit | **en stormansdräkt**<br>= a 'chieftain-costume' |

Accent 2 can also have a 'distinctive function': there are about 350 homophones which are distinguished only by their accents. Many of these minimal pairs are inflected forms of originally monosyllabic (accent 1) and originally bisyllabic (accent 2) words:

| Accent 1 | Accent 2 |
|---|---|
| **and-en**<br>(< **and** 1 syllable)<br>= the duck | **ande-n**<br>(< **ande** 2 syllables)<br>= the spirit |
| **brunn-en**<br>(< **brunn** 1 syllable)<br>= the well | **brunnen**<br>(< **brinna** 2 syllables)<br>= burned |
| **Polen**<br>= Poland | **pålen (< påle)**<br>= the pole |
| **komma**<br>= comma | **komma**<br>= come |

## 20   RULES FOR ACCENT 2

| Accent 1 is found: | Accent 2 is found: |
|---|---|
| 1 In all *monosyllabic* words:<br><br>**bok   bil   kallt   först** | 1 In most *compounds*:<br><br>**järnväg   lastbil   bokhylla**<br><br>**sjukhus** |
| 2 In some *bisyllabic words* detailed below. | 2 In most other *polysyllabic words with stress on the first syllable*:<br><br>**flicka   pojke   sexton   börjar**<br><br>**bilar   katterna   pratat   skrivet**<br><br>**lättast** |

| A *The following features 'block' accent 2* | *Exceptions to this blocking: (i.e. with accent 2)* |
|---|---|
| (i) Endings in a *vowel* + **l**:<br><br>*Nouns:*<br><br>**cykel   segel   fågel   medel** | <br><br><br><br>**nyckel** |
| *Adjectives*:<br><br>**enkel   simpel** | <br><br>– |

| A *The following features 'block' accent 2* | *Exceptions to this blocking: (i.e. with accent 2)* |
|---|---|

(ii) Endings in a *vowel* + **n**:

*Nouns:* cf.

öken   socken   tecken   vatten

fruktan   tävlan

*Adjectives:*

–

egen   ledsen   öppen   skriven
(and other Conjugation 4 participles)

(iii) Endings in a *vowel* + **r**:

*Nouns:*

vinter   teater   nummer   fönster

moder   syster   sommar

Plurals with *mutation* + **er**:

böcker   fötter   händer

nätter   städer

Plurals *without mutation*:

(cf. flickor   stolar   katter)

*Adjectives*:

vacker   mager   läcker

–

*Verbs in* -**er** (present tense):

ringer   läser   skriver   äter

*Verbs in* -**ar** (present tense)

tittar   målar   badar   lagar

(iv) Adjective comparative endings in
  -**re**, superlative endings in -**erst**:

längre   yngre   lägre   större

överst   ytterst

(cf. lättare   lättast)

(v) Adjective endings in -**isk**, -**sk**:

typisk   komisk   engelsk

(vi) Noun endings in -**is**, -**iker**:

dagis   kompis   godis   gratis

musiker   tekniker

(vii) Verbs with unstressed initial syllables:

betalar   förstår

(vii) Verbs ending in -**era**:

fotograferar   studerar   socialiserar

**B** All nouns with end articles have the same accent as in the form without end article:

en bil  bilen                          en klocka  klockan

en polis  polisen                      en invandrare  invandraren

**C** Notice however that the verb accents often change through the paradigm:

läsa  läs!  läser  läste  läst

dricka  drick!  dricker  drack  druckit

# 3  NOUNS

## GENDER AND NOUN TYPE

### 21  GENDER

Swedish nouns are divided into non-neuter gender (sometimes called **en**-words or **N**-words or common gender) and neuter gender (sometimes called **ett**-words or **T**-words). This division is expressed in the choice of the indefinite article (see **24**):

| *Non-neuter* | | *Neuter* | |
|---|---|---|---|
| *en* **bil** | *en* **flicka** | *ett* **hus** | *ett* **äpple** |
| a car | a girl | a house | an apple |

Gender determines the end (definite) article singular and plural (see also **37f**):

| | *Non-neuter* | | *Neuter* | |
|---|---|---|---|---|
| *Singular* | **bil***en* | **flicka***n* | **hus***et* | **äpple***t* |
| | the car | the girl | the house | the apple |
| *Plural* | **bilar***na* | **flickor***na* | **hus***en* | **äpple***na* |
| | the cars | the girls | the houses | the apples |

Gender is also important for the selection of a plural ending (see **25ff**) and for the agreement of pronouns, adjectives and past participles (see **47, 68, 98**):

| **hus***et* **är stor***t* | **flicka***n* **är stor**⊗ |
|---|---|
| the house is big | the girl is big |

| *ett* **grönt äpple** | *en* **stor**⊗ **flicka** |
|---|---|
| a green apple | a big girl |

### 22  GENDER RULES

Gender is only partly predictable for Swedish, i.e. the meaning or form (often suffixes) of some nouns may tell us whether we are dealing with a non-neuter or neuter noun, but in many cases we cannot predict gender accurately by either form or meaning. What follows is a guide to those clues available to us for predicting gender by the meaning or form of a word:

1 Non-neuter by meaning:

(a) Most human beings:      **en far, en lärare**, *not*: **ett barn, ett biträde**
(b) Most animals:      **en fisk, en höna**, *not*: **ett djur, ett får, ett bi, ett lejon**
(c) Days, parts of the day:      **en fredag, en timme**, *not*: **ett dygn**
(d) Festivals:      **julen, påsken, midsommaren**
(e) Months, seasons:      **januari var kall; hösten, våren**
(f) Trees:      **granen, apeln**, *not*: **ett träd** or compounds in **-träd**

2 Non-neuter by form:

| | |
|---|---|
| **-a** | **en gata, en krona, en människa**, *not*: **ett drama, ett öga** |
| **-are** | **en lärare, en stockholmare**, *not*: **ett altare** |
| **-dom** | **en sjukdom, kristendomen** |
| **-else** | **en rörelse, en styrelse**, *not*: **ett fängelse** |
| **-het** | **en svaghet, en personlighet** |
| **-ing/-ning** | **en ordning, en höjning** |
| **-ion** | **en station, en religion** |
| **-ism** | **realismen, socialismen** |
| **-nad** | **byggnaden, tystnaden** |

3 Neuter by meaning:

(a) Continents:      **Asien är överbefolkat.**
(b) Countries:      **Sverige är avlångt.**
(c) Provinces:      **Småland är bergigt.**
(d) Towns:      **Stockholm är stort.**

Notice the 'hidden agreement' in these four cases where there is no article on the noun to indicate gender.
(e) Letters of the alphabet:      **ett a, ett b.**
(f) Nouns from other parts of speech:      **nuet, jaget, ett nej.**

4 Neuter by form:

| | |
|---|---|
| **-ande** | **ett antagande**, *not*: people – **en sökande, en studerande** |
| **-ende** | **ett leende, ett utseende** |
| **-um** | **ett faktum, ett museum, ett gymnasium** |

## 23 TYPES OF NOUN

The three main types of noun are:

1 Common nouns:      **katt** (cat), **stol** (chair), **pojke** (boy)
2 Abstract nouns:      **glädje** (joy), **sjukdom** (illness), **mjukhet** (softness)
3 Proper nouns:      **Gustav, Stockholm, Sverige** (Sweden), **Volvo**

A further important distinction is made between count nouns and non-count nouns (see also **36**, **67.3**):

Count nouns are often concrete things and creatures:

**bulle** (bun), **träd** (tree), **student** (student).

Some abstracts are count nouns: **skratt** (laugh), **färg** (colour)

Non-count nouns are often substances:

**vatten** (water), **bensin** (petrol), **luft** (air)

Some abstracts are non-count nouns: **vithet** (whiteness), **lycka** (happiness)

## INDEFINITE DECLENSION

### 24   INDEFINITE FORMS

Like most major languages Swedish has indefinite and definite forms of the noun. The indefinite singular form is often indicated by the use of the indefinite article – either **en** or **ett** – before the noun, depending on the gender of the noun:

| | | | |
|---|---|---|---|
| *Non-neuter* | *en* **mor** | a mother | For constructions with adjectives, |
| | *en* **timme** | an hour | see **47**ff. |
| *Neuter* | *ett* **hus** | a house | |
| | *ett* **äpple** | an apple | |

As in English a whole species or family may be denoted by either definite singular or indefinite plural:

**Ekorrar/Ekorren finns överallt**    Squirrels are/The squirrel is found
**i Europa.**    throughout Europe.

The indefinite article is the same as the numeral **en**, **ett**, 'one'. The indefinite plural of Swedish nouns is formed by adding one of several different endings to the noun, see **25**ff.

### 25   PLURALS

Regular plurals are expressed by the addition of one of the following endings:

**-or   -ar   -er   -r   -n** -zero (i.e. no plural ending)

Nouns are often grouped by their plural ending in declensions which correspond to these endings:

Declension

| | | | |
|---|---|---|---|
| 1 **en gata** | a street | **två gat*or*** | two streets |
| 2 **en sjö** | a lake | **två sjö*ar*** | two lakes |
| 3 **en park** | a park | **två park*er*** | two parks |
| **en sko** | a shoe | **två sko*r*** | two shoes |
| 4 **ett yrke** | a job | **två yrke*n*** | two jobs |
| 5 **ett barn** | a child | **två barn** | two children |

Plurals of Swedish nouns are very largely predictable. The decisive factors in the choice of a plural ending are:

1 Gender – whether it is a non-neuter or neuter noun:

| | | | |
|---|---|---|---|
| *en* **arm** | **två arm*ar*** | *ett* **hus** | **två hus**⊗ |
| *en* **krona** | **två kron*or*** | *ett* **stycke** | **två stycke*n*** |

2 Whether the neuter noun ends in a vowel or a consonant:

| | | | |
|---|---|---|---|
| **ett kvitt*o*** | **två kvitt*on*** | **ett papp*er*** | **två papp*er*⊗** |
| **ett part*i*** | **två parti*er*** | | |

3 Whether the neuter noun ending in a vowel has stress on the last syllable:

| | | | |
|---|---|---|---|
| **ett 'ställe̥** | **två 'ställe*n*** | **ett bage'ri̠** | **två bage'ri*er*** |

4 Whether the non-neuter noun has stress on the last syllable. Those with end stress take **-er**:

| | |
|---|---|
| **en sta'ti̠on** | **två sta'tion*er*** |

5 Which of the following suffixes the non-neuter noun without stress on the last syllable possesses:

| | | |
|---|---|---|
| **-e** | **en pojke** | **två pojk*ar*** |
| **-a** | **en krona** | **två kron*or*** |
| **-are** | **en läkare** | **två läkare⊗** |
| **-er** | **en indier** | **två indier⊗** |
| **-(n)ing** | **en tidning** | **två tidning*ar*** |
| **-tion** | **en lektion** | **två lektion*er*** |
| **-het** | **en nyhet** | **två nyhet*er*** |
| **-nad** | **en byggnad** | **två byggnad*er*** |

**26** below shows these factors both as rules and in diagrammatic form.

## 26 PLURALS – PREDICTABILITY

There are six main rules for predicting the plural forms of nouns:

1 Non-neuter nouns ending in unstressed **-a** have a plural in **-or** (and drop **-a**).

| en flicka | två flick*or* |
|---|---|

2 Non-neuter nouns ending in unstressed **-e** have a plural in **-ar** (and drop **-e**).

| en pojke | två pojk*ar* |
|---|---|

3 Non-neuter nouns with stress on the last syllable have a plural in **-er**.

| en armé | två armé*er* |
|---|---|

4 Neuter nouns ending in a stressed vowel have a plural in **-er**.

| ett geni | två geni*er* |
|---|---|

5 Neuter nouns ending in an unstressed vowel have a plural in **-n**.

| ett yrke | två yrke*n* |
|---|---|

6 Neuter nouns ending in a consonant have a plural in -zero (i.e. no plural ending, shown below as ⊗).

| ett barn | två barn⊗ |
|---|---|

It is possible to formulate a number of additional rules for prediction:

7 Non-neuter nouns ending in suffix **-are** have a plural in -zero.

| en lärare | två lärare⊗ |
|---|---|

8 Non-neuter nouns ending in suffix **-er** have a plural in -zero.

| en tekniker | två tekniker⊗ |
|---|---|

9 Nouns (always non-neuter) ending in suffix **-ing** have a plural in **-ar**.

| en tidning | två tidning*ar* |
|---|---|

10 Nouns (always non-neuter) ending in the stressed suffixes **-het**, **-nad**, **-tion** have a plural in **-er**.

| en nyhet | två nyhet*er* |
|---|---|
| en byggnad | två byggnad*er* |
| en station | två station*er* |

*Notes:*

1 It is often difficult to predict the plurals of monosyllabic non-neuter nouns ending in a consonant. Such nouns add either **-ar** or **-er**:

| cf.  en bil | två bil*ar* |
|---|---|
| en färg | två färg*er* |
| en hund | två hund*ar* |
| en park | två park*er* |

2 Nouns ending in **-el**, **-en**, **-er** tend to drop the **-e** and add **-ar**:

| en fågel | två fågl*ar* |
|---|---|
| en vinter | två vintr*ar* |
| en fröken | två frökn*ar* |

Notice, however, that some loanwords take **-er**:

| en muskel | två muskl*er* |
|---|---|
| en neger | två negr*er* |

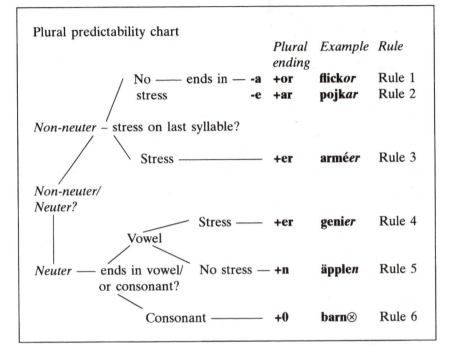

Plural predictability chart

## PLURAL FORMS

Whilst plurals in the majority of cases are predictable from the form or pronunciation of the noun (see **25**ff), it is also useful to gather nouns into groups (often called 'declensions') according to their plural ending:

### 27   PLURALS IN **-or** (FIRST DECLENSION)

These comprise only non-neuter nouns, which include:

1 All nouns of two or more syllables ending in **-a**. These drop the **-a** before adding the plural ending:

| en blomma | +*or* | > två blommor | flower(s) |
|---|---|---|---|
| en människa | +*or* | > två människor | person(s) |

2  Very few others:

| en toffel | +*or* | > två tofflor | slipper(s) |
| en ros | +*or* | > två rosor | rose(s) |

## 28   PLURALS IN -ar (SECOND DECLENSION)

These comprise only non-neuter nouns, which include:

1  Most monosyllabic nouns ending in a consonant:

| en hund | +*ar* | > två hundar | dog(s) |
| en arm | +*ar* | > två armar | arm(s) |

2  Some monosyllabic nouns ending in a vowel:

| en sjö | +*ar* | > två sjöar | lake(s) |
| en å | +*ar* | > två åar | river(s) |

3  Nouns ending in unstressed -e:
These drop the -e before adding the plural ending:

| en pojke | +*ar* | > två pojkar | boy(s) |

4  Any nouns ending in unstressed -en, -el, -er:
These drop the -e of the last syllable before adding the plural ending:

| en fågel | +*ar* | > två fåglar | bird(s) |
| en vinter | +*ar* | > två vintrar | winter(s) |

5  Many nouns ending in -(n)ing:

| en övning | +*ar* | > två övningar | exercise(s) |
| en tävling | +*ar* | > två tävlingar | competition(s) |

6  Notice the following irregular nouns:

| ett finger | +*ar* | > två fingrar | finger(s) |
| en dotter | +*ar* | > två döttrar | daughter(s) |
| en mo(de)r | +*ar* | > två mödrar | mother(s) |
| en mun | +*ar* | > två munnar | mouth(s) |
| en morgon | +*ar* | > två morgnar | morning(s) |
| en sommar | +*ar* | > två somrar | summer(s) |

## 29   PLURALS IN -er (THIRD DECLENSION)

These comprise both non-neuter and neuter nouns, which include:

1  Some monosyllabic non-neuter nouns ending in a consonant:

| en park | +*er* | > två parker | park(s) |
| en färg | +*er* | > två färger | colour(s) |

2 Many nouns of both genders with stress on the final syllable (often loans):

| en miljö | +*er* | > två miljöer | environment(s) |
| en restaurang | +*er* | > två restauranger | restaurant(s) |
| en student | +*er* | > två studenter | student(s) |
| ett myteri | +*er* | > två myterier | mutiny(-ies) |

3 Some nouns ending in unstressed **-en, -el, -er**:
These drop the **-e-** of the last syllable before adding the plural ending:

| en möbel | +*er* | > två möbler | piece(s) of furniture |
| en neger | +*er* | > två negrer | negro(es) |

4 A number of nouns which change their root vowel:

**A > Ä**:

| en hand | +*er* | > två händer | hand(s) |
| en tand | +*er* | > två tänder | tooth (teeth) |
| en strand | +*er* | > två stränder | beach(es) |
| ett land | +*er* | > två länder | country(-ies) |
| en stad | +*er* | > två städer | town(s) |

**O > Ö**:

| en son | +*er* | > två söner | son(s) |
| en ledamot | +*er* | > två ledamöter | member(s) |

**O > Ö** + *vowel shortening*:

| en fot | +*er* | > två fötter | foot/feet |
| en bok | +*er* | > två böcker | book(s) |
| en rot | +*er* | > två rötter | root(s) |

## 30   PLURALS IN **-r** (THIRD DECLENSION)

These comprise mostly non-neuter nouns ending in a vowel, which include:

1 Nouns ending in **-e, -ie, -je, -else**:

| en linje | +*r* | > två linjer | line(s) |
| en bakelse | +*r* | > två bakelser | cream cake(s) |
| ett fängelse | +*r* | > två fängelser | prison(s) |
| Notice: | | | |
| en bonde | +*r* | > två bönder | farmer(s) |

2 Nouns ending in **-o, -u, -å, -ö**: (see also **33.1**)

| en sko | +*r* | > två skor | shoe(s) |
| en tå | +*r* | > två tår | toe(s) |

## 31  PLURALS IN -n (FOURTH DECLENSION)

1 These comprise only neuter nouns ending in an unstressed vowel:

| | | | |
|---|---|---|---|
| ett ansikte | +*n* | > två ansikten | face(s) |
| ett leende | +*n* | > två leenden | smile(s) |
| ett bi | +*n* | > två bin | bee(s) |
| ett konto | +*n* | > två konton | account(s) |

2 Notice the following irregular **n**-plurals:

| | | |
|---|---|---|
| ett öga | > två ögon | eye(s) |
| ett öra | > två öron | ear(s) |
| ett huvud | > två huvuden | head(s) |

## 32  PLURALS IN -ZERO (NO PLURAL ENDING, FIFTH DECLENSION)

These comprise both neuter and non-neuter nouns, which include:

1 Many neuter nouns ending in a consonant:

| | | | |
|---|---|---|---|
| ett hus | +zero | > två hus⊗ | house(s) |
| ett barn | +zero | > två barn⊗ | child(ren) |
| ett fönster | +zero | > två fönster⊗ | window(s) |

2 Most non-neuter nouns ending in **-are**, **-er** (see also **29.3**), **-ande**, **-ende** denoting people(s) and professions:

| | | | |
|---|---|---|---|
| en läkare | +zero | > två läkare⊗ | doctor(s) |
| en väljare | +zero | > två väljare⊗ | voter(s) |
| en studerande | +zero | > två studerande⊗ | student(s) |
| en musiker | +zero | > två musiker⊗ | musician(s) |

3 A few non-neuter nouns with vowel change in the plural:

| | | | |
|---|---|---|---|
| en man | +zero | > två män⊗ | man/men |
| en bro(de)r | +zero | > två bröder⊗ | brother(s) |
| en mus | +zero | > två möss⊗ | mouse, mice |
| en gås | +zero | > två gäss⊗ | goose, geese |

4 Nouns of measurement of both genders:

| | | | |
|---|---|---|---|
| en meter | +zero | > två meter⊗ | metre(s) |
| en kilometer | +zero | > två kilometer⊗ | kilometre(s) |
| en mil | +zero | > två mil⊗ | Swedish mile(s) |
| ett ton | +zero | > två ton⊗ | tonne(s) |
| en liter | +zero | > två liter⊗ | litre(s) |

## 33   PLURALS IN -s

The plural in **-s** often represents a transitional form. Loanwords in **-s** are usually quickly assimilated into one of the regular Swedish inflexional types. Such nouns often possess an alternative Swedish plural. They comprise:

1 Words ending in unstressed vowels other than **-a**, **-e**:

| | |
|---|---|
| **en hobby** | **två hobbies/hobby***er* |
| **en duo** | **två duos/duo***r* |
| **en studio** | **två studios/studio***r* |

2 Words with unstressed final syllables (often **-er**) and/or un-Swedish sound combinations:

**en cowboy**                      **två cowboys/cowboy***er*
(Like **cowboy** goes: **bungalow**)

**en outsider**                    **två outsiders/outsider**⊗
(Like **outsider** go: **designer, thriller, bestseller, partner**)

**en gangster**                    **två gangsters/gangstr***ar*
(Like **gangster** go: **blinker, reporter, supporter**)

**en peso**                        **två peso***s*
**en musical**                     **två musicals/musikal***er*

3 Words for pairs:

**pumps, boots, jeans, slacks, shorts, goggles**

4 Words for collectives:

**scones, muffins, chips** (= potato crisps), **blues**

## 34   PLURALS IN -a

These comprise a number of Latin and Greek loanwords of both genders which often possess alternative Swedish plurals in zero (marked ⊗).

| | |
|---|---|
| **ett centrum** | **två centrum**⊗**/centrer/centra** |
| **ett faktum** | **två faktum**⊗**/fakta** |
| **ett lexikon** | **två lexikon**⊗**/lexika** |

## 35   NOUNS WITH NO PLURAL FORM

These comprise:

1 Some nouns possess no plural form because of their meaning.

|   |   |
|---|---|
| Abstract nouns: | **fattigdom, glädje, köld** |
| Some names of substances: | **guld, snö, kol, luft** |
| Some collective nouns: | **boskap, folk** |

2 Non-neuter nouns ending in unstressed **-an** which occasionally 'borrow' a plural from other synonymous words:

|   |   |
|---|---|
| **en önskan** | **(två önskningar)** |
| **en början** | **(två inledningar)** |
| **en tävlan** | **(två tävlingar)** |
| **en anmälan** | **(två anmälningar)** |

## DIFFERENCES BETWEEN SWEDISH AND ENGLISH NUMBER

### 36  DIFFERENCES IN NUMBER

Swedish may have a plural where English has a singular and vice versa.

1 Non-count singular in English, count plural in Swedish:

| | | | |
|---|---|---|---|
| advice | **råd** | furniture | **möbler** |
| business | **affärer** | news | **nyheter** |
| income | **inkomst(er)** | applause | **applåder** |
| information | **upplysningar** | homework | **läxor** |
| knowledge | **kunskap(er)** | cash | **kontanter** |
| money | **pengar** | | |

Notice: **en nyhet** a piece of news, **en möbel** a piece of furniture

2 Count plural in English, often non-count singular in Swedish:

| | | | |
|---|---|---|---|
| contents | **innehåll** | stairs | **trappa** |
| drugs | **narkotika, knark** | wages | **lön** |

3 Count plural in English, count singular in Swedish:

| | | | |
|---|---|---|---|
| scissors | **sax** | scales | **(en) våg** |
| tweezers | **pincett** | pincers | **(en) tång** |

## DEFINITE DECLENSION

### 37  FORMS WITH END ARTICLE SINGULAR

The definite form of the noun is indicated by the use of the end (definite) article, **-en** for singular non-neuter nouns, **-et** for singular neuter nouns (cf. indefinite **en**, **ett**, **24**). If a noun ends in a vowel the end article is **-n** (non-neuter) or **-t** (neuter). The end article in Swedish is not a separate word but a suffix which is added to the end of the noun:

| *Indefinite* | | *Definite* | |
| | | *(Form with end article)* | |
| a car | *en* **bil** | the car | **bil**en |
| a house | *ett* **hus** | the house | **hus**et |

The form of the noun with end article singular (i.e. the singular definite) can be predicted from the gender and ending of the noun as shown in the following rules:

1 Non-neuter ending in a consonant: (other than **-l** or **-r**)

   **arm**   +*en*  > **armen**

2 Non-neuter ending in a vowel (stressed or unstressed):

   **flicka**  +*n*  > **flickan**
   **industri**  +*n*  > **industrin**

3 Non-neuter ending in an unstressed vowel +**l/r**:

   **fågel**  +*n*  > **fågeln**
   **moder**  +*n*  > **modern**
   **doktor**  +*n*  > **doktorn**

4 Neuter ending in a consonant:   **hus**  +*et*  > **huset**

5 Neuter ending in an unstressed vowel:  **yrke**  +*t*  > **yrket**

6 Neuter ending in a stressed vowel:  **geni**  +*et*  > **geniet**

Notice that the stem of the following nouns in **-el**, **-en**, **-er** drops an **-e-** before adding the end article:

   **öken**  +*en*  > **öknen**
   **tecken**  +*en*  > **tecknen**
   **exempel** +*et*  > **exemplet**
   **finger**  +*et*  > **fingret**

Notice that neuters ending in **-eum**, **-ium** drop the letters **-um** before adding the end article:

   **museum** +*et*  > **museet**

Notice also some short forms in spoken Swedish that are increasingly found in written Swedish:

   **stan** (from **staden**), **dan** (from **dagen**), **sommarn** (from **sommaren**),
   **knät** (from **knäet**), **idén** (from **idéen**), **direktörn** (from **direktören**),
   **lärarn** (from **läraren**)

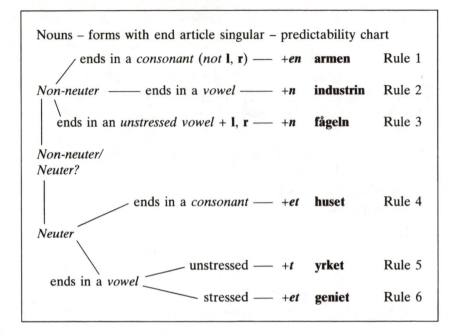

Nouns – forms with end article singular – predictability chart

| | | |
|---|---|---|
| ends in a *consonant* (*not* **l, r**) —— **+en armen** | Rule 1 |
| *Non-neuter* —— ends in a *vowel* —— **+n industrin** | Rule 2 |
| ends in an *unstressed vowel* + **l, r** — **+n fågeln** | Rule 3 |

*Non-neuter/*
*Neuter?*

| | | |
|---|---|---|
| ends in a *consonant* —— **+et huset** | Rule 4 |
| *Neuter* | |
| ends in a *vowel* — unstressed —— **+t yrket** | Rule 5 |
| stressed —— **+et geniet** | Rule 6 |

## 38   FORMS WITH END ARTICLE PLURAL

The end article plural is either **-na**, **-a** or **-en**. The form of the noun with end article plural (i.e. plural definite) can be predicted from the following rules:

1 Plurals ending in a *vowel* + **r** (both genders):

| | | |
|---|---|---|
| **flickor** | **+na** | > **flickorna** |
| **armar** | **+na** | > **armarna** |
| **filmer** | **+na** | > **filmerna** |
| **viner** | **+na** | > **vinerna** |

Notice that plurals of nouns in **-are** drop the final **-e**:

| | | |
|---|---|---|
| **arbetare** | **+na** | > **arbetarna** |
| **läkare** | **+na** | > **läkarna** |

2 Plurals ending in a *consonant other than* **-r** (both genders):

| | | |
|---|---|---|
| **barn** | **+en** | > **barnen** |
| **män** | **+en** | > **männen** |

Notice that stems of nouns in **-el**,  **-en**, **-er** drop an **-e-**:

| | | |
|---|---|---|
| **exempel** | **+en** | > **exemplen** |
| **tecken** | **+en** | > **tecknen** |
| **fönster** | **+en** | > **fönstren** |

3 Plurals of neuter nouns ending in a vowel which have added +**n** to form their plural:

**yrken**   +*a*   > **yrkena**

Nouns – forms with end article plural – predictability chart

|  |  |  |
|---|---|---|
| | — **flickorna** | |
| *vowel* + **r** ————— +*na* | — **armarna** | Rule 1 |
| | — **filmerna** | |

Plural indefinite
ending in:

|  |  |  |  |
|---|---|---|---|
| *vowel* + **n** (neuters) +*a* | — | **yrkena** | Rule 3 |
| *consonant* (*not* **r**) +*en* | — | **barnen** | |
| | | **borden** | |
| | | **exemplen** | Rule 2 |
| | | **husen** | |

# ARTICLE USE

In many cases usage is similar in the two languages, e.g. both use definite articles for familiar ideas and indefinite articles for new ideas. The paragraphs below outline major *differences* in usage.

## 39   END ARTICLE IN SWEDISH, NO ARTICLE IN ENGLISH

1 Abstract nouns and nouns in a general sense:

| | |
|---|---|
| **Svenskarna älskar naturen.** | Swedes love nature. |
| **Historien upprepar sig.** | History repeats itself. |
| **Sådant är livet.** | Such is life. |
| **Han fruktar döden.** | He fears death. |
| **Priserna stiger jämt.** | Prices are always rising. |

2 Locations:

| | |
|---|---|
| **Olle går i kyrkan/skolan.** | Olle goes to church/school. |
| **Eva åker till staden.** | Eva is going to town. |
| **Eva är i staden.** | Eva is in town. |
| **Lars studerar vid universitetet.** | Lars is /studying/ at university. |

3 Days, seasons, festivals, mealtimes:

| | |
|---|---|
| **På fredagarna åker vi bort.** | On Fridays we go away. |
| **På vintern spelar de ishockey.** | In winter they play ice hockey. |
| **Vi ses på nyårsdagen!** | Be seeing you on New Year's Day! |
| **Efter middagen läste jag en bok.** | After dinner I read a book. |

See also **139**.

## 40   END ARTICLE IN SWEDISH, INDEFINITE ARTICLE IN ENGLISH

1 Prices:

| | |
|---|---|
| **Osten kostar 30 kronor kilot.** | The cheese costs 30 kronor a kilo. |

2 Frequency of occurrence:

| | |
|---|---|
| **Jag tjänar 50 kronor i timmen,** | I earn 50 kronor an hour, i.e. 400 |
| **dvs 400 kronor om dagen.** | kronor a day. |

## 41   NO ARTICLE IN SWEDISH, DEFINITE ARTICLE IN ENGLISH

1 Instruments, machines:

| | |
|---|---|
| **Han spelar piano.** | He is playing the piano. |
| **De lyssnar på radio.** | They are listening to the radio. |
| **Vi tittar på tv.** | We are watching /the/ TV. |

2 Proper names:

| | |
|---|---|
| **Jag har bjudit hit Janssons.** | I've invited the Janssons round. |

3 Nouns after **nästa, samma, fel, rätt, följande, föregående** (cf. **55.6**):

| | |
|---|---|
| **De bor i nästa hus.** | They live in the next house. |
| **Samma dag kom vi hem.** | The same day we came home. |
| **Det var rätt/fel hus.** | It was the right/wrong house. |
| **Följande år hade vi en fin vår.** | The following year we had a fine spring. |

## 42   NO ARTICLE IN SWEDISH, INDEFINITE ARTICLE IN ENGLISH

1 Nationality, profession, religious and political belief:

| | |
|---|---|
| **Per är norrman.** | Per is a Norwegian. |
| **Han är lärare.** | He is a teacher. |
| **Moberg var socialist.** | Moberg was a Socialist. |
| **Hon är katolik.** | She is a Catholic. |

*Exceptions:*

(a) When the noun is qualified by an adjective:

**Hon är en god katolik.**  She is a good Catholic.

(b) When the noun is preceded by a preposition:

**Hon är gift med en lärare.**  She is married to a teacher.

(c) When the noun is qualified by a relative clause:

**Hon är en lärare som kan sin sak.**  She is a teacher who knows her stuff.

2 Count nouns in a general sense when only one is inferred:

**De väntar barn och söker bostad/lägenhet.**  They are expecting a child and looking for somewhere to live/ a flat.

**Hon har inte körkort/bil.**  She has not got a driving licence/ a car.

**Han var utan arbete.**  He was without a job.

3 Nouns after the words **vilken**, **mången** (many a), **hur ... än**:

**Vilken skön dag!**  What a beautiful day!

**Hur fint hus de än har, är det inte lika bra som vårt.**  However nice a house they may have, it is not as nice as ours.

## 43 END ARTICLE IN SWEDISH, POSSESSIVE PRONOUN IN ENGLISH

Parts of the body, clothing:

**Hon ska tvätta håret/händerna.**  She is going to wash her hair/ hands.

**Hon tog av sig skorna/kappan.**  She took off her shoes/coat.

**Han har ont i ryggen/magen.**  He has a pain in his back/ stomach.

## 44 ARTICLE USE WITH DEMONSTRATIVE PRONOUNS

|  | **Den här** etc. <br> *+ End article* | **Den** etc. <br> *+ End article* | **Denna** etc. <br> *No end article* |
|---|---|---|---|
| *Non-neuter* | **den här filmen** <br> **den där filmen** <br> this/that film | **den filmen** <br><br> this/that film | **denna film**⊗ <br><br> this/that film |

| *Neuter* | **det här kortet** | **det kortet** | **detta kort**⊗ |
|---|---|---|---|
| | **det där kortet** | | |
| | this/that card | this/that card | this/that card |
| *Plural* | **de här filmerna** | **de filmerna** | **dessa filmer**⊗ |
| | **de där filmerna** | | |
| | these/those films | these/those films | these/those films |
| | **de här korten** | **de korten** | **dessa kort**⊗ |
| | **de där korten** | | |
| | these/those cards | these/those cards | these/those cards |

*Exception:* where **den/det/de** are determinative pronouns, see **76**.

## 45   NO ARTICLE AFTER THE POSSESSIVE

See also **72, 55.2**.

As in English, nouns following a possessive *never* take an end article:

| **pennan** | the pen | **min penna**⊗ | my pen |
|---|---|---|---|
| **bordet** | the table | **mitt bord**⊗ | my table |

This also applies to constructions with noun + adjective:

| **min röda penna**⊗ | my red pen |
|---|---|
| **mitt stora bord**⊗ | my big table |

# GENITIVES

## 46   THE GENITIVE

See **141** for the translation of English 'of' expressions.

1 The genitive is formed by adding **-s** to the noun. Notice that there is no apostrophe:

| **en flickas** | **flickans** | **flickors** | **flickornas** |
|---|---|---|---|
| a girl's | the girl's | girls' | the girls' |

*Exceptions:*
– no **-s** after a noun ending in **-s**, **-x**:

| **Marx skrifter** | Marx's writings |
|---|---|
| **en kaktus taggar** | a cactus's spines |

– no **-s** after place names ending in a vowel:

| **Uppsala slott** | Uppsala Castle |
|---|---|
| (cf. **Gripsholms slott**) | |

2 Some old genitive case endings remain in a few set phrases:

| | |
|---|---|
| **gå till fots/skogs/bords/sängs** | go on foot/into the forest/to table/ to bed |
| **gå till väga; vara till salu** | set about (something); be for sale |

3 Latin genitive endings are found in some names:

| | |
|---|---|
| **Jesu liv (< Jesus)** | Jesus' life |
| **Kristi himmelsfärd (< Kristus)** | Christ's ascension |

4 The genitive **-s** is usually placed on the last word of the group:

| | |
|---|---|
| **mannen på gatans åsikter** | the view of the man in the street |
| **Karl den tolftes död** | the death of Charles XII |

5 The noun following a genitive *never* takes an end article:

| | |
|---|---|
| **gårdens ägare**⊗ | *the* owner of the farm |
| **Sveriges huvudstad**⊗ | *the* capital of Sweden |
| **årets sista dag**⊗ | *the* last day of the year |

6 The genitive usually denotes possession or belonging in a wide sense, but is also used:

(a) In measurement:

| | |
|---|---|
| **ett par timmars sömn** | a couple of hours' sleep |
| **ett fyrtifem minuters program** | a 45-minute programme |

(b) To express a 'kind/sort of':

| | |
|---|---|
| **en sorts fisk** | a kind of fish |
| **alla sorters mat** | all kinds of food |
| **ett slags fisk** | a kind of fish |
| **alla slags mat** | all kinds of food |

(c) In names:

| | |
|---|---|
| **Jag handlar alltid hos Olssons.** | I always shop at Olsson's. |
| **Vi bor mitt emot Perssons.** | We live opposite the Perssons. |

# 4  ADJECTIVES

## 47  ADJECTIVES IN OUTLINE

Swedish adjectives inflect. In the indefinite declension they agree with the noun in gender (singular only) and number both attributively and predicatively. They also add inflexional endings in the definite declension.

INDEFINITE FORMS

|             | Non-neuter | Neuter | Plural |
|-------------|-----------|--------|--------|
| *Attributive* | **en stor⊗ bil** | **ett stort hus** | **stora bilar/hus** |
|             | a big car | a big house | big cars/ houses |
|             | **god⊗ mat** | **varmt vatten** | **raka vägar** |
|             | good food | hot water | straight roads |
| *Predicative* | **bilen är stor⊗** | **huset är stort** | **bilarna/husen är stora** |
|             | the car is big | the house is big | the cars/houses are big |

DEFINITE FORMS

|  | **den stora bilen** | **det stora huset** | **de stora bilarna/ husen** |
|--|---------------------|---------------------|------------------------------|
|  | the big car | the big house | the big cars/houses |

*Notes:*

1 For the inflexion of adjectives and past participles, see **48**ff, **97**.

2 An alternative form of the adjective, in **-e**, is found in the definite singular before non-neuter nouns indicating a male person (cf. **53.2**):

| **den gamle mannen** | the old man |
| **den store ledaren Napoleon** | the great leader Napoleon |

3 The definite ending in **-e** also occurs, as a compulsory form on the adjective ending in **-ad**, superlative in **-ast** (cf. **53.2**):

| **den nymålade stugan** | the newly painted cottage |
| **det billigaste huset** | the cheapest house |

# INDEFINITE DECLENSION

## 48 INDEFINITE FORMS – REGULAR

*Main rule*: Most adjectives including all ending in **-(l)ig**:

| *Non-neuter* | *Neuter* | *Plural* |
|---|---|---|
| +⊗ (*no ending*) | **+t** | **+a** |

| | | |
|---|---|---|
| **en fin⊗ tavla** | **ett fint hus** | **fina tavlor/hus** |
| a fine picture | a fine house | fine pictures/houses |
| **en rolig⊗ film** | **ett roligt skämt** | **roliga filmer/skämt** |
| a funny film | a funny joke | funny films/jokes |

## 49 INDEFINITE FORMS – VARIATIONS

| *Non-neuter* | *Neuter* | *Plural* |
|---|---|---|

Adjectives ending in:

| 1 | *long vowel* | *short vowel* | *long vowel* | |
|---|---|---|---|---|
| | | **+tt** | **+a** | |
| | **fri** | **fritt** | **fria** | free |
| | **blå** | **blått** | **blå/a/** | blue (**-a** is optional) |
| | **grå** | **grått** | **grå/a/** | grey (**-a** is optional) |

Like **fri** go: **ny** (new), **rå** (raw), **slö** (blunt)

| 2 | *long vowel* | *short vowel* | *long vowel* | |
|---|---|---|---|---|
| | **+t** | **+tt** | **+t+a** | |
| | **vit** | **vitt** | **vita** | white |

Like **vit** go: **het** (hot), **fet** (fat), **våt** (wet)

| 3 | *short vowel* | *short vowel* | *short vowel* | |
|---|---|---|---|---|
| | **+tt** | **+tt** | **+tt+a** | |
| | **lätt** | **lätt** | **lätta** | easy |

Like **lätt** go: **rätt** (right), **trött** (tired), **mätt** (replete)

| 4 | *consonant* | *consonant* | *consonant* | |
|---|---|---|---|---|
| | **+t** | **+t** | **+t+a** | |
| | **intressant** | **intressant** | **intressanta** | interesting |

Like **intressant** go: **abstrakt, elegant, intelligent, perfekt**

| 5 | *long vowel* | *short vowel* | *long vowel* | |
|---|---|---|---|---|
| | **+d** | **+tt** | **+d+a** | |
| | **glad** | **glatt** | **glada** | happy |

Like **glad** go: **bred** (wide), **död** (dead), **god** (good), **röd** (red)

| 6 | *cons.* | *cons.* | *cons.* | |
|---|---------|---------|---------|---|
| | *+d* | *+t* | *+d+a* | |
| | **hård** | **hår**t | **hård**a | hard |

Like **hård** go: **ond** (evil), **vild** (wild), **mild** (mild), **värd** (worth), **stängd** (closed), **berömd** (famous), **bestämd** (definite)

| 7 | *-ad* | *-at* | *-ad+e* | |
|---|-------|-------|---------|---|
| | **älskad** | **älska**t | **älska**de | loved |

Like **älskad** go: all first conjugation past participles, e.g. **kortfattad** (concise), **koncentrerad** (concentrated). See **98**.

| 8 | *short vowel* | *short vowel* | *short vowel* | |
|---|--------------|--------------|--------------|---|
| | *+m* | *+m+t* | *+mm+a* | |
| | **dum** | **dum**t | **dum**ma | stupid |

Like **dum** go: **tom** (empty), **grym** (cruel), **hjälpsam** (helpful), **långsam** (slow), **våldsam** (violent). See **177**.

| 9 | *short vowel* | *short vowel* | *short vowel* | |
|---|--------------|--------------|--------------|---|
| | *+nn* | *+n+t* | *+nn+a* | |
| | **sann** | **san**t | **san**na | true |

Like **sann** go: **grann** (pretty), **noggrann** (careful), **tunn** (thin). See **177**.

| 10 | *-el/-er* | *-el+t/-er+t* | *-l+a/-r+a* | |
|----|-----------|---------------|-------------|---|
| | **enkel** | **enkel**t | **enk**la | simple |
| | **vacker** | **vacker**t | **vack**ra | pretty |

Like **enkel** go: **acceptabel** (acceptable), **flexibel** (flexible)
Like **vacker** go: **säker** (sure), **mager** (thin), **nykter** (sober)

| 11 | *-en* | *-e+t* | *-n+a* | |
|----|-------|--------|--------|---|
| | **mogen** | **moge**t | **mog**na | ripe |
| | **skriven** | **skrive**t | **skriv**na | written |

Like **mogen** go: **egen** (own), **ledsen** (sad), **nyfiken** (curious), **öppen** (open), **vaken** (awake), **erfaren** (experienced) and past participles of fourth conjugation verbs. See **97f**.

| 12 | **gammal** | **gammalt** | **gamla** | old |
|----|------------|-------------|-----------|-----|
| 13 | **liten** | **litet** | **små** | little |
| | (definite: | | | |
| | **lilla** | **lilla** | **små**) | |

## 50    INDECLINABLE ADJECTIVES

Some adjectives do not inflect in either definite or indefinite declension, unlike those in **48f**. These include those ending in **-s**, **-e**, **-a** and some others:

1 Adjectives ending in **-s**:

**ett medelålders biträde**      a middle-aged assistant

Includes: **gammaldags** (old-fashioned), **stackars** (poor), **utrikes** (foreign), **avsides** (remote).

*Exceptions*:  adjectives ending in **-ös**: **nervös nervöst nervösa** nervous
            adjectives ending in **-is**: **vis**     **vis*t***     **vis*a*** wise

2 Adjectives ending in **-e**:

**ett gyllene tak**      a golden roof

Includes: **främmande** (foreign), **öde** (deserted), **ense** (agreed), **ordinarie** (regular) and all present participles and comparatives in **-are**, **-re**:

**omfattande kunskaper**      wide knowledge
**ett större hus**      a bigger house

3 Adjectives ending in **-a**:

**ett bra tag**      a good while

Includes: **sakta** (slow), **stilla** (peaceful), **äkta** (genuine), **extra**, **samma** (the same), **nästa** (the next), **förra** (/the/ last), **nutida** (present day)

Some indeclinable adjectives are only used attributively:

**de stackars flickorna**      the poor girls
**i fjärran länder**      in foreign parts
**det dåtida Stockholm**      the Stockholm of that time

Some indeclinable adjectives are only used predicatively:

**Arbetet var slut för dagen.**      Work had finished for the day.
**Bilen är sönder.**      The car is unserviceable.
**Jag är ense med dig.**      I agree with you.

Some indeclinable adjectives may be used either attributively or predicatively:

**Jag slog fel nummer.**      I dialled the wrong number.
**Du har fel.**      You are wrong.
**en öde ö**      a desert island
**Ön var öde och obebodd.**      The island was deserted.

## 51 INDEFINITE CONSTRUCTIONS

The indefinite noun phrase (in this case: indefinite premodifier + adjective + noun) usually expresses something general and non-specific.

| *Non-neuter* | *Neuter* | *Plural* |
|---|---|---|

1  When no word precedes adjective + noun:

| **god**⊗ **mat** | **vacker***t* **väder** | **rak***a* **vägar** |
|---|---|---|

2  When one of the following premodifiers precedes adjective + noun:

| en | | ett | | två | | a/two |
|---|---|---|---|---|---|---|
| någon | | något | | några | | a/some/any |
| ingen | | inget | | inga | | no |
| en enda | | ett enda | | – | | a single |
| en annan | stor⊗ | ett annat | stor*t* | andra | stor*a* | (an)other |
| | pojke | | hus | | pojkar/hus | |
| en likadan | | ett likadant | | likadana | | (a) similar |
| en sådan | | ett sådant | | sådana | | such /a/ |
| vilken | | vilket | | vilka | | which |
| varje | | varje | | – | | each |
| | | | | många | | many |
| | | | | flera | | several |
| | | | | alla | | all |
| | | | | få | | few |
| | | | | olika | | different |
| | | | | somliga | | some |
| | | | | åtskilliga | | several |

## 52   AGREEMENT AND LACK OF AGREEMENT

Generally speaking Swedish adjectives in the indefinite agree with the noun which they qualify:

> **Gård***en* **är stor**⊗**, men hus***et* **är lit***et* **med mörk***a* **rum.**
> The farm is big but the house is small with dark rooms.

Notice, however, the following special cases where there is lack of agreement:

1  Constructions according to meaning:

| **Folk är mer intresserad***e* **av** | People are more interested in |
|---|---|
| **idrott än politik.** | sport than politics. |

Cf. **lite/t/ folk**  few people

**Statsrådet var säker**⊗ **på sin sak.**  The minister was sure of her case.

Notice also:  **paret ... de; affärsbiträdet ... han/hon; barnet ... det**
the couple; the shop assistant; the child

2  Some nouns in a general, abstract or collective sense take the neuter:

**Ärter är go*tt*.**                    Peas are good /to eat/.
ç̧f.  **Att äta ärter är gott.**
     **Det är gott med ärter.**

**Danska är svår*t*.**                  Danish is difficult.
cf.  **Att lära sig danska är svårt.**
     **Det är svårt att lära sig danska.**

This only occurs with nouns without articles:

cf:  **De här ärterna är goda.**        These peas are good.
     **Danskan är svår.**               The Danish is difficult.

## DEFINITE DECLENSION

**53**  DEFINITE FORM OF THE ADJECTIVE: **-e** OR **-a**?

1 Forms in **-a** are used:

(a) With non-neuter nouns in the singular:  **den vackr*a* flickan**
                                            **den ny*a* stolen**

(b) With adjectival nouns in the singular referring to a female person:
                                            **den sjuk*a* (damen)**

(c) With plural nouns of both genders      **de fin*a* blommorna**
    (except those in 2(a), (b) below):     **de ung*a* pojkarna, de billig*a***
                                           **husen**

(d) With neuter nouns in the singular      **det hög*a* trädet**
    (except those in 2(a), (b) below):

2 Forms in **-e** are used:

(a) With past participles ending in **-ad**:
                                            **den nymålad*e* stugan**
                                            **det nymålad*e* huset**
                                            **de nymålad*e* husen/stugorna**

(b) With superlatives ending in **-ast**:  **den vackrast*e* flickan**
    (cf. **61**)                           **det billigast*e* huset**
                                            **de billigast*e* husen**

(c) With singular nouns referring to a male person:
    (*Preferred form*, see 1(a) above):    **den lång*e* pojken**
                                            **den berömd*e* poeten**

(d) With singular adjectival nouns referring to a male person:
    (*Compulsory*, see **59**):            **den sjuk*e* (mannen)**

Notice that: **äkta** (genuine, married), **före detta** (former, ex-) have no **e**-form:

**Evas äkta man**

**Barbros före detta man**

Remember: **e**-forms are used with adjectives in **-ad**, **-ast** and with masculine singulars.

The definite noun phrase (i.e. definite premodifier + adjective + noun) usually expresses something specific (cf. indefinite noun phrase, **51**).

## 54   DEFINITE CONSTRUCTION Type 1 – DEN NYA BILEN

This is the basic type of definite construction. The noun is defined in three ways, by:

(1) the front (adjectival) article: **den**, **det**, or **de**
(2) the definite ending on the adjective: **-a/(-e)**
(3) the end article on the noun: **-(e)n**, **-(e)t**, **-na**, **-a**, or **-en**

| Non-neuter | Neuter | Plural |
|---|---|---|
| *den* nya bil*en* | *det* nya hus*et* | *de* nya bilar*na*/hus*en* |
| (1)  (2)   (3) | (1) (2)  (3) | (1) (2)  (3)       (3) |
| the new car | the new house | the new cars/houses |

This is sometimes called 'double definition'. The construction with the demonstrative **den här** etc. (see **75**) is an extension of this type:

| *den här* nya bil*en* | *det här* nya hus*et* | *de här* nya bilar*na*/hus*en* |
|---|---|---|
| this new car | this new house | these new cars/houses |

## 55   DEFINITE CONSTRUCTION Type 2 – FIRMANS NYA BIL

In many cases the adjective has a definite ending **-a/-e** while there is no end article on the noun (cf. **54**). This occurs after the following types of word:

1 The genitive:

| Non-neuter | Neuter | Plural |
|---|---|---|
| **firmans** ny*a* bil | **mannens** ny*a* hus | **barnets** ny*a* kamrater |
| the firm's new car | the man's new house | the child's new friends |
| **Olles** ny*a* bil | **Olles** ny*a* hus | **Olles** ny*a* kamrater |
| Olle's new car | Olle's new house | Olle's new friends |

NB *Exceptions* (which take the indefinite endings in -⊗, **-t**, **-a**):

– the genitive of measurement:   **ett trettiminuters lång*t* program**
– with **en sorts/ett slags**:   **en sorts dyrbar⊗ stereo, ett slags grön*t* tyg**

2 The possessive:

| *Non-neuter* | *Neuter* | *Plural* |
|---|---|---|
| **min söta flickvän** | **mitt nya hus** | **mina nya skor** |
| my pretty girlfriend | my new house | my new shoes |

NB *Exceptions:*

– **egen** takes an indefinite ending after the possessive and genitive:

| **mammas egen⊗ Olle** | Mummy's very own Olle |
|---|---|
| **deras eget fina hus** | their own nice house |

– after **var sin, var sitt** the adjective is often found in the indefinite form:

**Pojkarna fick var sin ny/a/ cykel.**  The boys each got a new bicycle.

3 The demonstratives **denna, detta, dessa** (cf. **den här** etc. **54, 75**):

| *Non-neuter* | *Neuter* | *Plural* |
|---|---|---|
| **denna mörka skog** | **detta vackra träd** | **dessa mörka skogar** |
| this dark forest | that beautiful tree | these dark forests |
| | | **dessa vackra träd** |
| | | these beautiful trees |

**Denna** etc. is usually found only in written Swedish.

4 The determinative pronoun **den, det, de** (see **76**):

**Den unga student som inte pluggade blev underkänd i skrivningen.**
That young student who didn't study failed the exam.

5 The relative pronoun **vars** (see **77**):

**Mannen vars lilla dotter är sjuk, är mycket orolig.**
The man whose little daughter is ill is very worried.

**Vars** is usually found only in written Swedish.

6 Others:

| **samma** | **samma dumma fråga** | the same stupid question |
|---|---|---|
| **nästa** | **nästa vackra helg** | the next fine weekend |
| **följande** | **följande svåra problem** | the following difficult problem(s) |
| **föregående** | **föregående långa brev** | the previous long letter(s) |

**56**   DEFINITE CONSTRUCTION Type 3 – **SVENSKA SPRÅKET**

The front article in Type 1 (see **54**) is often omitted:

| *Non-neuter* | *Neuter* | *Plural* |
|---|---|---|
| **Svenska akademien** | **Röda korset** | **Förenta staterna** |
| the Swedish Academy | the Red Cross | the United States |

This happens:

1 When the expression becomes a set phrase and the adjective loses its stress:

| | |
|---|---|
| Cf. **det 'vita 'huset** | the white house |
| **Vita 'huset** | the White House (in Washington) |
| Cf. **det 'röda 'korset** | the red cross |
| **Röda 'korset** | the Red Cross (aid organization) |

2 In some cases when a contrast is expressed or implied and the noun is unstressed:

**Det är 'stora flickan som fyller år, inte 'lilla flickan.**
It is the big girl who is having a birthday, not the little girl.

3 In some cases when the (stressed) adjective provides stylistic marking to the phrase (in spoken Swedish):

**Det är ju 'rena smörjan!**     It is complete rubbish!

The main kinds of Type 3 construction are found:

(a) In geographical locations:

| | |
|---|---|
| **Gamla stan** | the Old Town |
| **Döda havet** | the Dead Sea |
| **Förenta staterna** | the United States |

(b) With nationality adjectives:

| | |
|---|---|
| **franska revolutionen** | the French Revolution |
| **brittiska flottan** | the British navy |

(c) With colours:

| | |
|---|---|
| **Vita huset** | the White House |
| **Röda korset** | the Red Cross |

(e) With words for location:

| | |
|---|---|
| **på högra sidan** | on the right hand side |
| **i mellersta lådan** | in the middle drawer |

(e) With compass points:

| | |
|---|---|
| **södra stambanan** | the main (railway) line to the south |
| **västra halvklotet** | the western hemisphere |

(f) With ordinal numbers:

| | |
|---|---|
| **första hjälpen** | first aid |
| **för andra gången** | for the second time |

(g) With the words **båda, förra, hela, halva, själva, ena, enda, rena rama, blotta**:

**hela året om** (all year round); **gå halva vägen** (walk half the way); **själva tanken är briljant** (the thought itself is brilliant); **ha ont i ena benet** (have a pain in one leg); **det var rena rama skojet** (it was a complete joke)

(h) In some forms of address:

| | |
|---|---|
| **snälla rektorn!** | dear headmaster/headmistress! |
| **lilla gumman!** | my dear old girl! |

## 57 DEFINITE CONSTRUCTION Type 4 – **FÖRSTA KLASS**

This is a relatively infrequent construction in which there is neither front article nor end article (nor necessarily any word preceding the adjective). It is used:

1 In forms of address and with proper nouns:

| | |
|---|---|
| **Käre far!** | Dear father! |
| **Lilla vän!** | My little friend! |
| **Gamle herr Nilsson** | old Mr Nilsson |
| **Lille Albert** | Little Albert |

2 With some ordinal numbers:

**Vi ska resa med första tåg, och åka första klass.**
We're going by the first train and travelling first class.

**De kom i sista stund.**
They arrived at the last moment.

3 Often with superlatives:

**med största nöje**          with great pleasure

## 58 DEFINITE CONSTRUCTIONS – SUMMARY CHART

| Premodifier: | Non-neuter singular | Neuter singular | Plural |
|---|---|---|---|

*Type 1 Front article/Demonstrative + end article ('Double definition') See **54**.*

| | | | |
|---|---|---|---|
| Front article | **den** ⎫ | **det** ⎫ | **de** ⎫ |
| Demonstrative | **den här** ⎬ nya bilen | **det här** ⎬ nya huset | **de här** ⎬ nya bilarna/husen |
| Demonstrative | **den där** ⎭ | **det där** ⎭ | **de där** ⎭ |

| Premodifier: | Non-neuter singular | Neuter singular | Plural |
|---|---|---|---|

*Type 2 No end article See 55.*

| *Genitive:* | Åkes | | Åkes | | Åkes | |
|---|---|---|---|---|---|---|
| | firmans | | firmans | | firmans | |
| *Possessive:* | min | | mitt | | mina | |
| *Demonstrative:* | denna | nya bil | detta | nya hus | dessa | nya bilar/hus |
| *Determinative:* | den | | det | | de | |
| *Relative:* | vars | | vars | | vars | |
| *Others:* | samma | | samma | | samma | |
| | nästa | | nästa | | nästa | |
| | följande | | följande | | följande | |
| | föregå- | | föregå- | | föregå- | |
| | ende | | ende | | ende | |

*Type 3 No front article See 56.*

| *In set phrases:* | Gamla testamentet | Röda korset | Förenta nationerna |
|---|---|---|---|
| *Locations:* | högra sidan | Vita huset | Klippiga bergen |
| *Nationality adjectives:* | engelska kyrkan | svenska språket | Brittiska öarna |
| *Compass points:* | östra stadsdelen | södra korset | |
| *Ordinal numbers:* | första gången | andra steget | |
| *Certain words:* | hela dagen | förra seklet | |
| | halva kakan | i själva verket | |
| | | enda barnet | |

*Type 4 Neither front nor end article See 57.*

With some forms of·address, ordinals and superlatives:

      **Käre far!**           **med största nöje!**
      **första klass**

# ADJECTIVAL NOUNS AND NATIONALITY WORDS

## 59   ADJECTIVAL NOUNS

1 There are three cases where the adjective is used independently, as if it were a noun:

(a) When the noun may easily be supplied: (Adjective inflexion)

**Gamla bilar är billigare än nya /bilar/.**
Old cars are cheaper than new ones.

**Jag har en gammal bil och vill köpa en ny /bil/.**
I have an old car and want to buy a new one.

**Ett rött hus och ett vitt /hus/.**
A red house and a white one.

**Alla de äldre /människorna/ var trötta.**
All the elderly people were tired.

(b) When the noun is not usually supplied (Adjectival noun – *adjective* inflexion):

**en blind /människa/**                A blind person

**Man måste hjälpa de blinda, de döva och de handikappade.**
One must help the blind, the deaf and the handicapped.

Notice that, in the singular, the **e**-form is compulsory for masculines:

**den blinde /mannen/** cf. **den blinda /kvinnan/** (see **54**)

**Det sista han gjorde var att skratta.**
The last thing he did was laugh.

**Det bästa jag vet är inlagd sill.**
The best thing I can think of is pickled herring.

**Du är den ende jag älskar.**
You are the only one (i.e. the only man) I love.

**Du är den enda jag älskar.**
You are the only one (i.e. the only woman) I love.

**Det enda du kan göra är att vänta.**
The only thing you can do is wait.

(c) When the conversion to noun is complete: (Noun inflexion – takes end article)

| | |
|---|---|
| **lillan** | the small (female) child |
| **lillen** | the small (male) child |
| **högern** | the Right (in politics) |
| **vänstern** | the Left (in politics) |
| **vitan** | the white (of an egg) |
| **gulan** | the yolk (of an egg) |
| **djupet** | the deep |
| **grundet** | the shallows |

2 As in English, deletion of the noun is common in Swedish in the plural definite:

| | |
|---|---|
| **de unga** | the young |
| **de gamla** | the old |
| **de sjuka** | the sick |
| **de fattiga** | the poor |

But the noun is more often deleted in Swedish, as the number and gender are indicated by the article and adjectival ending:

Cf. 'the tall man' with:

**den långe** /mannen/
**den långa** /kvinnan/
**det långa** /tinget/
**de långa** /människorna, tingen/

3 Swedish adjectival nouns can be formed from the following:

(a) The indefinite:

**en blind** (a blind person)
**en bekant** (an acquaintance)
**en död** (a dead person)

(b) The non-neuter singular definite:

**den gamle** (the old man)
**den gamla** (the old woman)

(c) The neuter singular definite:

**det nya** (the new thing)
**det enda** (the only thing)

(d) The definite form of the superlative:

**Det var det bästa vi kunde göra.**
(It was the best we could do.)

(e) The present participle:

**de närvarande** (those present)
**den inneboende** (the lodger/ inmate)

(f) The past participle:

**en nygift** (a newly wed)
**en okänd** (a stranger)
**den sårade** (the wounded person)
**de skadade** (the injured)

4 'The English': Expressions of nationality such as 'the English /people/', 'the French /people/' are rarely translated by adjectival nouns. Common nouns indicating the male inhabitants are used instead (see 60 below).

The English lost the battle of Hastings.
**Engelsmännen förlorade slaget vid Hastings.**

The French drink a lot of wine.
**Fransmännen dricker mycket vin.**

## 60 NATIONALITY WORDS

| Male inhabitant | Female inhabitant | Language | Adjective | Country |
| --- | --- | --- | --- | --- |
| 1 Plurals in **-ar**: | Plurals in **-or**: | | | |
| **svensk (-ar)** | **svenska (-or)** | svenska | svensk | **Sverige** |
| **dansk (-ar)** | **danska (-or)** | danska | dansk | **Danmark** |
| **tysk (-ar)** | **tyska (-or)** | tyska | tysk | **Tyskland** |

| islänning (-ar) | isländska (-or) | isländska | isländsk | Island |
| finne (-ar) | finska (-or) | finska | finsk | Finland |
| ryss (-ar) | ryska (-or) | ryska | rysk | Ryssland |

2 Plurals in **-er**:    Plurals in **-or**:

| spanjor (-er) | spanjorska (-or) | spanska | spansk | Spanien |
| kines (-er) | kinesiska (-or) | kinesiska | kinesisk | Kina |
| grek (-er) | grekiska (-or) | grekiska | grekisk | Grekland |

3 Plurals in ⊗:    Plurals in **-or**:
   engelsman

| -(män) | engelska-or | engelska | engelsk | England |
| fransman (-män) | fransyska-or | franska | fransk | Frankrike |
| norrman (-män) | norska (-or) | norska | norsk | Norge |
| holländare | holländska (-or) | holländska | holländsk | Holland |
| amerikanare | amerikanska (-or) | engelska | amerikansk | Amerika |
| italienare | italienska (-or) | italienska | italiensk | Italien |

## COMPARISON OF ADJECTIVES

**61    COMPARISON WITH -are, -ast**

The comparative has one form only for both genders, definite and indefinite. The superlative has two forms, an indefinite and a definite form. For the definite forms of the superlative see **66**.

A large number of Swedish adjectives form their comparative and superlative forms by adding the endings **-are**, **-ast** to the positive form:

| *Positive:* | *Comparative:* | *Superlative:* |
| **glad** | **glad*are*** | **glad*ast*** |
| happy | happier | happiest |

This group includes all those adjectives in **49.1–5, 8–10** above, including the frequent group ending in **-(l)ig**:

| **rolig** | **rolig*are*** | **rolig*ast*** |
| funny | funnier | funniest |

Some adjectives compared in this way drop the **-e-** in their final syllable before adding **-are**, **-ast**:

| **vacker** | **vackrare** | **vackrast**    49.10, 11 |
| pretty | prettier | prettiest |

Adjectives in a short vowel **+m/n** double the vowel when adding the endings **-are**, **-ast** (see **177.3**):

| **grym** | **grymmare** | **grymmast** |
| cruel | crueller | cruellest |

Notice that many adjectives which in English compare with 'more, most' in Swedish add **-are**, **-ast**:

*Comparative:*          *Superlative:*

| | | |
|---|---|---|
| **intelligentare** | **intelligentast** | more, most intelligent |
| **intressantare** | **intressantast** | more, most interesting |
| **modernare** | **modernast** | more, most modern |
| **skickligare** | **skickligast** | more, most skilful |
| **svårare** | **svårast** | more, most difficult |

*Notes:*

1 Past participles in **-d**, **-t** may either compare with **mer/a/**, **mest** or with **-are**, **-ast**:

   **en mer/a/ bortskämd flicka/en bortskämdare flicka**
   a more spoilt girl

2 Those adjectives in **-d**, **-dd**, **-t**, **-en** which appear to be past participles tend to add **-are**, **-ast**:

   **en vidsyntare lärare**                a more broad-minded teacher

3 Past participles ending in **-en** compare most often with **-are**, **-ast**:

   **en frusnare brevbärare**              a colder postman

## 62   COMPARISON WITH -re, -st

There is a small but rather frequent group of monosyllabic adjectives which, with the exception of **hög**, change the stem vowel in the comparative and superlative forms as well as adding **-re**, **-st**:

| | *Positive* | *Comparative* | *Superlative* | *Meaning* |
|---|---|---|---|---|
| O > Ö: | **stor** | **större** | **störst** | big, bigger, biggest |
| | **grov** | **grövre** | **grövst** | coarse, coarser, coarsest |
| Å > Ä: | **låg** | **lägre** | **lägst** | low, lower, lowest |
| | **lång** | **längre** | **längst** | long, longer, longest |
| | **trång** | **trängre** | **trängst** | narrow, narrower, narrowest |
| | **få** | **färre** | – | few, fewer |
| | **små** | **smärre** | – | small, smaller |
| U > Y: | **ung** | **yngre** | **yngst** | young, younger, youngest |
| | **tung** | **tyngre** | **tyngst** | heavy, heavier, heaviest |
| Ö: | **hög** | **högre** | **högst** | high, higher, highest |

## 63   IRREGULAR COMPARISON

There is a small group of adjectives which compares by adopting a different stem:

| Positive | Comparative | Superlative | Meaning |
|---|---|---|---|
| god/bra | bättre | bäst | good, better, best |
| dålig | sämre | sämst | bad, worse, worst |
| dålig/ond | värre | värst | bad, worse, worst |
| gammal | äldre | äldst | old, older, oldest |
| liten | mindre | minst | small, smaller, smallest |
| mången/många | fler | flest | many, more, most |
| mycken/mycket | mer/a/ | mest | much, more, most |

**Mången** and **mycken** etc. could also be termed 'adjectival pronouns'. See also **67**.

## 64   COMPARISON WITH mer, mest

A large and varied group of adjectives compares using the adverbs **mer** and **mest** rather than an ending. This group includes:

1 Most past participles:

| Positive | Comparative | Superlative |
|---|---|---|
| **komplicerad** | *mer* **komplicerad** | *mest* **komplicerad** |
| complicated | more complicated | most complicated |
| **ansträngd** | *mer* **ansträngd** | *mest* **ansträngd** |
| strained | more strained | most strained |

*Exceptions*: Past participles ending in **-en** often add an inflexional ending:

| **frusen** | **frusn*are*** | **frusn*ast*** |
|---|---|---|
| cold (lit. frozen) | colder | coldest |

2 All present participles:

| **omfattande** | *mer* **omfattande** | *mest* **omfattande** |
|---|---|---|
| wide-ranging | more wide-ranging | most wide-ranging |

3 All adjectives with 2+ syllables ending in **-isk**:

| **fantastisk** | *mer* **fantastisk** | *mest* **fantastisk** |
|---|---|---|
| fantastic | more fantastic | most fantastic |

Notice that all adjectives compared using **mer** and **mest** also inflect according to the indefinite and definite declensions (see **66**):

| **en mest fantastisk⊗ match** | a most fantastic match |
|---|---|
| **ett mest fantastisk*t* slott** | a most fantastic castle |
| **den mest fantastisk*a* matchen** | the most fantastic match |

## 65   COMPARISON (INDEFINITE) – SUMMARY CHART

| Positive | Comparative | Superlative | Meaning |
|---|---|---|---|
| 1 Comparative with **-are, -ast**: See **61**. | | | |
| **glad** | **gladare** | **gladast** | happy |
| **rolig** | **roligare** | **roligast** | funny |
| Notice:   **mager** | **magrare** | **magrast** | thin |
| 2 Comparative with (vowel change and) **-re, -st**. See **62**. | | | |
| **stor** | **större** | **störst** | big |
| **lång** | **längre** | **längst** | long |
| **ung** | **yngre** | **yngst** | young |
| But notice also | | | |
| **hög** | **högre** | **högst** | high |
| 3 Irregular comparison – new stem: See **63**. For use, see **67**. | | | |
| **god/bra** | **bättre** | **bäst** | good |
| **dålig** | **sämre** | **sämst** | bad |
| **dålig/ond** | **värre** | **värst** | bad |
| **gammal** | **äldre** | **äldst** | old |
| **liten** | **mindre** | **minst** | little |
| **mången/många** | **fler** | **flest** | many |
| **mycken/mycket** | **mer** | **mest** | much |

4 Comparison with **mer, mest**: See **64**.
All present and past participles and adjectives with suffixes in **-isk, -ad, -e**:

| | | | |
|---|---|---|---|
| **befogad** | **mer befogad** | **mest befogad** | justified |
| **glädjande** | **mer glädjande** | **mest glädjande** | pleasing |
| **typisk** | **mer typisk** | **mest typisk** | typical |

## 66   COMPARISON (INDEFINITE AND DEFINITE)

1 The comparative formed without **mer/mest** (see **64**) does not inflect:

| Non-neuter | Neuter | Plural |
|---|---|---|
| *Indefinite* | | |
| **en vackrare flicka** | **ett större hus** | **vackrare flickor/större hus** |
| a prettier girl | a bigger house | prettier girls/bigger houses |
| *Definite* | | |
| **den vackrare flickan** | **det större huset** | **de vackrare flickorna/större husen** |
| the prettier girl | the bigger house | the prettier girls/bigger houses |

2 The superlative inflects in the definite form when used attributively, but does not inflect when used predicatively:

| Non-neuter | Neuter | Plural |
|---|---|---|
| *Predicative* | | |
| **flickan är vackrast**⊗ | **huset är nyast**⊗ | **bilarna är dyrast**⊗ |
| the girl is prettiest | the house is newest | the cars are dearest |

**flickan är äldst⊗    slottet är äldst⊗    flickorna är äldst⊗/slotten är äldst⊗**
the girl is oldest    the castle is oldest    the girls/castles are oldest

**pojken är äldst⊗**
the boy is oldest

**kungen är mest älskad⊗**
the king is most beloved

*Attributive*

**den vackraste flickan**    **det nyaste huset**    **de dyraste bilarna**
the prettiest girl    the newest house    the dearest cars

**den äldsta flickan**    **det äldsta slottet**    **de äldsta flickorna/slotten**
the oldest girl    the oldest castle    the oldest girls/castles

**den äldste/äldsta pojken**
the oldest boy

**den mest älskade kungen**
the most beloved king

See also **53** for **e-/a**-forms.


**67**  USE OF COMPARATIVES AND SUPERLATIVES

1 **god, bra: godare, godast** = pleasant-tasting. **Bättre** and **bäst** are used in a general sense.

    **den godaste middagen**        the best dinner
Cf. **den bästa uppstatsen**        the best essay

2 **dålig – värre/sämre**:

**värre** = more of a bad property:

    **den värsta lögn jag hört**    the worst lie I have heard

**sämre** = less of a good property:

    **byxor av sämre kvalitet**    trousers of worse quality

3 **mer** and **mest** are only used with non-count nouns:

    **Vill du ha mer kaffe?**    Would you like more coffee?

4 **fler** and **flest** are only used with count nouns:

    **De flesta svenskar gillar sill.**    Most Swedes like pickled herring.

If a comparison is implied when using **de flesta** the noun following takes the end article:

    **Vem fick de flesta rösterna?**    Who received most votes?

5 Absolute comparative (i.e. the comparative element is lost, the adjective indicates a high degree):

**Han har vunnit en större summa.** He has won a fairly large sum.
**(= en ganska stor summa)**

Cf. relative comparative:

**Summan var större än han trodde.**
The sum was larger than he thought.

Notice: **flera** = several (cf. 4 above):

**Jag har varit här flera gånger.** I have been here several times.

6 Absolute superlative (i.e. the comparative element is lost, the adjective indicates a very high degree):

**De var de bästa vänner.** They were the best of friends.
**(mycket goda vänner)**

Cf. relative superlative:

**De bästa vännerna i vår klass var Per och Ulf.**
The best friends in our class were Per and Ulf.

# 5 PRONOUNS

## 68 PERSONAL AND REFLEXIVE PRONOUNS – FORM

| Subject pronouns | | Object pronouns | | Reflexive pronouns | |
|---|---|---|---|---|---|
| *Singular* | | | | | |
| 1 **jag** | I | **mig** | me | **mig (mej)** | me/myself |
| 2 **du** | you | **dig** | you | **dig** | you/yourself |
| **ni** | you | **er** | you | **er** | you/yourself |
| 3 **han** | he | **honom** | him | **sig (sej)** | him/himself |
| **hon** | she | **henne** | her | **sig (sej)** | her/herself |
| **den** | it | **den** | it | **sig (sej)** | it/itself |
| **det** | it | **det** | it | **sig (sej)** | it/itself |
| *Plural* | | | | | |
| 1 **vi** | we | **oss** | us | **oss** | we/ourselves |
| 2 **ni** | you | **er** | you | **er** | you/yourselves |
| 3 **de (dom)** | they | **dem (dom)** | them | **sig (sej)** | them/themselves |

*Notes:*

1 Unlike English 'I', **jag** does not have a capital letter except at the beginning of a sentence. **Jag** is pronounced [ja] unless stressed.

2 **Du/ni**, **dig/er** etc. occasionally have capital initial letters in official communications.

3 The spoken forms **mej**, **dej**, **sej** and the use of the spoken form **dom** for both subject and object forms of the third person plural pronoun are now becoming accepted even in less formal written Swedish.

4 **Det** is pronounced [de:].

## 69 USE OF PERSONAL PRONOUNS

1 **du/ni**: In the singular most people now use the familiar **du**; **ni** is old-fashioned and may sound distant. Sometimes a person's title is used rather than a second-person pronoun (see **74**). Note also the following idiomatic expressions:

**Du, kan du hjälpa mig?**
I say/Hey there, can you give me a hand?

**Snälla du, hjälp mig!**
Will you/Please help me!

2 **han/hon**: **han** is also used to refer to so-called 'higher animals' irre-spective of their true gender. **Hon** is used to refer to the clock when telling the time and also to the noun **människa** (human being):

**Hur mycket är klockan? Hon är fyra.**
What's the time? It's four o'clock.

3 **den/det/de**: In addition to serving as personal pronouns, these words may also be used as demonstrative pronouns (see **75**).

**Det** also has a number of idiomatic usages:

(a) as a complement of **vara/bli** when the verb is followed by a noun or pronoun, irrespective of gender or number:

**Vad var det? Det var en katt/jag.** What was that? It was a cat/me.
**Vem är hon? Det är min mamma.** Who's she? She's my mum.

**Bröderna Olsson. Det är två fina killar.**
The Olsson brothers, they're a couple of fine lads.

(b) as a formal subject (see **151, 166**):

**Det är svårt att lära sig tyska.**    It's hard to learn German.
**Det finns ingen matta på golvet.**    There's no carpet on the floor.

**Det bor många svenskar här.**    There are a lot of Swedes living
here.

Note that Swedish may use **det** + any intransitive verb in this way. English generally uses only the verb 'to be'.

(c) in passive constructions without a real subject (see **118**):

**Det skrivs/pratas mycket om det där.**
There's a lot written/said about it.

**Det hörs att du inte är svensk.**
One can hear that you're not Swedish.

(d) as an impersonal subject:

**Det blåste, det snöade och det kändes mycket kallt.**
It was windy, snowing and it felt very cold.

**Det syns att han är sjuk.**
You can see he's ill.

**Hur står det till?**
How are you? / How are things going?

**Hur gick det?**
What happened?

(e) as an object of verbs expressing 'think/believe/hope/say' etc. (cf. English 'so'):

**Är han död? De fruktar/tror/hoppas/säger det.**
Is he dead? They fear/think/hope/say so.

Note also:

**Olle var hungrig. Och det var vi också.**
Olle was hungry. And so were we.

(f) in answer to questions, without an English equivalent, as a complement of **vara/bli** or an object of auxiliary verbs:

**Är du rik? Nej, det är jag inte.**
Are you rich? No, I'm not.

**Kan du svenska? Ja, det kan jag.**
Do you speak Swedish? Yes, I do.

Note also:

**Hon ser snäll ut, och det är hon.**   She looks kind, and she is too.

(g) when referring back to a whole clause:

**Han säger att han bor i Amerika, men det gör han inte.**
He says he lives in America, but he doesn't.

| *Summary of the major uses of **det**:* | | |
|---|---|---|
| *Function* | *Used with* | *English equivalent* |
| personal pronoun | any verb to refer back to neuter noun in singular | it |
| demonstrative pronoun | cf. **75** | that/it/that one |
| complement of **vara/bli** | **vara/bli** + noun/pronoun | it/he/she/they |
| formal subject | **vara/bli** + adjective | it |
| | any intransitive verb | there |
| | any passive verb | there |
| impersonal subject | impersonal verb | it |
| object | verbs expressing say/think/ hope/believe etc. | so |
| answering questions | **vara/bli** or auxiliary verb | – |
| refers back to clause or infinitive | any verb | –/it/that |

## 70  REFLEXIVE PRONOUNS

The reflexive pronoun is used when the object of a sentence or clause is also the subject. Reflexive forms are identical to object forms for all but the third person:

| | |
|---|---|
| **Jag har skurit mig.** | I have cut myself. |
| **Han har skurit sig.** | He has cut himself. |
| **Stäng dörren efter dig!** | Close the door behind you. |
| **Han stängde dörren efter sig.** | He closed the door behind him. |
| **De hade inga pengar på sig.** | They had no money on them. |

Note that the reflexive forms must be used in Swedish. There is a great deal of difference between **Han sköt honom** and **Han sköt sig!**

There is one important and frequent exception to the main rule. After verbs followed by object and infinitive constructions (see **102.3**) the reflexive pronoun idiomatically refers to the object, and the personal pronoun to the subject of the main clause:

**Han** (S) **bad doktorn** (O) **tvätta sig** (RP).
He asked the doctor to wash himself.

**Han** (S) **bad doktorn** (O) **tvätta honom** (PP).
He asked the doctor to wash him.

The reflexive pronouns are used with a number of verbs (see **115**) regarded as expressing reflexive actions in Swedish, but where the reflexive idea is absent in English:

**gifta sig** (get married), **raka sig** (have a shave)

## 71  SJÄLV

**Själv** (-t, -a) is only used for emphasis. It is not itself reflexive (cf. **70** above):

**Jag kan göra det själv.**
I can do it myself.

**Studenterna själva ordnade festen.**
The students themselves arranged the party.

**Han älskar bara sig själv.**
He only loves himself.

## 72  POSSESSIVE PRONOUNS

In Swedish the possessive pronoun and possessive adjective have the same form:

| **Boken är min.** | The book is mine. |
|---|---|
| **Det är min bok.** | It is my book. |

First and second person possessives agree with the noun:

**Det är *din* hatt, *ditt* paraply och *dina* stövlar.**

Third person possessives ending in **-s** do not inflect:

**Det är *hans* hatt, *hans* paraply och *hans* stövlar.**

Reflexive possessives are given in brackets in the following table. These forms are explained more fully in **73**.

|  | *Non-neuter* | *Neuter* | *Plural* | |
|---|---|---|---|---|
| *Singular* | | | | |
| 1 | **min** | **mitt** | **mina** | my, mine |
| 2 familiar | **din** | **ditt** | **dina** | your, yours |
| formal | **er** | **ert** | **era** | |
| 3 | **hans** | **hans** | **hans** | his |
| | **(sin** | **sitt** | **sina)** | |
| | **hennes** | **hennes** | **hennes** | her, hers |
| | **(sin** | **sitt** | **sina)** | |
| | **dess** | **dess** | **dess** | its |
| | **(sin** | **sitt** | **sina)** | |
| *Plural* | | | | |
| 1 | **vår** | **vårt** | **våra** | our, ours |
| 2 | **er** | **ert** | **era** | your, yours |
| 3 | **deras** | **deras** | **deras** | their, theirs |
| | **(sin** | **sitt** | **sina)** | |

*Notes:*

1 Possessive pronouns have no genitive form:

| **min brors böcker** | my brother's books |
|---|---|

2 Noun + 'of' before a possessive pronoun in English is usually rendered in Swedish by **till** and object pronoun (see **141.1**(c)):

| a friend of mine | **en vän till mig/en av mina vänner** |
|---|---|

3 The possessive pronoun **dess** is reserved almost exclusively for written Swedish. The definite article is often used as a Swedish equivalent to 'its':

| **Bilen tappade ett av hjulen.** | The car lost one of its wheels. |
|---|---|
| **Filmen minns jag men inte titeln.** | I recall the film but not its title. |

4 English possessive adjectives with parts of the body, clothing etc. are generally rendered by the Swedish definite article if there is no doubt as to ownership:

| **Aj! Jag har stukat foten.** | Ouch! I've twisted my ankle. |
|---|---|
| **Ta av er skorna!** | Take off your shoes! |

## 73   NON-REFLEXIVE AND REFLEXIVE POSSESSIVES: **HANS** OR **SIN**?

1 The reflexive possessives **sin/sitt/sina** (according to the gender/number of the noun qualified) refer to possession by the subject of the clause:

He loves his wife, his child and his parents.
**Han älskar *sin* fru, *sitt* barn och *sina* föräldrar.**
S ←———————|————|—————————|

**Sin/sitt/sina** cannot be used to qualify the subject of the clause:

His wife loves him.
**Hans fru älskar honom.**
S

2 The non-reflexive forms do not refer back to the subject of the clause:

| Olle is cross. Why? | Åke went out with his wife. |
|---|---|
| **Olle är sur. Varför det?** | **Åke gick ut med hans fru.** |
| S | S                   O |

The non-reflexive possessive pronouns **hans**, **hennes**, **dess**, **deras** (indeclinable) may qualify the subject or object of a clause:

| His wife is a teacher. | I've seen his wife at school. |
|---|---|
| **Hans fru är lärare.** | **Jag har sett hans fru på skolan.** |
| S | O |

There are two ways of maintaining the clear distinction necessary between the areas of usage of these different forms:

(a) Draw an arrow to the 'possessor'. Is the 'possessor' the subject of the clause?

(b) Can you insert the word 'own' before the object in English? If so, use a form of **sin/sitt/sina**. If not, then use a non-reflexive form.

3 A problem arises when there is more than one clause in the sentence:

They think that their teacher is boring.
S          /SC        S

Here 'their teacher' is the subject of the subordinate clause and 'their' does not refer back, but qualifies the subject. Therefore use **deras**.

**De tycker att deras lärare är tråkig.**
S          /SC        S

4 A confusing case occurs when the possessive precedes the subject:

Despite his appearance he was very young.
**Trots sitt utseende var han mycket ung.**
|————————————→ S

5 In ellipted (object + infinitive) clauses, when there is no finite verb in the clause, **sin/sitt/sina** may refer to the *implied subject* of the clause:

I heard her call her husband.     **Jag hörde henne ropa på sin man.**
I saw him kick his dog.           **Jag såg honom sparka sin hund.**
                                  S      IS ←——————— O

To test this, expand the ellipted clause into a full clause and apply the basic rules (see 1, 2 above):

**Jag såg att han sparkade sin hund.**
S    /SC S ←——————— O

6 Note the idiomatic use of **sin/sitt/sina** in such phrases as:

**Det är inte lätt att älska sin nästa.**
Loving your neighbour is not easy.

**Att offra sin hälsa på cigaretter är dumt.**
It's stupid to sacrifice your health for cigarettes.

7 Note the idiomatic use of **sin/sitt/sina** in abbreviated comparisons:

**Han är längre än sin fru.**        He is taller than his wife.
**Han är längre än hans fru är.**    He is taller than his wife is.

8 Note the use of **sin/sitt/sina** in expressions with **var sin** etc.:

**Vi fick var sin banan.**           We got a banana each.
**Flickorna fick var sitt äpple.**   The girls got an apple each.

Notice that **var** is indeclinable in such phrases, and that the choice of **sin/sitt/sina** is determined by the gender/number of the noun qualified.

## 74 FORMS OF ADDRESS

For personal pronouns see **68f**.

1 By far the most common forms of address in modern Swedish are **du** (you, singular) and **ni** (you, plural). There are, however, a number of alternative conventions.

2 Formal or polite **ni** is used for both singular and plural 'you' in more conservative circles, amongst older people who are not on first-name terms, and in formal business and official communications.

3 Titles: Addressing a person by his/her title and a third person construction is sometimes used to convey formal deference. (English has a similar – though far less common – construction).

**Har fröken bokat rum?**             Have you booked a room, miss?
**Skulle damen vilja prova kappan?**  Would madam like to try on the
                                      coat?

4 Impersonal constructions: Especially when asking a question, impersonal constructions provide a very neutral – but by no means unfriendly or impolite – form of address between people not personally acquainted.

| | |
|---|---|
| **Hur var namnet?** | What is your name? |
| **Vad får det lov att vara?** | What can I do for you? |
| **Önskas socker?** | Do you take/Would you like sugar? |

5 Pejorative expressions: Swedish uses the possessive not the personal pronoun in pejorative expressions such as:

| | |
|---|---|
| **Din dumbom!** | You fool! |
| **Era idioter!** | You idiots! |

Note also:

| | |
|---|---|
| **Era stackare!** | You poor things! |

A modification of this possessive construction is used when addressing royalty (cf. English):

**Eders majestät/Hans majestät har besök från ambassaden.**
Your/His Majesty has a visitor from the Embassy.

## 75   DEMONSTRATIVE PRONOUNS

| Non-neuter | Neuter | Plural |
|---|---|---|
| *den* **flickan**<br>this/that girl | *det* **huset**<br>this/that house | *de* **flickorna/husen**<br>these/those girls/houses |
| *den här* **flickan**<br>this girl | *det här* **huset**<br>this house | *de här* **flickorna/husen**<br>these girls/houses |
| *den där* **flickan**<br>*that girl* | *det där* **huset**<br>*that house* | *de där* **flickorna/husen**<br>those girls/houses |
| *denna* **flicka**⊗<br>this/that girl | *detta* **hus**⊗<br>this/that house | *dessa* **flickor**⊗**/hus**⊗<br>these/these girls/houses |
| *samma* **flicka**⊗<br>the same girl | *samma* **hus**⊗<br>the same house | *samma* **flickor**⊗**/hus**⊗<br>the same girls/houses |
| *en sådan* **flicka**⊗<br>such a girl | *ett sådant* **hus**⊗<br>such a house | *sådana* **flickor**⊗**/hus**⊗<br>such girls/houses |

*Notes:*

1 **Den** etc. is preferred with abstract nouns:

**Det året kom vi till Sverige.**       That year we arrived in Sweden.

2 **Den här, den där** etc. are found in both speech and writing, and require an end article on the noun.

3 **Denna, detta** etc. are only found in writing and have no end article.

4 As in English, the demonstratives may be used predicatively (i.e. independently of a noun). They then take the number/gender of the noun to which they refer:

**De här tavlorna är dyrare än de där.**     These pictures are more expensive than those.

**Detta är något nytt.**     This is something new.

**Jag tar det här, inte det där.**     I'll take this one, not that one.

(a) Note that **de** (these, those) has an object form when used predicatively:

**Jag tar de här skorna, inte dem.**     I'll take these shoes, not those.

(b) There is no equivalent in Swedish to English 'one' in phrases like 'this one/that one' etc.

5 **Samma** is only used attributively; **densamma** etc. is used predicatively and in more formal Swedish. There is neither front nor end article with **samma**.

6 **Sådan** is preceded by the singular indefinite article, not followed by it as in English. In colloquial Swedish it is combined with **här/där**:

**en sådan /här/ flicka**     such a girl/a girl like this

Notice:

**Jag tar fem sådana.**     I will have five of those.

**En sådan stor bil han hade!**     What a big car he had!

## 76 DETERMINATIVE PRONOUNS

| *Non-neuter* | *Neuter* | *Plural* |
|---|---|---|
| *den* flicka⊗ som | *det* hus⊗ som | *de* flickor⊗ /hus⊗ som |

1 The determinative is a kind of demonstrative that directs attention to a following relative clause. When the determinative qualifies a noun, the noun has *no* end article (cf. demonstratives **75** above):

Cf. Demonstrative:

*De turisterna* **därborta fick mycket sol.**
Those tourists over there got a lot of sun.

    Determinative:

*De turister som* **åkte till Island fick mycket sol, medan** *de turister som* **åkte till Italien fick regn varje dag.**
Those/The tourists who went to Iceland got a lot of sun, whilst those/the tourists who went to Italy had rain every day.

2 Determinatives are used when the following relative clause is essential to the sentence ('restrictive clause'). Notice that a contrast is often implied. If the relative clause is merely an afterthought and may be deleted ('non-restrictive clause'), then a demonstrative or an end article may be used:

Cf.

**De fabriker som anställer ungdomar bör hjälpas.** (restrictive)
/Only/ those firms employing young people should be helped.

**/De/ fabrikerna som anställer ungdomar bör hjälpas.**
The firms, which employ young people, should be helped.

3 When the determinative is used without a noun **de som** is now accepted as an object form for **dem som**:

**Jag kände ingen av de som/dem som var där.**
I knew none of those who were there.

**Samhället straffar de som/dem som bryter mot lagen.**
Society punishes those who break the law.

## 77   RELATIVE PRONOUNS

Relative pronouns introduce a subordinate (relative) clause, referring back to a correlative in the main clause:

**Han är en vän     som man kan lita på.**
    *correlative* ←——┘
He is a friend whom one can rely on.

Relative pronouns include:

| | | |
|---|---|---|
| **som** | – the most frequent relative pronoun | which, who, what |
| **vars** | – genitive of **som**, sing. and plural (written only) | whose |
| **vilkas** | – genitive of **som**, plural only (written only) | whose |
| **vilken** n-n. | | |
| **vilket** n. | = **som** | who, which, what |
| **vilka** pl. | | |
| **vad** | | what |

Examples of use:

**Ser du pojken som leker därborta?**
Do you see the boy who is playing over there?

**Mannen, vars dotter ska gifta sig, är sjuk.**
The man whose daughter is getting married is ill.

**Föräldrarna, vars/vilkas dotter ska gifta sig, är sjuka.**
The parents whose daughter is getting married are ill.

**Det är allt, vad jag vet.**
That's all that I know.

*Notes:*

1 **Vilken** etc. is rarely used other than in formal Swedish, but note that **vilket** (*not* **som**) must be used to refer back to a whole clause:

**Hon ska bli student, vilket gläder mig.**    She's going to be a student, which
                                                pleases me.

2 **Som** may be omitted when it does not serve as a subject in a subordinate clause:

**Han är den intelligentaste student /som/ jag har träffat.**
              O                              S
He's the most intelligent student /that/ I've met.

But:

**Ser du pojken som står därborta?**
                S
Can you see the boy /who is/ standing over there?

3 In contrast to English, a preposition does not appear in the same clause directly before **som**:

**Den man som du pratar om ...**         The man of whom you speak ...

4 When used as the subject of a relative clause **vad** is followed by **som** (See **78.4**):

**Vi vet inte vad som hände honom.**     We don't know what happened to him.
              S

# 78  INTERROGATIVE PRONOUNS (**V**-WORDS)

Interrogative pronouns introduce a direct or indirect question.

Interrogative pronouns (**v**-words) include:

| | |
|---|---|
| **vem, vilka** | who (sg.), who (pl.) |
| **vad** [vɑːd] or [va] | what |
| **vad ... för något/någonting** | what |
| (spoken Swedish) | |
| **vilken** n-n. ⎫ | |
| **vilket** n.     ⎬ | which |
| **vilka** pl.   ⎭ | |
| **när** | when |
| **var** | where |
| **hur** | how |
| **varför** | why |

*Notes:*

1 When rendering English 'who' remember that **vem** is only used in the singular, **vilka** is only used in the plural:

**Vem var det som ringde?**        Who was it that phoned?
**Vilka är det som kommer ikväll?**   Who are coming tonight?

2 'What kind of' is often rendered in spoken Swedish by **vad för en/ett** + singular noun or **vad för** + plural noun:

| | |
|---|---|
| **Vad köpte du för /en/ bil?** | What kind of car did you buy? |
| **Vad köpte du för /ett/ hus?** | What kind of house did you buy? |
| **Vad köpte du för böcker?** | What kind of books did you buy? |

3 **Vilken** etc. may be used attributively and predicatively:

| | |
|---|---|
| **Vilken dikt har ni läst?** | Which poem have you read? |
| **Vilken vill du läsa nu?** | Which one do you want to read now? |

4 Notice that **som** is inserted after **vad, vilken** etc. + noun when this is the subject of a subordinate clause (indirect question):

| | |
|---|---|
| **Jag undrar** *vad* **(O)** *han* **(S) gör.** | I wonder what he's doing. |
| **Jag undrar** *vad* **(O) som (S) händer.** | I wonder what's happening. |
| **Jag undrar** *vem som* **(S) kommer.** | I wonder who's coming. |
| **Jag undrar** *vilka böcker* **(S) som är dina.** | I wonder which books are yours. |

5 Notice the use of **vilken** etc. in exclamations:

| | |
|---|---|
| **Vilken härlig dag!** | What a lovely day! |
| **Vilket dåligt väder!** | What awful weather! |

6 Notice other interrogatives using **hur**: **hur länge?** (how long?); **hur långt?** (how far?); **hur mycket?** (how much?); **hur många** (how many?); **hur dags?** (what time?)

## 79   INDEFINITE PRONOUNS

Indefinite pronouns include:

| *Non-neuter* | *Neuter* | *Plural* | |
|---|---|---|---|
| **någon** | **något** | **några** | some, any, someone, anything |
| **ingen** | **inget** | **inga** | no, none, no-one, nothing |
| **all** | **allt** | **alla** | all, everything |
| **varje** | **varje** | | each, every |
| **varenda** | **vartenda** | | each and every |
| **var** | **vart** | | each, every |
| **var och en** | **vart och ett** | | each and every one |
| **varannan** | **vartannat** | **varandra** | every other, each other |
| **vem som helst** | **vad som helst** | **vilka som helst** | anyone at all, anything at all |

| | | |
|---|---|---|
| **man** | | one, you |
| Possessive form of **man**: | **ens** | one's |
| Object form of **man**: | **en** | one, you |
| Reflexive form of **man**: | **sig** | oneself See **70** |
| Reflexive possessive form of **man**: | **sin** | one's own See **73** |

Note also the pronominal adverbs:

**någonsin**                                        sometime, ever
**någonstans**                                      somewhere

*Notes:*

1 (a) **Ingen** etc./**inte någon** etc. are alternatives as object in a main clause with simple tense (present, past):

**De** (S) **såg** *ingen/inte någon* (O) **i skogen.**    They saw no-one in the forest.

(b) **Inte någon** etc. must be used as the object in a main clause with complex tense (perfect, pluperfect, modal + main verb) or in a subordinate clause. When **inte någon** constructions are found in the subordinate clause, **inte** precedes the finite verb (see also **164**):

**Jag har** *inte* **sett** *någon* (O) **i skogen.**     I haven't seen anyone in the forest.
**Jag kan** *inte* **se** *någon* (O).                    I can't see anyone.

**De sa, att de** *inte* **hade sett** *någon* (O) **i skogen.**
They said that they hadn't seen anyone in the forest.

2(a) **All** etc. may be used with or without an end article on the noun following in much the same way as in English:

**Alla böcker är dyra.**                            All books are expensive.
**Alla böckerna hade sålts.**                       All the books had been sold.

(b) English 'all' = 'the whole (of)' is usually rendered by **hela** + the noun with end article singular:

**Har du läst hela boken?**                         Have you read all the book?

(c) **Allt** corresponds to 'everything'; **alla** corresponds to 'everyone':

**Han berättade allt för alla.**                    He told everyone everything.

3(a) **Varje**, **var** and **vart** are synonymous but not always interchangeable: **varje** is common in spoken Swedish, and is used pronominally only after a preposition:

**Fem påsar med 12 kg i varje.**                    Five bags with 12 kilos in each.

(b) **Var/vart** is preferred before ordinals:

**Han kommer var tredje vecka.**
He comes every third week/every three weeks.

4(a) **Varenda/vartenda** and **var och en/vart och ett** are more emphatic than **varje/var**. **Varenda** is used attributively before the indefinite form of the noun:

**Vartenda fel ska rättas.**                        Every single error must be corrected.

(b) **Var och en** is used predicatively, but is often followed by **av** + plural noun or pronoun:

**Var och en gick hem till sig.**                   Each one /of us/ went home.
**Var och en av bilarna var rostig.**               Every single one of the cars was rusty.

5 **Varandra** is restricted in meaning to 'one another/each other':

**Vi känner inte varandra.**                    We don't know each other.

6(a) **Man** is used far more commonly in Swedish than the rather stilted English 'one'. It occasionally replaces **jag**. Note the form **en** used as an object or after prepositions:

**Man vet aldrig vad som kan hända en.**
You never know what might happen to you.

(b) The possessive forms **ens** and **sin/sitt/sina** are non-reflexive and reflexive respectively (cf. **73**):

**Ens ord kan missförstås.**                    One's words may be misunderstood.
**Man måste göra sin plikt.**                    One must do one's duty.

# 6 NUMERALS

**80** CARDINAL AND ORDINAL NUMBERS

| | *Cardinal numbers* | *Ordinal numbers* |
|---|---|---|
| 0 | **noll** | |
| 1 | **ett/en** | **första** |
| 2 | **två** | **andra** |
| 3 | **tre** | **tredje** |
| 4 | **fyra** | **fjärde** |
| 5 | **fem** | **femte** |
| 6 | **sex** | **sjätte** |
| 7 | **sju** | **sjunde** |
| 8 | **åtta** | **åttonde** |
| 9 | **nio** [niːɷ] or [niːə] | **nionde** |
| 10 | **tio** [tiːɷ] or [tiːə] | **tionde** |
| 11 | **elva** | **elfte** |
| 12 | **tolv** | **tolfte** |
| 13 | **tretton** | **trettonde** |
| 14 | **fjorton** [fjɷːtɔn] | **fjortonde** |
| 15 | **femton** | **femtonde** |
| 16 | **sexton** | **sextonde** |
| 17 | **sjutton** | **sjuttonde** |
| 18 | **arton** | **artonde** |
| 19 | **nitton** | **nittonde** |
| 20 | **tjugo** [ɕʉːgɷ], [ɕʉːgu] or [ɕʉːgi] | **tjugonde** |
| 21 | **tjugoett (tjugoen)** | **tjugoförsta** |
| 22 | **tjugotvå** | **tjugoandra** |
| 30 | **trettio** | **trettionde** |
| 40 | **fyrti/o/** [føti] | **fyrtionde** |
| 50 | **femti/o/** | **femtionde** |
| 60 | **sexti/o/** | **sextionde** |
| 70 | **sjutti/o/** | **sjuttionde** |
| 80 | **åtti/o/** | **åttionde** |
| 90 | **nitti/o/** | **nittionde** |
| 100 | **/ett/hundra** | **hundrade** |
| 101 | **/ett/ hundraett (-en)** | **hundraförsta** |
| 1 000 | **/ett/tusen** | **tusende** |
| 1 001 | **/ett/ tusenett (-en)** | **tusenförsta** |

| | | |
|---|---|---|
| 1 000 000 | **en miljon** | **miljonte** |
| 1 000 000 000 | **en miljard** | |

*Notes:*

1 **Miljon, miljard** have plurals in **-er**.

2 **-en** is used before non-neuter nouns: **tjugoen bilar** cf. **tjugoett hus, hundraen bilar**
BUT: **ett hundra hus/ett hundra bilar**

3 423 = **fyrahundratjugotre** = four hundred *and* twenty-three

## 81   MAJOR USES OF CARDINAL AND ORDINAL NUMBERS

1 Cardinal numbers as nouns

(a) **En etta, en tvåa, en trea** etc.:

| | |
|---|---|
| (i)   The number itself, position in a race: | **Hon kom tvåa.** |
| (ii)  Bus, tram number: | **Det är en femtifyra.** |
| (iii) Size of flat (number of rooms): | **De har en trea i Åby.** |
| (iv)  Size of clothes, shoes: | **Fyrtiettorna passar bäst.** |

(b) **En femma, en tia**:   A five-kronor coin/ten-kronor coin.

2 Ordinal numbers

(a) Ordinal numbers are frequently found after the front article, possessive adjective or noun in the genitive:

**Det är den första idag.** (i.e. first of the month)
**Det är Olles tredje bil. Hon är min andra fru.**

(b) **1:a, 2:a, 3:e** etc. are common abbreviations for **första, andra, tredje** etc. In Swedish the number alone is often sufficient to indicate an ordinal:

| | |
|---|---|
| **måndagen 4 juni** | = **måndagen den fjärde juni** |
| **3 pers. sing.** | = **tredje person singularis** |

3 Fractions, decimals etc.

Fractions are largely formed from ordinal numbers by adding **-del**:

¼ = **en fjärdedel**, ⅗ = **tre femtedelar** etc.

Note that the **-de** of ordinals ending in **-onde** is assimilated:

| | |
|---|---|
| ⅛ | **en åttondel** |
| ⅒ | **en tiondel** etc. |
| ½ | **en halv** |
| 1½ | **en och en halv/halvannan** – (in e.g. **halvannan timme**) |
| | **ett och ett halvt/halvtannat** – (in e.g. **halvtannat år**) |
| 2½ | **två och en halv** |

| | | |
|---|---|---|
| ⅔ | **två tredjedelar** | |
| ¼ | **en fjärdedel** | |
| ⅕ | **en femtedel** | |
| ⅙ | **en niondel** | |
| 3,5 | **tre komma fem** | English 3.5 |
| 3 000 | **tretusen** | English 3,000 |
| 3 000 000 | **tre miljoner** | English 3,000,000 |

Half = **halv** (**-t, -a**) i.e. an adjective which inflects:

| | |
|---|---|
| **en halv sida** | half a page |
| **halva sidan** | half the page |
| **ett halvt äpple** | half an apple |
| **fem och ett halvt år** | five and a half years |
| **två och ett halvt äpple** | two and a half apples |

Notice    (i) The word order in Swedish in e.g. **en halv sida**
(ii) Half past one = **halv två** (see **82**)

4 **-tal**: Neuter nouns may be formed by adding **-tal** to cardinal numbers to render:

(a)  An approximate number:

**Ett hundratal brev har sänts ut.**
A hundred or so letters have been sent out.

**Tusentals sjöfåglar dödades.**
Thousands of seabirds were killed.

(b)  A decade or century:

**Almqvist är en författare från 1800-talet.**
Almqvist is an author from the 19th century.

**EU på 90-talet**
the EU in the /19/90s

**Lagerlöf debuterade på 90-talet.**
Lagerlof made her debut in the /18/90s.

5 Dates

(a) Years are usually given in figures, but if written out in full are written as one word. The word **hundra** is not omitted in spoken or written Swedish but there is no **och** between the hundreds and tens:

1984                                        **nittonhundraåttifyra**

(b) The English preposition 'in' before years has no equivalent in Swedish (see **138**):

**Han är född /år/ 1944.**          He was born in 1944.

(c) Days of the month: see 2(b) above.

6 Telephone numbers. The digits are frequently given in pairs:

**12 34 56**                              **tolv trettifyra femtisex**

7 Temperature

− 5°C          **Det är fem grader kallt** or: **Det är minus fem grader.**
+ 15°C        **Det är femton grader /varmt/** or: **Det är plus femton /grader/.**

8 Money:

**3:00**          **tre kronor**
**3:50**          **tre och femti/tre kronor och femti öre**

## 82   TIME BY THE CLOCK

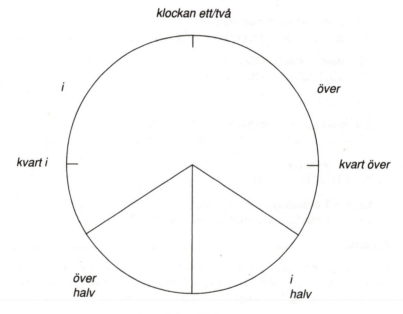

*halv ett/två*

(a) What is the time? etc.

| | |
|---|---|
| **Hur mycket är klockan?** | What time is it? |
| **Vad är klockan?** | |
| **Klockan/Hon är ett/tolv.** | It is one o'clock/twelve o'clock |
| **Klockan är en minut över/i ett.** | It is one minute past/to one. |
| **Klockan är fem /minuter/ över tre.** | It is five/minutes/past three. |
| **Klockan är /en/ kvart över fyra.** | It is/a/quarter past four. |
| **Klockan är fem /minuter/ i halv sex.** | It is 25 past five. |
| **Klockan är halv sex.** | It is half past five. |
| **Klockan är fem /minuter/ över halv sex.** | It is 25/minutes/to six. |

(b) 'What time ...?' etc.

| | |
|---|---|
| **Hur dags/När går tåget?** | What time does the train leave? |
| **Klockan tre.** | At three o'clock. |
| **Klockan fem och fyrtifem.** | At five forty-five. |
| **Klockan kvart i sex.** | At a quarter to six. |
| **kl. 05.45 (/noll/ fem fyrtifem)** | /At/ 05.45 (in timetables etc.) |

*Notes:*

1 'Half past' an hour in English is always expressed as 'half to' the next hour in Swedish:

| | |
|---|---|
| **halv fem** | half past four |
| **halv ett** | half past twelve |

2 Swedes have a special way of expressing time in the period between 21 minutes past the hour and 21 minutes to the hour (see clock diagram):

| | |
|---|---|
| **sex minuter i halv fyra** | 3.24 |
| **tre minuter över halv två** | 1.33 |

3 The word **minuter** is often omitted, but as a general rule it is best retained.

# 7 VERBS

## 83 VERB FORMS IN OUTLINE

In modern Swedish there is only one form for all persons, singular and plural, in each of the various tenses of the verb (cf., however **90** Note 2).

Swedish has no continuous form of the verb (cf. **106.3**) but, like English, employs auxiliary verbs to help form the future, perfect and pluperfect tenses (**108**ff).

For learning purposes it is a convenient simplification to consider the formation of the tenses as the addition of an ending to the basic part of the verb – the *stem* (see below).

There are four principal types or conjugations of Swedish verbs. Conjugations I, II and III are *weak* conjugations, forming the past tense by the addition of an ending, and all their forms can be built up simply on the basis of their infinitive/present forms. Conjugation IV is *strong*, forming its past tense by changing the stem vowel. The table summarizes generalized endings for each conjugation and tense:

| Conjugation | Imperative | Infinitive | Present | |
|---|---|---|---|---|
| | = stem | =stem + a/⊗ | =stem + **er/r** | |
| I | **arbeta** | **arbeta** | **arbetar** | work |
| IIa | **ring** | **ringa** | **ringer** | ring |
| IIb | **köp** | **köpa** | **köper** | buy |
| III | **sy** | **sy** | **syr** | sew |
| IV | **bit** | **bita** | **biter** | bite |
| | **bjud** | **bjuda** | **bjuder** | invite |

| Conjugation | Past | Supine |
|---|---|---|
| | stem + **de/te/dde** | stem + **t/tt** |
| I | **arbetade** | **arbetat** |
| IIa | **ringde** | **ringt** |
| IIb | **köpte** | **köpt** |
| III | **sydde** | **sytt** |
| IV | stem with *vowel change* | stem with *vowel change* + **it** |
| | **bet** | **bitit** |
| | **bjöd** | **bjudit** |

| Conjugation | Present participle | Past participle |
|---|---|---|
| | stem + (a)nde/ende | stem + d/t/dd/en |
| I | arbeta*nde* | arbeta*d* |
| IIa | ring*ande* | ring*d* |
| IIb | köp*ande* | köp*t* |
| III | sy*ende* | sy*dd* |
| IV | bit*ande* | bit*en* |
| | bjud*ande* | bjud*en* |

# THE FOUR CONJUGATIONS

## 84 FIRST CONJUGATION

| Infinitive | Present | Past | Supine | Past participle | |
|---|---|---|---|---|---|
| + ⊗ | +r | +de | +t | +d | |
| arbeta | arbetar | arbeta*de* | arbeta*t* | arbeta*d* | work |
| studera | studerar | studera*de* | studera*t* | studera*d* | study |

Includes: two-thirds of all verbs (a quarter of all active verbs) and all new verbs, e.g. **jobba** (work), **lifta** (hitch), **parkera** (park), **nationalisera** (nationalize).

Some very frequent conjugation I verbs are:

**berätta** (tell), **bruka** (use), **börja** (begin), **fråga** (ask), **förklara** (explain), **handla** (shop), **kalla** (call), **kosta** (cost), **lämna** (leave), **mena** (think, mean), **spela** (play), **svara** (answer), **tala** (speak), **verka** (seem), **visa** (show), **öka** (increase), **öppna** (open).

## 85 IRREGULAR VERBS OF THE FIRST CONJUGATION

Irregular forms are marked * Forms within brackets ( ) are less common.

| Infinitive | Present | Past | Supine | Past participle | |
|---|---|---|---|---|---|
| besluta | beslutar/ | beslutade/ | beslutat/ | beslutad/ | decide |
| | besluter | beslöt | beslutit | besluten | |
| betala | betalar | betalade | betalt* | betald* | pay |
| | | (betalde) | (betalat) | (betalad) | |
| koka | kokar/ | kokade/ | kokat/ | kokad/ | boil |
| | | kokte | kokt | kokt | |

## 86 SECOND CONJUGATION

The second conjugation is divided into two types:

IIa – past tense in **-de**, stem in voiced consonant

IIb – past tense in **-te**, stem in voiceless consonant (i.e. **-k/-p/-s/-t/-x**) and in **-n**

IIa

| Infinitive | Present | Past | Supine | Past participle | |
|------------|---------|------|--------|-----------------|---|
| +a | +er | +de | +t | +d | |
| följ*a* | följ*er* | följ*de* | följ*t* | följ*d* | follow |
| bygg*a* | bygg*er* | bygg*de* | bygg*t* | bygg*d* | build |

The following patterns vary slightly from the main paradigm:

1 Stem in **-r**. No ending in present tense:

| kör*a* | kör | kör*de* | kör*t* | kör*d* | drive |
|--------|-----|---------|--------|--------|-------|

Like **köra**: **lära** (learn), **höra** (hear), **röra** (move), **störa** (disturb), **begära** (demand), **föra** (lead), **hyra** (rent).

2 Stem in *-vowel* + **d**. Doubling of final consonant in supine and past participle:

| betyd*a* | betyd*er* | betyd*de* | betyt*t* | betyd*d* | mean |
|----------|-----------|-----------|----------|----------|------|

Like **betyda**: **föda** (feed/bear), **träda** (step), **antyda** (hint), **lyda** (obey).

3 Stem in *-consonant* + **d**. Add only **-e** in past tense:

| använd*a* | använd*er* | använd*e* | använt | använd | use |
|-----------|------------|-----------|--------|--------|-----|

Like **använda**: **tända** (light), **sända** (send), **hända** (happen)

4 Stem in **-l**. No ending in present tense:

| tål*a* | tål | tål*de* | tål*t* | tål*d* | put up with |
|--------|-----|---------|--------|--------|-------------|

Like **tåla**: **mala** (grind)

5 Stem in **-mm**. Single **m** before consonant or in final position. See **177**:

| glömm*a* | glömm*er* | glöm*de* | glöm*t* | glöm*d* | forget |
|----------|-----------|----------|---------|---------|--------|

Like **glömma**: **drömma** (dream), **gömma** (hide), **skrämma** (frighten)

6 Stem in **-nn**. Single **n** before consonant. See **177**:

| känn*a* | känn*er* | kän*de* | kän*t* | kän*d* | know |
|---------|----------|---------|--------|--------|------|

Like **känna**: **bränna** (burn), **påminna** (remind)

7 Stem in *mutated vowel* + **j**. Mutation and **j** in infinitive, present tense only:

| välj*a* | välj*er* | val*de* | val*t* | val*d* | choose |
|---------|----------|---------|--------|--------|--------|
| dölj*a* | dölj*er* | dol*de* | dol*t* | dol*d* | conceal |

Like **välja**: **vänja** (get used to), **svälja** (swallow)

Like **dölja**: **spörja** (ask), **smörja** (lubricate)

Notice also:

| | | | | | |
|---|---|---|---|---|---|
| **skilj**a | **skilj**er | **skil**de | **skil**t | **skil**d | separate |

8 Infinitive, present only in *mutated vowel*:

| | | | | | |
|---|---|---|---|---|---|
| **bö**ra | **bö**r | **bor**de | **bor**t | – | ought, should |

Like **böra**: **töra** (be likely)

IIb

| *Infinitive* | *Present* | *Past* | *Supine* | *Past participle* | |
|---|---|---|---|---|---|
| +a | +er | +te | +t | +t | |
| **köp**a | **köp**er | **köp**te | **köp**t | **köp**t | buy |
| **tryck**a | **tryck**er | **tryck**te | **tryck**t | **tryck**t | press |

The following patterns vary slightly from the main paradigm:

1 Stem in *-vowel* + **t**. Doubling of final consonant in supine and past participle:

| | | | | | |
|---|---|---|---|---|---|
| **möt**a | **möt**er | **möt**te | **möt**t | **möt**t | meet |

Like **möta**: **byta** (exchange), **mäta** (measure), **sköta** (look after)

2 Stem in *-consonant* + **t**. Add only **-e** in past tense, no ending in supine and past participle:

| | | | | | |
|---|---|---|---|---|---|
| **gift**a | **gift**er | **gift**e | **gift** | **gift** | marry |

Like **gifta**: **mista** (lose), **lyfta** (lift), **smälta** (melt), **fästa** (attach)

## 87   IRREGULAR VERBS OF THE SECOND CONJUGATION

Irregular forms are marked *

| *Infinitive* | *Present* | *Past* | *Supine* | *Past participle* | |
|---|---|---|---|---|---|
| **bringa***  | **bringar*** | **bragte** | **bragt** | **bragt** | bring about |
| **glädja** | **gläder*** | **gladde*** | **glatt*** | – | please |
| **göra*** | **gör*** | **gjorde** | **gjort** | **gjord** | do, make |
| **ha** | **har*** | **hade** | **haft*** | **-havd*** | have |
| **heta** | **heter** | **hette** | **hetat*** | – | be called |
| **kunna** | **kan*** | **kunde** | **kunnat*** | – | can, be able |
| **lägga** | **lägger** | **la/de/*** | **lagt*** | **lagd*** | lay (tr.) |
| – | **måste** | **måste** | **måst** | – | must |
| **skola*** | **ska/ll/*** | **skulle** | **skolat*** | – | shall |

| | | | | | |
|---|---|---|---|---|---|
| stödja* | stöder | stödde | stött | stödd | support |
| säga | säger | sa/de/* | sagt* | sagd* | say |
| sälja | säljer | sålde* | sålt* | såld* | sell |
| sätta | sätter | satte* | satt* | satt* | place |
| (varda) | – | vart* | – | – | become |
| veta* | vet* | visste | vetat* | – | know |
| vilja* | vill* | ville | velat* | – | want |
| växa | växer | växte | växt/ vuxit | vuxen* | grow |

## 88   THIRD CONJUGATION

| Infinitive | Present | Past | Supine | Past participle | |
|---|---|---|---|---|---|
| -vowel (not **a**) | +r | +dde | +tt | +dd | |
| sy | syr | sydde | sytt | sydd | sew |
| bo | bor | bodde | bott | -bodd | live |

Includes: most verbs with stems ending in a long stressed vowel other than **-a**. The stem vowel is shortened before the past tense ending in **-dde** and supine ending in **-tt**. This is a small and non-productive group. Vowels involved are:

- **-e**   ske (occur), **bete** (behave)
- **-o**   tro (believe), **ro** (row), **bero** (depend)
- **-y**   bry (care), **fly** (flee), **avsky** (hate), **gry** (dawn)
- **-ö**   strö (strew)
- **-ä**   klä (dress)
- **-å**   rå (be able to, manage)

*Note:* Several verbs of this group possess longer forms which are now formal or archaic:

| Infinitive | | Present | | | |
|---|---|---|---|---|---|
| klä | (kläda) | klär | (kläder) | dress | |
| bre | (breda) | brer | (breder) | spread | |
| spä | (späda) | spär | (späder) | dilute | |
| trä | (träda) | trär | (träder) | step | |

## 89   IRREGULAR VERBS OF THE THIRD CONJUGATION

Irregular forms are marked *

| Infinitive | Present | Past | Supine | Past participle | |
|---|---|---|---|---|---|
| be | ber | bad* | bett | -bedd | ask |
| dö | dör | dog* | dött | – | die |
| få | får | fick* | fått | – | get |
| ge | ger | gav* | gett/givit | given | give |

| gå | går | gick* | gått | -gången | walk, go |
|----|-----|-------|------|---------|----------|
| le | ler | log*  | lett | –       | smile    |
| se | ser | såg*  | sett | sedd    | see      |
| stå | står | stod* | stått | stådd  | stand    |

*Note:* Two verbs of this group possess longer forms which are now formal or archaic:

| *Infinitive* | | *Present* | |
|--------------|--|-----------|--|
| ge | (giva) | ger | (giver) |
| be | (bedja) | ber | (beder) |

## 90 FOURTH CONJUGATION: INTRODUCTION

| *Infinitive* | *Present* | *Past* | *Supine* | *Past participle* | |
|--------------|-----------|--------|----------|-------------------|--|
| -a | -er | Vowel change | Vowel change + it | -en | |
| dricka | dricker | drack | druckit | drucken | drink |

This conjugation includes only strong verbs, i.e. those whose past tense is formed not by adding an ending but by changing the stem vowel. This vowel change often applies also to the supine:

| flyga | flyger | flög | flugit | flugen | fly |
|-------|--------|------|--------|--------|-----|

Strong verbs are best learned individually, but many follow the same vowel change sequence or gradation series. The vowel is often the same in the infinitive/present and supine/past participle and forms are largely predictable.

*Notes:*

1 Several strong verbs in this group possess longer forms now formal or archaic:

| *Infinitive* | | *Present* | | |
|--------------|--|-----------|--|--|
| dra | (draga) | drar | (drager) | pull |
| ta | (taga) | tar | (tager) | take |
| bli | (bliva) | blir | (bliver) | be, become |

2 The past tense of strong verbs until the 1900s possessed a separate plural form in written Swedish which often had a different stem vowel from the singular. These forms (given in brackets) have now almost entirely fallen out of use:

**blev (blevo), bjöd (bjödo), fann (funno), bar (buro), bad (bådo), var (voro).**

## 91 FOURTH CONJUGATION: GRADATION SERIES i – e – i

Irregular forms are marked *

| *Infinitive* | *Present* | *Past* | *Supine* | *Past participle* | |
|--------------|-----------|--------|----------|-------------------|--|
| bita | biter | bet | bitit | biten | bite |
| bli* | blir* | blev | blivit | bliven | be, become |
| driva | driver | drev | drivit | driven | drive, drift |

| | | | | | |
|---|---|---|---|---|---|
| glida | glider | gled | glidit | – | glide |
| gnida | gnider | gned | gnidit | gniden | rub |
| kliva | kliver | klev | klivit | -kliven | step, climb |
| knipa | kniper | knep | knipit | – | pinch |
| kvida | kvider | kved | kvidit | – | whimper |
| lida | lider | led | lidit | liden | suffer |
| niga | niger | neg | nigit | – | curtsy |
| pipa | piper | pep | pipit | – | chirp |
| rida | rider | red | ridit | riden | ride |
| riva | river | rev | rivit | riven | tear |
| skina | skiner | sken | skinit | – | shine |
| skrida | skrider | skred | skridit | skriden | glide |
| skrika | skriker | skrek | skrikit | – | shout |
| skriva | skriver | skrev | skrivit | skriven | write |
| slita | sliter | slet | slitit | sliten | wear out |
| smita | smiter | smet | smitit | – | run away |
| sprida | sprider | spred | spritt* | spridd* | spread |
| stiga | stiger | steg | stigit | stigen | step, climb |
| strida | strider | stred | stritt* | stridd* | struggle |
| svida | svider | sved | svidit | – | smart |
| svika | sviker | svek | svikit | sviken | fail, desert |
| tiga | tiger | teg | tigit | -tegen* | be silent |
| vika | viker | vek | vikit | viken | fold, yield |
| vina | viner | ven | vinit | – | whine |
| vrida | vrider | vred | vridit | vriden | twist |

## 92    FOURTH CONJUGATION: GRADATION SERIES y/(j)u – ö – u

Irregular forms are marked *

| Infinitive | Present | Past | Supine | Past participle | |
|---|---|---|---|---|---|
| bjuda | bjuder | bjöd | bjudit | bjuden | invite |
| bryta | bryter | bröt | brutit | bruten | break |
| drypa | dryper | dröp | drupit/ drypt* | – | drip |
| duga | duger | dög | dugt* | – | be suitable |
| dyka | dyker | dök | dykt* | – | dive |
| flyga | flyger | flög | flugit | flugen | fly |
| flyta | flyter | flöt | flutit | -fluten | float |
| frysa | fryser | frös | frusit | frusen | freeze (itr), be cold |
| cf. | fryser | fryste | fryst | -fryst | freeze (tr) |
| gjuta | gjuter | göt* | gjutit | gjuten | cast (metal) |

| | | | | | |
|---|---|---|---|---|---|
| hugga | hugger | högg | huggit | huggen | chop |
| klyva | klyver | klöv | kluvit | kluven | cleave, split |
| knyta | knyter | knöt | knutit | knuten | tie, knot |
| krypa | kryper | kröp | krupit | krupen | creep |
| ljuda | ljuder | ljöd | ljudit | – | sound |
| ljuga | ljuger | ljög | ljugit | -ljugen | tell a lie |
| njuta | njuter | njöt | njutit | njuten | enjoy |
| nypa | nyper | nöp/ (nypte)* | nupit/ (nypt)* | nupen | pinch |
| nysa | nyser | nös | nyst* | – | sneeze |
| rysa | ryser | rös | ryst* | – | shudder |
| ryta | ryter | röt | rutit | – | roar |
| sjuda | sjuder | sjöd | sjudit | sjuden | simmer |
| sjunga | sjunger | sjöng | sjungit | sjungen | sing |
| sjunka | sjunker | sjönk | sjunkit | sjunken | sink (itr) |
| skjuta | skjuter | sköt* | skjutit | skjuten | shoot |
| skryta | skryter | skröt | skrutit | -skruten | boast |
| sluta | sluter | slöt | slutit | sluten | close |
| cf. | slutar | slutade | slutat | -slutad | end |
| smyga | smyger | smög | smugit | -smugen | slink |
| snyta | snyter | snöt | snutit | snuten | blow one's nose |
| stryka | stryker | strök | strukit | struken | stroke |
| suga | suger | sög | sugit | sugen | suck |
| supa | super | söp | supit | -supen | drink |
| tjuta | tjuter | tjöt | tjutit | – | howl |
| tryta | tryter | tröt | trutit | – | run short |

## 93  FOURTH CONJUGATION: GRADATION SERIES i – a – u

| Infinitive | Present | Past | Supine | Past participle | |
|---|---|---|---|---|---|
| binda | binder | band | bundit | bunden | bind, tie |
| brinna | brinner | brann | brunnit | brunnen | burn (itr) |
| brista | brister | brast | brustit | brusten | burst |
| dricka | dricker | drack | druckit | drucken | drink |
| finna | finner | fann | funnit | funnen | find |
| finnas | finns | fanns | funnits | – | be (located) |
| försvinna | försvinner | försvann | försvunnit | försvunnen | disappear |
| hinna | hinner | hann | hunnit | – | have time |
| rinna | rinner | rann | runnit | runnen | run, flow |
| sitta | sitter | satt | suttit | -sutten | sit |
| slinka | slinker | slank | slunkit | – | slink |
| slinta | slinter | slant | (sluntit) | – | slip |

| slippa | slipper | slapp | sluppit | -sluppen | avoid |
|--------|---------|-------|---------|----------|-------|
| spinna | spinner | spann | spunnit | spunnen | spin, purr |
| spricka | spricker | sprack | spruckit | sprucken | crack, burst |
| springa | springer | sprang | sprungit | sprungen | run |
| spritta | spritter | spratt | (spruttit) | – | give a start |
| sticka | sticker | stack | stuckit | stucken | sting |
| cf. | stickar | stickade | stickat | stickad | knit |
| stinka | stinker | stank | – | – | stink |
| vinna | vinner | vann | vunnit | vunnen | win |

## 94    FOURTH CONJUGATION: GRADATION SERIES a̲ – o̲ – a̲

Irregular forms are marked *

| Infinitive | Present | Past | Supine | Past participle | |
|------------|---------|------|--------|-----------------|------|
| dra* | drar* | drog | dragit | dragen | pull |
| fara | far* | for | farit | faren | travel |
| gala | gal* | gol | galt/galit | – | crow |
| ta* | tar* | tog | tagit | tagen | take |

## 95    FOURTH CONJUGATION: GRADATION SERIES ä̲ – a̲ – u̲

Irregular forms are marked *

| Infinitive | Present | Past | Supine | Past participle | |
|------------|---------|------|--------|-----------------|------------|
| bära | bär* | bar | burit | buren | carry |
| skära | skär* | skar | skurit | skuren | cut |
| stjäla* | stjäl* | stal | stulit | stulen | steal |
| svälta | svälter | svalt | svultit | svulten | starve (itr) |
| cf. | | svälte | svält | svält | starve (tr) |

## 96    FOURTH CONJUGATION: MINOR GRADATION SERIES (MIXED)

| Infinitive | Present | Past | Supine | Past participle | |
|------------|---------|------|--------|-----------------|-------|
| falla | faller | föll | fallit | fallen | fall |
| gråta | gråter | grät | gråtit | -gråten | weep |
| hålla | håller | höll | hållit | hållen | hold |
| komma | kommer | kom | kommit | kommen | come |
| ligga | ligger | låg | legat* | -legad* | lie |
| låta | låter | lät | låtit | -låten | allow |
| slå | slår | slog | slagit | slagen | hit |
| slåss | slåss | slogs | slagits | – | fight |

| sova | sover | sov | sovit | – | sleep |
|------|-------|-----|-------|---|-------|
| svära | svär | svor | svurit | svuren | swear |
| vara | är* | var | varit | – | be |
| äta | äter | åt | ätit | -äten | eat |

# PARTICIPLES AND SUPINE

## 97  SUPINE AND PAST PARTICIPLE FORMS

| Conj. | Supine | Past participle | | | |
|-------|--------|-----------------|---|---|---|
| | | *Non-neuter* | *Neuter* | *Plural/Definite* | |
| I | älska*t* | älska*d* | älska*t* | älska*de* | loved |
| IIa | böj*t* | böj*d* | böj*t* | böj*da* | bent |
| IIb | köp*t* | köp*t* | köp*t* | köp*ta* | bought |
| III | sy*tt* | sy*dd* | sy*tt* | sy*dda* | sewn |
| IV | bit*it* | bit*en* | bit*et* | bit*na* | bitten |
| | bjud*it* | bjud*en* | bjud*et* | bjud*na* | invited |

*Notes:*

1 The supine is the same as the neuter form of the past participle in conjugations I, II, III.

2 In conjugation IV the supine ends in **-it** and the neuter past participle in **-et**.

3 The non-neuter form of the conjugation IIb past participle in **-t** may seem confusing.

## 98  USE OF THE SUPINE AND PAST PARTICIPLE

1 The supine is used with **har/hade** to form the perfect and pluperfect tenses respectively. No other verbs are used before the supine. It does *not* inflect.

**Olle har tvättat bilen.**        Olle has washed the car.

**Han hade tvättat den innan det började regna.**
He had washed it before it began to rain.

2 The past participle is used as an adjective and inflects as follows (see also **48**ff, **97**):

| *Indefinite attributive* | *Indefinite predicative* | *Definite attributive* |
|---------------------------|---------------------------|-------------------------|
| **en nytvätta*d* bil** | **bilen är nytvätta*d*** | **den nytvätta*de* bilen** |
| a newly washed car | the car is newly washed | the newly washed car |
| **ett nymåla*t* hus** | **huset är nymåla*t*** | **det nymåla*de* huset** |
| a newly painted house | the house is newly painted | the newly painted house |

| **en nyköpt lampa** | **lampan är nyköpt** | **den nyköpta lampan** |
|---|---|---|
| a newly bought lamp | the lamp was newly bought | the newly bought lamp |

| **ett nyköpt bord** | **bordet är nyköpt** | **det nyköpta bordet** |
|---|---|---|
| a newly bought table | the table is newly bought | the newly bought table |

| **en omskriven bok** | **boken är omskriven** | **den omskrivna boken** |
|---|---|---|
| a rewritten book | the book is rewritten | the rewritten book |

| **ett omskrivet brev** | **brevet är omskrivet** | **det omskrivna brevet** |
|---|---|---|
| a rewritten letter | the letter is rewritten | the rewritten letter |

*Note:* The past participle is also used with forms of **vara** or **bli** to construct one type of passive. See **118**.

## 99 PRESENT PARTICIPLE

Form:

| Verbs with *stem* ending in: | *Present participle* consists of: |
|---|---|
| – a *consonant* or **-a** (Conj. I, II, IV): | stem + /**a**/**nde**: **ropande, ringande, skrivande** |
| – a *long vowel* (Conj. III and many irregular verbs): | stem + **ende**: **troende, gående** |

Use:

1 Present participles are only rarely used in Swedish like the English '-ing' forms, notably after the verbs **komma, gå, bli** and verbs of motion:

**De kom springande.**    They came running.
**Han blev sittande/liggande.**    He remained sitting/lying.

**Sjungande Internationalen marscherade studenterna genom gatorna.**
Singing the Internationale the students marched through the streets.

2 Normally the present participle is one of the following:

(a) An adjective:    **en heltäckande matta, en genomgripande förändring**
(b) A noun:    **ett erbjudande, ett påstående, en ordförande, en studerande**
(c) An adverb:    **Han var påfallande lat. Vädret var övervägande mulet.**
(d) A preposition:    **Angående det här fallet ...**

# TRANSLATING VERBS

**100** SOME PROBLEMS IN TRANSLATING ENGLISH VERBS

Arrive 1 **anlända, komma** of people: **Lasse kommer imorgon.**
2 **ankomma** of trains, boats, planes: **Tåget ankommer kl.6.**

Ask 1 **fråga** ask someone a question: **Vi frågade honom om läget.**
2 **be** ask someone to do something: **Vi bad dem gå.**

Change 1 **ändra, förändra** alter: **Lagen har ändrats nyligen.**
2 **ändra sig** change one's mind: **Olle ändrade sig.**
3 **byta** exchange: **Man byter tåg i Katrineholm.**
4 **växla** money, gear: **Man växlar pund i kronor. Föraren växlade ner.**

Feel 1 **känna** (transitive): **Han kände smärtan.**
2 **känna sig** (reflexive): **Han kände sig trött.**
3 **kännas** (impersonal passive): **Det känns kallt ute.**

Go 1 **åka, resa, fara** by vehicle: **Jag reser till Amerika.**
2 **åka** ski, skate, cycle: **Han åkte skidor.**
3 **gå** walk, leave: **Jag måste verkligen gå nu.**

Grow 1 **växa** (intransitive): **Ris växer i Kina.**
2 **odla** (transitive): **De odlar ris i Kina.**
3 **öka** increase: **Antalet studenter har ökat.**

Have 1 **äga, ha** possess: **Jag har en gammal bil.**
2 **äta** eat: **Vad åt du till lunch?**
3 **måste** have to: **Jag måste verkligen gå nu.**
4 **behöver inte** not have (need) to: **Jag behöver inte gå genast.**
5 **få** receive: **Har du fått mitt brev?**

Know 1 **veta** facts: **Vet du vad detta kallas?**
2 **känna** people: **Känner du honom?**
3 **kunna** languages, subjects: **Han kan ryska.**

Leave 1 **resa, åka, gå** (intransitive): **De gick tidigt.**
2 **lämna** (transitive): **De lämnade sin bil hemma.**

Live 1 **bo** reside: **Han bor i Södertälje.**
2 **leva** be alive: **Bellman levde på 1700-talet.**

Put 1 **lägga** flat: **Han lade en penna på bordet.**
2 **ställa** upright: **Han ställde en ljusstake på bordet.**

|          | 3 sätta | fix: **De satte upp tältet.** |
|          | 4 stoppa | put in/to/: **Stoppa din portmonnä i väskan!** |
| See      | 1 se | see: **Kan du se huset härifrån?** |
|          | 2 träffa | meet: **Det är en herr Jansson som vill träffa dig.** |
| Stop     | 1 stanna | movement: **Stanna bilen!** |
|          | 2 sluta | cease doing: **Han slutade prata.** |
| Think    | 1 tycka, mena | hold an opinion: **Jag tycker att det är tråkigt.** |
|          | 2 tänka, fundera | ponder: **Han satt och tänkte på det.** |
|          | | intend: **Han tänker gå.** |
|          | 3 ämna | intend: **Jag ämnar stämma tidningen.** |
|          | 4 tro | believe: **Jag tror att han vinner valet.** |
| Want     | 1 vilja | want + verb: **Jag vill köpa en bil.** |
|          | 2 vilja ha | want + noun: **Jag vill ha en ny bil.** |

## 101  TRANSLATING THE ENGLISH VERB 'TO BE'

No less than six Swedish verbs are used to translate different senses of the English verb 'to be'.

In order to indicate location three verbs are often used in preference to **vara**, namely **sitta** (main meaning = sit), **ligga** (main meaning = lie) and **stå** (main meaning = stand).

### 1 ligga

(a) Used of towns, buildings and places:

| | |
|---|---|
| **Sverige ligger i Skandinavien.** | Sweden is in Scandinavia. |
| **Staden ligger vid en liten sjö.** | The town is/lies by a little lake. |
| **I centrum ligger många banker.** | In the centre there are many banks. |

(b) Used of objects which lie horizontally:

**Var ska tidningen ligga?**
Where should the newspaper be/go?

**Kläderna låg utströdda över hela golvet.**
The clothes were/lay strewn across the floor.

(c) Notice also:

| | |
|---|---|
| **Hans son låg vid universitetet.** | His son was at university. |
| **Jag låg och läste. ( = Jag läste)** | I was (lay) reading. |

## 2 sitta

(a) Used of objects that are fixed in position:

| | |
|---|---|
| **Tavlorna sitter snett.** | The pictures are crooked. |
| **Sitter nyckeln i låset?** | Is the key in the lock? |
| **Muttern sitter fast.** | The nut is stuck. |
| **Dina glasögon sitter på näsan.** | Your glasses are on your nose. |

(b) Notice also:

**Olle sitter i fängelse/i sammanträde/i en kommitté.**
Olle is in prison/at a meeting/on a committee.

**Jag satt och drack te.**
I was/sat drinking tea.

## 3 stå

(a) Used of objects that stand vertically:

**Du ska bestämma var skåpet ska stå.**
You decide where the cupboard should be/stand.

| | |
|---|---|
| **Bordet står i hörnet.** | The table is/stands in the corner. |
| **Står inte boken på hyllan?** | Isn't the book on the shelf? |

(b) = be (written):

| | |
|---|---|
| **Detta står på sidan 10 i boken.** | That is on page 10 of the book. |

To indicate existence or transition (change of state) two verbs are used in preference to **vara**, namely **finnas** (meaning = existence) and **bli** (meaning = transition):

## 4 finnas

| | |
|---|---|
| **Det finns många sjöar i Sverige.** | There are a lot of lakes in Sweden. |
| **I Uppsala finns det en domkyrka.** | In Uppsala there is a cathedral. |
| **Älgar finns överallt i Sverige.** | There are elk everywhere in Sweden. |

## 5 bli-transition

**Vad tänker du bli när du har tagit din examen?**
What do you intend to be when you have graduated?

**Han blir sju år idag.**
He will be seven today.

**Han blev förvånad över att höra nyheten.**
He was surprised to hear the news.

| | |
|---|---|
| **Bli inte arg!** | Don't get angry! |
| **Vad blev resultatet?** | What was the result? |

# THE USE OF THE INFINITIVE AND DIFFERENT VERBAL CONSTRUCTIONS

## 102 INFINITIVE – VERBAL USE

1 In two-verb constructions after the modal auxiliaries **kan, ska, vill, måste** etc. (**112f**):

| | |
|---|---|
| **Han kan komma ikväll.** | He can come tonight. |
| **Måste du göra det?** | Do you have to do that? |
| **Får jag följa med?** | May I come along? |
| **Ska du åka bort över jul?** | Are you going away over Christmas? |
| **Vill du åka bort?** | Do you want to go away? |

2 In two-verb constructions after modal equivalents:

| | |
|---|---|
| **De brukar åka bort.** | They usually go away. |
| **Jag hoppas kunna åka.** | I hope to be able to go away. |
| **Hon tänker inte gifta sig.** | She doesn't intend to get married. |
| **Det verkar vara sant.** | It appears to be true. |

Modal equivalents include:

| | | | |
|---|---|---|---|
| **behöva** | need | **råka** | happen to |
| **bruka** | usually do | **slippa** | avoid |
| **börja** | begin | **sluta** | stop |
| **fortsätta** | continue | **tyckas** | seem |
| **försöka** | try to | **tänka** | intend |
| **hoppa** | hope to | **våga** | dare to |
| **lova** | promise (to) | **vägra** | refuse to |
| **lycka** | succeed in | **ämna** | intend |
| **låtsas** | pretend to | **önska** | wish |
| **orka** | manage to | | |

3 In object + infinitive constructions, often with the verbs **se** (see), **höra** (hear), **låta** (allow, let), **tillåta** (permit), **anse** (consider):

| | |
|---|---|
| **Vi såg honom göra det.** | We saw him do it. |
| **Jag hörde henne sjunga.** | I heard her sing. |
| **Han lät kaffet kallna.** | He allowed the coffee to cool. |

4 In reflexive object + infinitive constructions, often with the verbs **säga sig** (say), **påstå sig** (claim), **förklara sig** (declare), **tro sig** (consider), **anse sig** (consider):

| | |
|---|---|
| **Hon säger sig vara lycklig.** | She says that she is happy. |

## 103 INFINITIVE – NOMINAL USE

Infinitive phrases (**att** + infinitive) often function as if they were noun phrases:

1 As the subject:

**Att spela piano är svårt.**      Playing the piano is difficult.
**Det är svårt att spela piano.**      (see **166**)

2 As the object:

**Hon älskar att köra bil.**      She loves driving/to drive.

3 After a preposition or a stressed verb particle:

**Han gick hem utan att säga någonting.**
He went home without saying anything.

**Han stannade tåget genom att dra i nödbromsen.**
He stopped the train by pulling the communication cord.

**Jag tycker om att läsa rysare.**
I like reading thrillers.

**Du måste tänka på att byta jobb.**
You must think of changing jobs.

Notice that in expressions indicating an intention **för att** is used:

**Han kom hit för att vila sig.**      He came here /in order/ to rest.

4 When qualifying a noun:

**Konsten att skriva.**      The art of writing.

## 104 USE OF THE INFINITIVE IN ENGLISH AND SWEDISH

1 English infinitive = Swedish infinitive, notably in two-verb constructions (see **102**).

2 Swedish often has a full clause when English has object + infinitive (NB. **att** is a conjunction here) and after an interrogative:

| | |
|---|---|
| What do you want me to do? | **Vad vill du att jag skall göra?** |
| They waited for the rain to stop. | **De väntade på att regnet skulle upphöra.** |
| They don't know what to do. | **De vet inte vad de ska göra.** |

## 105   TRANSLATING '-ING' FORMS

1 For the English continuous (or progressive) tense see **106.3**.

2 English infinitive or gerund (-ing form) = Swedish infinitive:

He began to write/writing.   **Han började skriva.**
It's no use trying.   **Det är inte värt att försöka.**
He left without saying goodbye.   **Han gick utan att säga adjö.**

3 English gerund (-ing form) = Swedish full clause

He admits having stolen the money.
**Han medger att han har stulit pengarna.**

We thanked him for coming.
**Vi tackade honom för att han kom.**

## 106   PRESENT TENSE

1 The present tense is used much as in English. It has five main uses:

(a) Present action:   **Jag sitter hemma nu och läser tidningen.**
   I'm sitting at home reading the paper.

(b) Universal action:   **Jorden går runt solen.**
   The Earth goes round the Sun.

(c) Repeated action:   **Lektionerna börjar kl. 9.**
   Lessons start at 9 o'clock.

(d) Future action:   **Om en vecka reser jag bort.** (see also **110.**)
   In a week's time I'm going away.

(e) Historic present (to create an illusion of present):

**27 november bryter Strindberg upp från Klam och reser över Berlin
och Danmark hem.**
On 27 November Strindberg leaves Klam and travels home via
   Berlin and Denmark.

2 Notice the following minor difference of usage:
Present in Swedish = past in English when an action is completed in the past:

**När är du född?**   When were you born?
**Jag är född 1951.**   I was born in 1951.
(cf. **När *var* Napoleon född?** – when a person is dead)
**Slottet är byggt på 1300-talet.**   The castle was built in the 14th century.

3 The English continuous (or progressive) tense with forms in '-ing' corresponds in Swedish to:

(a) Simple present tense

I am sitting in my study. **Jag sitter på arbetsrummet.**
I am sitting reading. **Jag sitter och läser.**

(b) **Håller på att** + infinitive, which is used to stress the continuity of an action:

The house is /in the process of/ being built.
**Huset håller på att byggas.**

He is /busy/ painting the bathroom.
**Han håller på att måla badrummet.**

## 107 PAST TENSE

Sometimes known as the imperfect or preterite tense, the past tense in Swedish is used much as in English, namely to express an action completed at a point of time in the past.

1 The past tense is often used in conjunction with a time marker, often an adverb:

**I fjol/Då reste vi till Grekland.** Last year/Then we went to Greece.

2 The past tense may express a repeated action:

**Som liten skrek han ofta.** As a small child he yelled a lot.

3 The past tense may inject a note of politeness or caution into a demand or intention, especially with the modal auxiliary (see **112**):

**Jag skulle vilja ha en sådan, tack.** I would like one of those, please.
(Cf. **Jag vill ha ...** I want ...)

4 The past tense may possess a modal sense (see **112**):

**Om jag hade tid skulle jag skriva en bok.**
If I had time I would write a book.

5 Swedish past tense = English present tense in exclamations and on first impressions:

**Det var snällt av dig att komma.** It is kind of you to come.
**Detta var verkligen gott!** This is really good!

## 108  PERFECT TENSE

The perfect tense is formed by using **har** with the supine (see **98**). The verb **har** is often omitted in the subordinate clause in written Swedish:

**Då jag inte /har/ fått svar på mitt brev, skriver jag igen.**
As I have not received a reply to my letter, I am writing again.

The perfect tense in Swedish is, as in English, a non-narrative tense used to indicate a link between past and present, the relevance of a completed action in the past to a present situation:

**Vi har rest till Spanien förr, men nu föredrar vi Grekland.**
We have gone to Spain before, but now we prefer Greece.

The tense indicates an indeterminate length of time or point in time.

1 Time markers are used to indicate present time:

**Nu har jag avslutat boken.**        Now I have finished the book.

2 The perfect may indicate that an action has taken place and is still taking place:

**De har varit gifta i många år.**
They have been married for many years.

3 The perfect may express future:

**Om en månad har vi glömt / kommer vi att ha glömt / allting.**
In a month we will have forgotten everything.

4 Perfect in Swedish = past in English, when the present result is emphasized rather than the action in the past:

**Vem har skrivit Röda rummet?**      Who wrote 'The Red Room'?
**Var har du lärt dig svenska?**      Where did you learn Swedish?
**Det har jag aldrig tänkt på.**      I never thought of that.

## 109  PLUPERFECT TENSE

The pluperfect tense is formed by using **hade** with the supine (see **98**). The verb **hade** is often omitted in the subordinate clause in written Swedish:

**Om jag inte /hade/ hittat boken vet jag inte vad jag hade gjort.**
If I hadn't found the book I don't know what I would have done.

The pluperfect tense is used much as in English. It expresses an action taking place before an action expressed by the past tense:

**Innan han kom hit hade han köpt blommor.**
Before he came here he had bought some flowers.

Other uses:

1 The pluperfect tense may express the result of a completed action:

**Då hade vi redan gett upp allt hopp.**
Then we had already given up all hope.

2 The pluperfect may indicate that an action had taken place and at some point in the past was still taking place:

**De hade varit gifta i många år när de skildes.**
They had been married for many years when they got divorced.

3 The pluperfect may have a modal sense (see **112**) indicating an unreal situation:

**Om det bara inte varit så halt på vägen hade jag klarat mig.**
If only it hadn't been so icy on the road I would have been all right.

## 110  FUTURE TENSE

There are three ways of expressing the future in Swedish:

1 Present tense + time marker is the most common construction. **Blir** is often used instead of **är** in this instance:

| | |
|---|---|
| **Jag åker snart.** | I'll be going soon. |
| **I år reser vi utomlands.** | This year we are going abroad. |
| **Det gör jag imorgon.** | I'll do that tomorrow. |
| **Det blir ljust om en timme.** | It will be light in an hour. |

2 **Kommer att** + infinitive is objective and often (but not always) found with an impersonal subject:

| | |
|---|---|
| **Det kommer att regna ikväll.** | It is going to rain tonight. |
| **Ni kommer att bli förvånade.** | You will be surprised. |

3 **Ska** + infinitive often indicates intention and is often found with a personal subject:

| | |
|---|---|
| **Jag ska titta på TV ikväll.** | I am going to watch TV tonight. |
| **Ska du resa imorgon?** | Are you leaving tomorrow? |
| **Du ska icke dräpa.** | Thou shalt not kill. |

Notice, however, that **ska** + infinitive may on occasion be objective and used with an impersonal subject:

| | |
|---|---|
| **Det ska bli auktion.** | There is going to be an auction. |
| **(= Det blir/kommer att bli auktion.)** | |

## 111   MOOD AND MODAL VERBS

The attitude of the speaker to the activity contained in the verb is
expressed by one of the following:

Modal verb + main verb (infinitive, **102**):

**Vi måste springa.**    We must run.

Subjunctive (**113**):

**Det vore roligt att träffa honom.**    It would be nice to meet him.

Imperative (**114**):

**Gå ut härifrån!**    Get out of here!

Modal verbs have irregular forms:

| Infinitive | Present | Past | Supine | |
|---|---|---|---|---|
| **kunna** | **kan** | **kunde** | **kunnat** | be able |
| **skola** | **ska(ll)** | **skulle** | **skolat** | shall, will |
| **vilja** | **vill** | **ville** | **velat** | will, want to |
| – | **måste** | **måste** | **måst** | must, have to |
| **böra** | **bör** | **borde** | **bort** | should, ought to |
| **(töra)** | **(tör)** | **torde** | **(tort)** | is probably |
| – | **må** | – | – | may, must |
| – | **måtte** | – | – | may, must |
| – | **lär** | – | – | is said to |
| **låta** | **låter** | **lät** | **låtit** | let |
| **få** | **får** | **fick** | **fått** | may, be allowed to, must, have to |

## 112   USE OF MODAL VERBS

1 **ska** (or **skall**), **skulle**

(a) Future: see **110**.

(b) Conditional:

**Om jag hade tid, skulle jag resa.**    If I had time, I would go away.
**Jag skulle knappast tro det.**    I would scarcely believe it.

(c) Polite use (use past tense)

**Jag skulle be dig om en tjänst.**    I would like to ask a favour.

NB **Ska** often translates English 'will':

**Ska du följa med på bio?**
Will you be coming/Are you coming to the cinema?

**(Nej, jag vill inte!**    No, I don't want to!)

## 2 vill, ville

(a) "want to, will": *Never* simple future, cf. **110**.

**Jag vill åka till Frankrike på semestern.**
I want to go to France on holiday.

But, note:

Will you give me a hand with this?
**Vill du hjälpa mig med detta?**

(b) 'would like':

**Vill du ha ett glas öl?**          Would you like a glass of beer?

(c) Polite use (use past tense)

**Jag ville helst inte stanna.**          I would rather not stay.

## 3 måste

(a) Compulsion – 'must/have to' in positive expressions:

**Jag måste tyvärr sluta nu.**          I have to finish now, unfortunately.

(b) Concession – 'do not have/need to' in negative expressions:

**Du måste ju inte äta så mycket!**
You don't have/need to eat so much.

NB 'Must not' (prohibition) is expressed by **får inte**:

**Du får inte äta så mycket!**          You must not eat so much!

## 4 bör, borde

Suitability:

**Du borde få lite frisk luft.**
You ought to/should get some fresh air.

Cf. **107.3**f

## 5 kan, kunde

(a) Possibility:

**Vi kan följa med ikväll.**
We can/are able to come along tonight.

(b) Ability:

**Eva kan köra bil.**          Eva can drive.

(c)  Concession:

**Det kan du ha rätt i.**            You may be right about that.

### 113  SUBJUNCTIVE

The subjunctive is rare now. It is found in fixed expressions and in **vore** (from **vara**):

**Det vore roligt om du kunde följa med.**
It would be nice if you could come.

| | |
|---|---|
| **Tack vare din hjälp ...** | Thanks to your help ... |
| **Leve konungen!** | Long live the King! |
| **Det vete fan!** | The Devil alone knows! |

### 114  IMPERATIVE

1 Form: The imperative is the same as the stem. This means that it is the same as the infinitive for conjugations I and III and the infinitive minus **-a** for conjugations II, IV and III irregular:

| | *Imperative* | | *cf. Infinitive* |
|---|---|---|---|
| I | **Arbeta hårdare!** | Work harder! | **arbeta** |
| IIa | **Släng bort den!** | Throw it away! | **slänga** |
| IIb | **Hjälp mig!** | Help me! | **hjälpa** |
| III | **Tro mig eller inte!** | Believe me or not! | **tro** |
| IV | **Skriv ett brev!** | Write a letter! | **skriva** |
| IV | **Var inte dum nu!** | Don't be stupid now! | **vara** |
| II irr. | **Gör något!** | Do something! | **göra** |
| III irr. | **Ge mig boken!** | Give me the book! | **ge** |

2 Use: The imperative expresses a command, wish or piece of advice. Occasionally the subject is inserted in spoken Swedish and especially to underline a contrast:

**Kom hit du, så ska vi dricka kaffe.**
You come here and we'll have coffee.

**Sitt kvar du, så städar jag.**
You sit there and I'll tidy up.

Notice the difference in the position of the subject, when inserted, between Swedish and English:

| **Sitt kvar du ...** | You sit there ... |
|---|---|
| FV       S | S    FV |

3 Notice the following polite uses of the imperative:

**Var snäll och ge mig ett äpple!**     Please give me an apple.
**Ge mig ett äpple är du snäll!**
**Var så god och stig in!**             Please come in!

## 115  TRANSITIVE, INTRANSITIVE AND REFLEXIVE VERBS

1 *Transitive* verbs have a direct object (**156**):

**John köpte huset.**          John bought the house.

*Intransitive* verbs do not have a direct object:

**John sov gott.**             John slept well.

*Ditransitive* verbs have both an indirect and direct object (**156**):

**John gav henne boken.**      John gave her the book.

*Reflexive* verbs are intransitive, as the subject does not direct the action outwards (cf. transitive) but at itself:

**Han tvättade sig.**          He washed /himself/.
**S ←——————**

2 Whereas Swedish makes firm distinctions between transitive and intransitive, many English verbs may be either:

They burn the paper.           **De bränner pappret.** tr.
The house burns down.          **Huset brinner ned.** itr.

Mary left the letter.          **Mary lämnade brevet.** tr.
Mary left early.               **Mary gick tidigt.** itr.

Other pairs of transitive/intransitive verbs in Swedish are:

| *Intransitive* | | *Transitive* | |
|---|---|---|---|
| **sitta** IV | sit | **sätta** IIirr | put |
| **ligga** IV | lie | **lägga** IIirr | lay |
| **falla** IV | fall | **fälla** IIa | fell |
| **kallna** I | grow cold, cool | **kyla** IIa | chill, cool |
| **vaka** I | stay awake | **väcka** IIb | awaken, arouse |
| **vakna** I | wake up | | |
| **ryka** IIb | /give off/ smoke | **röka** IIb | smoke |
| **tröttna** I | be tired, tire | **trötta** I | make tired, tire |

3 Many reflexive verbs in Swedish are not reflexive in English:

**Vi ska tvätta/raka/kamma oss.**
We shall wash/shave/comb our hair.

**De gifte sig förra året.**
They got married last year.

**Per reste sig och sedan satte han sig igen.**
Per got up and then he sat down again.

**Hon klädde sig i svart.**
She dressed in black.

For reflexive pronouns see **68**, **70**.

4 Many reflexive verbs indicate movement:

| | | | |
|---|---|---|---|
| **lägga sig** | lie down | **förkyla sig** | catch a cold |
| **röra sig** | move | **lära sig** | learn |
| **bege sig** | go | **känna sig** | feel |
| **vända sig** | turn round | **förirra sig** | get lost |
| **infinna sig** | present oneself | **skynda sig** | hurry up |
| **närma sig** | approach | | |

## 116   S-FORMS

| | *Infinitive* | *Present* | *Past* | *Supine* | |
|---|---|---|---|---|---|
| I | **bakas** | **bakas** | **bakades** | **bakats** | be baked |
| IIa | **böjas** | **böjs** | **böjdes** | **böjts** | be bent |
| IIb | **köpas** | **köps** | **köptes** | **köpts** | be bought |
| -stem in **-s**: | | | | | |
| | **läsas** | **läses** | **lästes** | **lästs** | be read |
| III | **sys** | **sys** | **syddes** | **sytts** | be sewn |
| IV | **bjudas** | **bjuds** | **bjöds** | **bjudits** | be invited |

In most cases the **-s** is simply added to the end of the existing form, but notice especially how to form the present tense:

| | | |
|---|---|---|
| **bakar** | + s > **bakas** | (i.e. delete present tense ending first) |
| **köper** | + s > **köps** | |
| **säljer** | + s > **säljs** | |

Formal written Swedish retains the **-e** however:

**köper**     + s > **köpes**

## 117   USES OF S-FORMS

1 Passive (see **118**):

**Huset målades.**                    The house was /being/ painted.

2 Deponent: The deponent is active and intransitive, i.e. it has passive
form but active meaning:

**Jag hoppas att de lyckas.**        I hope they succeed.
**Vi trivs här.**                    We like it here.

The deponent does not usually possess a form without **-s**. Deponents include:

| | | | |
|---|---|---|---|
| **minnas** IIa | remember | **kräkas** IIb | vomit |
| **finnas** IV | be, exist | **umgås** IV | be friendly with |
| **låtsas** I | pretend | **trängas** IIa | push |
| **synas** IIb | appear | **töras** IIa | dare |
| **tyckas** IIb | seem | **envisas** I | persist |
| **hoppas** I | hope | **trivas** IIa | like it |

3 Reciprocal: The reciprocal has a plural subject which both carries out
an action and is the object of an action:

**Vi träffas kl. 2.** (= **träffar varandra**)
We will meet at 2 o'clock.

**De kysstes bakom cykelstället.**
They kissed (one another) behind the bicycle shed.

Other reciprocal verbs:

| | | | |
|---|---|---|---|
| **brottas** I | wrestle | **höras** IIa | be in touch (with one another) |
| **enas** I | agree | **talas vid** I | talk over |
| **kramas** I | hug (one another) | **följas åt** IIa | accompany (one another) |
| **ses** IV | meet, rendezvous | **hjälpas åt** IIb | help (one another) |
| **slåss** IV | fight | **skiljas åt** IIa | part |

## 118    PASSIVE

Whereas active verbs often have a subject and an object, passive verbs
have a subject and an agent:

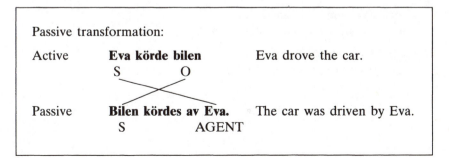

Passive transformation:

Active        **Eva körde bilen**          Eva drove the car.
              S        O

Passive       **Bilen kördes av Eva.**     The car was driven by Eva.
              S              AGENT

Many passive verbs have no agent, however:

**Bilen kördes vårdslöst.**          The car was driven carelessly.

The reason is that the agent in many cases is unknown, unimportant or obvious from the context, and it is the action expressed by the verb or the object of that action (subject of the passive) which is the dominating idea:

**Mat serveras i skolorna kl. 11.**
Lunch is served in schools at 11 o'clock.

**Han dödades i en bilolycka.**
He was killed in a car accident.

**Mötet hålls i den stora salen.**
The meeting is being held in the big hall.

Passives with an agent tend to appear in impersonal written Swedish:

**Skiftnyckeln uppfanns av en svensk.**
The adjustable spanner was invented by a Swede.

There are three ways of expressing the passive:

– S-passive:                        **Äpplena skalas.**
– Forms of **bli** + past participle:   **Äpplena blir skalade.**
– Forms of **vara** + past participle:  **Äpplena var skalade.**

Forms with **bli/vara** are sometimes called 'periphrastic forms'.

*Use of passive forms:*

1 **S**-passive
This is by far the most common form, especially in written Swedish, and stresses the action of the verb, often indicating a repetition, command or instruction:

**Frukost serveras kl. 9.**
Breakfast is served at 9 o'clock.

**Ordet uttalas med accent 1.**
The word is pronounced with accent 1.

**Felparkering straffas med böter.**
Illegal parking is punishable by fines.

**Öppnas här.**
Open here. (lit. To be opened here)

The s-passive construction often has no agent, and is often the equivalent of an active construction using **man**, **de**, **någon** or **folk**:

| | |
|---|---|
| **Man diskuterar nedrustning.** | = **Nedrustning diskuteras.** |
| **Man anser honom vara frisk.** | = **Han anses vara frisk.** |

2 **Bli**-passive

This form stresses the action of the verb and often indicates an isolated occurrence. The **bli**-passive often has an agent.

**Han blev påkörd av en bil.**
He was run down by a car.

**Herrarna blev avbrutna av servitrisen.**
The gentlemen were interrupted by the waitress.

**Tyskland blev slaget av Italien.**
Germany was beaten by Italy.

Notice that **blir** (present tense) indicates future action (see **110**):

**Saken blir avgjord imorgon.**
The matter will be decided tomorrow.

3 **Vara**-passive

This form stresses a state, the result of an action, and is adjectival. It provides a static picture.

| | |
|---|---|
| **Himlen är täckt av moln.** | The sky is covered in cloud. |
| **Han är bortrest för tillfället.** | He is away at present. |
| **Huset är sålt.** | The house is/has been sold. |
| **Väskan är stulen.** | The bag is/has been stolen. |

4 Tense equivalents

Notice the following different ways of expressing the same thing:

| *Vara*-passive | *Bli*-passive/*S*-passive |
|---|---|
| Present: | = Perfect: |
| **Middagen är förstörd.** | = **Middagen har blivit förstörd/ har förstörts.** |
| **Vi är bjudna på fest.** | = **Vi har blivit bjudna/ har bjudits på fest.** |
| | |
| Past: | = Pluperfect: |
| **Middagen var förstörd.** | = **Middagen hade blivit förstörd/ hade förstörts.** |

5 Verbs often found in the passive (given in the tenses in which they frequently occur):

**anses**, be considered; **betraktas**, be regarded; **byggdes**, was built; **diskuterades (diskuterats)**, was (has been) discussed, **dömdes**, was sentenced; **åtalas (åtalats)**, is (has been) charged; **gripits**, has been arrested; **nämnas (nämnts)**, is (has been) named; **publiceras**, be punished; **rapporteras**, be reported; **uppges**, be stated; **sändes**, was sent; **stängdes**, was closed; **såldes**, was sold; **utsågs**, was appointed

6 Differences in use between Swedish and English:

(a) English passive = Swedish active:

(i) 'There' + passive = Swedish active form:

There was nothing to be done. **Det var inget att göra.**

(ii) 'Be said to/reputed to' = Swedish **lär/ska**:

The food there is said to be good. **Maten där lär vara god.**

(iii) English passive = Swedish **man** + active:

It is more difficult than is generally supposed. **Det är svårare än man i allmänhet tror.**

(b) Swedish passive = English active:

(i) **Det** + passive ('impersonal passive') = 'There is/was' + gerundive (i.e. 'ing-'form):

**Det sjöngs och dansades hela natten.** There was singing and dancing all night.

(ii) Some Swedish agentless passives = English intransitive verbs:

**Dörren öppnades.** The door opened.

## 119   COMPOUND VERBS

Compound verbs are those prefixed by a particle.

In inseparable compounds the particle always remains attached:

**Han _be_talar räkningen.**     He pays the bill.

In separable compounds the particle may become separated from the verb:

**Värmen är _avstängd_.**     The heating is turned off.
**Han _stängde av_ värmen.**     He turned off the heating.

1 _Inseparable_ compounds include:

(a) Most verbs compounded with nouns, adjectives, other verbs and **själv-**:

**hungerstrejka, godkänna, brännmärka, självdö**

(b)  Verbs with the following prefixes:

Unstressed prefixes:    **betala**, **förklara**
Stressed prefixes:    **bistå, erhålla, föredra, missunna, närvara,
oroa, samtycka, umgås, undkomma,
vanhedra, välsigna**

2 *Separable* compounds include:
Many phrasal verbs with separable prefixes or particles. The particles, not
the verbs, are always stressed:

**resa** *bort*, **frysa** *fast*, **gå** *förbi*, **ta** *ifrån*, **känna** *igen*, **gå** *igenom*, **slå**
**ihjäl**, **räkna** *in*, **följa** *med*, **lägga** *ned*, **tycka** *om*, **falla** *omkull*, **slå**
**sönder**, **stryka** *under*, **slå** *upp*, **dricka** *ur*, **dö** *ut*, **gå** *vilse*

These verbs are always compounded in the participial forms:

| | |
|---|---|
| **Han blev** *ihjäl*slagen. | He was killed. |
| **Han är** *bort*rest. | He has gone away. |
| ett *igen*kännande leende | a smile of recognition |
| en *om*tyckt rektor | a popular headteacher |
| en *ned*lagd fabrik | a closed factory |

The same word may often be both a stressed particle and an unstressed
preposition:

| | |
|---|---|
| **Han satte** *på* **tvn.** | He put the TV on. |
| **Han satte** *tvn* **på bordet.** | He put the TV on the table. |

3 Stylistic differences between separable and inseparable compound verbs:
Often the separated form is used in everyday language and the integral
form in formal written style.

**Han lade ner böckerna på bordet.**
He laid the books on the table.

**Presidenten nedlade en krans på graven.**
The president laid a wreath on the grave.

| | |
|---|---|
| **Vi steg ner i gruvan.** | We went down into the mine. |
| **Kristus har nedstigit till dödsriket.** | Christ has descended into Hell. |

| | |
|---|---|
| **Hon lade fram hans pyjamas.** | She laid out his pyjamas. |
| **Hon framlade ett bra förslag.** | She put forward a good proposal. |

4 Semantic differences between separable and inseparable compound
verbs:
Often the separated forms are concrete and the integral forms abstract
in meaning. In some cases the semantic difference is so great as to warrant
regarding the forms as two distinct verbs.

| | |
|---|---|
| **Jag bryter av grenen.** | I break off the branch. |
| **Jag avbryter samtalet.** | I interrupt the conversation. |
| **Han strök under ordet.** | He underlined the word. |
| **Han underströk ordets betydelse.** | He emphasized the meaning of the word. |
| **Lampan lyste upp rummet.** | The lamp lit up the room. |
| **Vi upplyste honom om hans misstag.** | We enlightened him as to his mistake. |

5 Word order: (See also **157, 171.8**)
Notice that only a clausal adverbial (**154, 157, 159**) and/or a subject in inverted clauses may come between the verb and its separated particle, unlike English:

| | |
|---|---|
| **Kasta inte ut den!** | Don't throw it out! |
| **Kastade de inte ut den?** | Didn't they throw it out? |
| **Ring upp honom!** | Ring him up! |

# 8 ADVERBS

## 120 FORMS OF ADVERBS

1 Many adverbs derive from adjectives by adding the ending **-t**:

Cf.

**Hon var mycket vacker** (*adjective*). She was very beautiful.
**Hon sjöng mycket vackert** (*adverb*). She sang very beautifully.

The adverb in **-t** is identical to the neuter form of the adjective in **-t**:

**Huset var mycket vackert** (*adj*). The house was very beautiful.
**Huset var vackert** (*adv*) **målat**. The house was beautifully painted.

2 Some adjectives ending in **-lig** form adverbs by adding **-en** or **-tvis**:

**Han kommer möjligen imorgon.** He is probably coming tomorrow.
**Naturligtvis dricker han öl.** Naturally he drinks beer.

Notice that forms in **-en**, **-tvis** are often clausal adverbials (see **154**), whilst forms in **-t** are other adverbials (see **155**).

3 Other adverbs which are derivatives include those ending in:

| | | |
|---|---|---|
| **-städes/-stans** (location) : | **annorstädes, någonstans** | elsewhere, somewhere |
| **-ledes/-lunda** (manner) : | **således, annorlunda** | thus, differently |
| **-sin** (time) : | **någonsin** | ever |
| **-vart** (direction) : | **någonvart** | somewhere |

4 Many common adverbs are not derivatives, and these include:

(a) Adverbs of time: **aldrig** (never), **alltid** (always), **då** (then), **förr** (before), **genast** (immediately), **ibland** (sometimes), **igen** (again), **nu** (now), **ofta** (often)

(b) Adverbs of place: **här** (here), **hit** (here), **där** (there), **dit** (there), **var** (where), **vart** (where), **hem** (home), **bort** (away), **fram** (forward), **in** (in), **ner** (down) (for meanings see **122.**)

(c) Adverbs of manner: **bra** (well), **fort** (quickly), **ganska** (rather), **precis** (exactly)

(d) Modal adverbs: **ju, nog, väl** (for meanings see **123.7**), **inte** (not)

(e) Conjunctional adverbs: **alltså** (therefore), **också** (also), **så** (so)

5 Compound adverbs are formed from an adverb + preposition (or adverb):

**här** (*adv*) + **ifrån** (*prep*) > **härifrån**

Others are: **hemåt, norrut, hittills, härefter, därför, härmed, bortom, därvid**
Other frequent compound adverbs are: **ännu, ändå, ibland, numera, omkring, häromdagen, nuförtiden**

6 Some adverbs compare like the adjectives from which they derive (see also **61**ff):

| Positive | Comparative | Superlative | |
|---|---|---|---|
| tidigt | tidigare | tidigast | early, earlier, earliest |
| sent | senare | senast | late, later, latest |
| högt | högre | högst | loud, louder, loudest |
| långt | längre | längst | long, longer, longest (distance), far, further, furthest |
| länge | längre | längst | long, longer, longest (time) |
| väl | bättre | bäst | well, better, best |
| illa | sämre | sämst | badly, worse, worst |
| | värre | värst | See **67.2** for usage |
| mycket | mer/a/ | mest | a lot, more, most |
| fort | fortare | fortast | quickly, more quickly, most quickly |
| gärna | hellre | helst | willingly, more willingly, most willingly |
| ofta | oftare | oftast | often, more often, most often |
| nära | närmare | närmast | close, closer, closest |

## 121 USE OF ADVERBS

1 Adverbs may qualify:

(a) A verb: **Han sprang fort.**    He ran quickly.

(b) An adjective: **Sjön var otroligt vacker.**    The lake was incredibly beautiful.

(c) An adverb: **Hon sjöng ovanligt vackert.**    She sang unusually beautifully.

(d) A clause: **Det blir troligen regn ikväll.**    It will probably rain tonight.

2 Amplifiers

(a) These are adverbs that qualify an adjective or another adverb, especially one denoting degree or kind. They include:

**mycket** (very), **helt** (completely), **alldeles** (completely), **ganska**
(quite), **lagom** (suitably), **rätt** (very), **för** (too), **lite** (a little), **inte alls**
(not at all), **bra** (very)

| | |
|---|---|
| **Det var en mycket intressant film.** | It was a very interesting film. |
| **Det gick inte alls bra.** | It didn't go at all well. |

(b) **Mycket** = 'very' when qualifying an adjective in the positive or an
adverb:

| | |
|---|---|
| **Han var mycket lång.** | He was very tall. |
| **De gick mycket fort.** | They walked very fast. |

**Mycket** = 'much, a lot' when qualifying an adjective in the comparative
or a verb:

**Han var mycket längre än sin bror.**
He was much taller than his brother.

**Han sjöng mycket på den tiden.**
He sang a lot in those days.

**Väldigt mycket** . . . = 'very much . . .'

**Han är väldigt mycket rikare än alla sina bröder.**
He is very much richer than all his brothers.

(c) **Inte särskilt** . . . = 'not very . . .'

| | |
|---|---|
| **Han är inte särskilt rik.** | He is not very rich. |

**Inte mycket** . . . = 'not much . . .'

**Han är inte mycket rikare än sin bror.**
He isn't much richer than his brother.

(d) Adverbs formed from adjectives (see **120**) are often used as amplifiers:

| | |
|---|---|
| **Det blev förskräckligt varmt.** | It became awfully hot. |
| **Jag har hemskt bråttom.** | I am in a terrible hurry. |
| **Vi såg en fantastiskt bra match.** | We saw a fantastically good match. |

## 122    ADVERBS INDICATING LOCATION AND MOTION

1 Adverbs express this distinction in Swedish which is now no longer
found in English. One form is found with verbs indicating location at a
place, another with verbs indicating motion towards a place, and a third
with verbs indicating motion away from a place:

| | | |
|---|---|---|
| **Han bor här.** | He lives here. | LOCATION |
| **Han kom hit.** | He came here. | MOTION TOWARDS |
| **Han gick härifrån.** | He left here. | MOTION AWAY FROM |

English used to have this distinction in: here/hither/hence, there/thither/thence.

| *Location* *Where?* | | *Motion towards* *Where to?* | | *Motion away from* *Where from?* | |
|---|---|---|---|---|---|
| **var**/?/ | where | **vart**/?/ | where (to) | **varifrån**/?/ | where from |
| **här** | here | **hit** | (to) here | **härifrån** | from here |
| **där** | there | **dit** | (to) there | **därifrån** | from there |
| **inne** | in/side/ | **in** | in | **inifrån** | from inside |
| **ute** | out/side/ | **ut** | out | **utifrån** | from outside |
| **uppe** | up | **upp** | up | **uppifrån** | from above |
| **nere** | down | **ner** | down | **nerifrån** | from below |
| **hemma** | /at/ home | **hem** | (to) home | **hemifrån** | from home |
| **borta** | away | **bort** | away | **bortifrån** | from that direction |
| **framme** | forward | **fram** | forward | **framifrån** | from the front |

Notice the following idiomatic usages:

| | |
|---|---|
| **Jag ringde dit igår.** | I rang there yesterday. |
| **Vi längtar hem.** | We long for home. |
| **Han bor tre trappor upp.** | He lives on the third floor. |
| **Han satt längst bort.** | He sat furthest away. |
| Cf. **När är vi framme?** / | |
| **När kommer vi fram?** | When will we get there? |

---

2 How to translate where:

| | *Location* | *Motion* |
|---|---|---|
| Interrogative (V-word) | **var** | **vart** |
| | **Var är han?** | **Vart går han?** |
| | Where is he? | Where is he going? |
| Relative | **där** | **dit** |
| | **Jag vet ett kafé där vi kan äta.** | **Jag vet ett kafé dit vi kan gå.** |
| | I know a café where we can eat. | I know a café where we can go. |

---

\* The relative adverb **där/dit** follows a noun or noun phrase:

cf. **Jag vet ett kafé där vi kan äta. Jag vet var vi kan äta.**

It is generally possible to replace **där/dit** by **som** + preposition when it is used in this way:

**Jag vet ett kafé som vi kan äta på. Jag vet ett kafé som vi kan gå till.**

## 123  SOME DIFFICULT ADVERBS

### 1 **Då/sedan**

(a) As an adverb **då** = 'then', 'at that moment/time', 'in that case':

**Det blixtrade. Då började han springa.**
There was a flash of lightning. Then he began to run.

**Är du vaken? Då bör du stiga upp.**
Are you awake? Then you had better get up.

(b) As an adverb **sedan** = 'then', 'after that', 'subsequently':

**Först klippte vi gräsmattan. Sedan rensade vi ogräs.**
First we cut the lawn. Then we weeded.

(c) **Då** can also be:

(i)  a temporal conjunction = 'when':

**Då vi kom hem åt vi frukost.**
When we got home we ate breakfast.

(ii) a causal conjunction = 'as':

**Då jag hade pengar köpte jag en bil.**
As I had money I bought a car.

(d) **Sedan** can also be:

(i)  a temporal conjunction = 'after', 'since':

**Sedan han for är hon inte sig lik.**
Since he left she has not been herself.

(ii) a preposition = 'since':

**Jag har känt honom sedan kriget.** I have known him since the war.

### 2 **Därför/därför att**

(a) **Därför** is an adverb = 'for this reason', 'consequently', 'that is why', 'which is why':

**Det är varmt. Därför svettas jag.** It's hot. That's why I'm sweating.

(b) **Därför att** is a subordinating conjunction = 'because', 'on account of', 'owing to':

**Varför svettas du? /Jag svettas/ därför att det är varmt.**
Why are you sweating? /I'm sweating/ because it's hot.

## 3 Eller hur?

Like French 'n'est-ce pas?', German 'nicht wahr?' this phrase concludes
a sentence, corresponding to the English tag-question:

**Han har fått sina pengar, eller hur?**
He has got his money, hasn't he?

**De kommer hem ikväll, eller hur?**
They are coming home tonight, aren't they?

## 4 Först

(a) = 'first' (in time expressions):

**Jag följer med, men först måste jag byta om.**
I'll come, but first I have to change.

(b) = 'not until, only':

**Först igår fick jag veta det.**
It was not until yesterday that I found out.

| | |
|---|---|
| **Jag kom hem först igår.** | I only got home yesterday. |

## 5 Gärna

(a) = 'willingly', 'with pleasure', 'by all means':

**Tar du en öl? Ja, gärna.**
Will you have a beer? Yes, by all means.

(b) = 'like to':

| | |
|---|---|
| **Han badar gärna.** | He likes to swim. |

**Hellre**, comparative form of **gärna**, = 'prefers ... to ...', 'rather':

| | |
|---|---|
| **Han dricker hellre öl än vin.** | He prefers beer to wine. |
| **Te eller kaffe? Hellre kaffe, tack.** | Tea or coffee? I'd rather have coffee, please. |

(c) = 'certainly':

| | |
|---|---|
| **Han får gärna försöka.** | He can certainly try. |

## 6 Långt/länge

(a) **Långt** = 'far' (distance):

| | |
|---|---|
| **Hur långt är det till stan?** | How far is it to town? |

(b) **Länge** = 'long' (time):

**Hur länge har du bott i Sverige?**
How long have you lived in Sweden?

Notice, however, that the adjective is always **lång**:

**Hur lång tid tar det?**            How long will it take?

7 **Ju**, **nog**, **väl**, **nämligen**

As unstressed modal adverbs these words indicate the speaker's attitude
to the utterance. When stressed, **nog** = 'enough', **väl** = 'well', 'rather'

(a) **Ju** = 'you know', 'of course', 'to be sure', 'it is true'. You expect the
listener to agree.

**Det har jag ju aldrig sagt.**        I've never said that, you know.
**Du har ju aldrig varit här förr.**   You've never been here before, of
                                       course.

(b) **Nog** = 'probably', 'presumably', 'I expect', 'I daresay'. The speaker
injects a note of doubt or conciliation.

**Han kommer nog imorgon.**       He'll be here tomorrow, I expect.
**Hon klarar det nog.**           She'll manage it all right.

(c) **Väl** = 'surely', 'I hope', 'I suppose'. The speaker hopes the listener
will agree.

**Du är väl inte sjuk?**          You are not ill, surely?
**Du kommer väl?**                You'll be coming, I hope?

(d) **Nämligen** = 'you understand', 'you see'. New information is provided.

**Du måste komma idag. Imorgon är jag nämligen i Uppsala.**
You'll have to come today. Tomorrow, you see, I'll be in Uppsala.

Cf. **Du måste komma idag. Imorgon är jag ju i Uppsala.**
You'll have to come today. Tomorrow, as you know, I'll be in
   Uppsala.

8 **Redan**

(a) = 'already':

**Är du färdig redan?**           Have you finished already?

(b) = 'even':

**Redan en ytlig undersökning visade detta.**
Even a superficial investigation revealed this.

(c) = 'as early as':

**Redan på 1600-talet var Sverige en stormakt.**
As early as in the 17th century Sweden was a great power.

# 9 INTERJECTIONS

**124** INTERJECTIONS

Interjections are not inflected, and are often marked off by a comma, coming first in the sentence.

1 **Ja**, **nej**, **jo** etc.

(a) In answer to a positive yes/no question **ja/nej** is used:

**Tänker du gå på bio? Ja/Nej.**    Are you going to the cinema? Yes/No.

Strong agreement is indicated by **javisst**, surprise by **jaså!**

(b) If the question assumes a negative answer and the answer stresses a positive response, then **jo** is used:

**Tänker du inte gå på bio? Jo!**    Aren't you going to the cinema? Yes, I am!

2 Expressions of feeling, exclamations

| Pain: | **aj**, **o** | **Aj, vad det gör ont!** | Ow, that hurts! |
|---|---|---|---|
| Surprise: | **oj**, **o**, **å** | **Oj, vad vackert!** | Oh, how beautiful! |
| Disgust: | **usch**, **fy**, **hu** | **Usch, vad hemskt!** | Ugh, how horrible! |

3 Commands to animals, children

**kusch**, **hut** = down (to dogs), **ptro** = whoah (to horses), **hyssch** = shhh (to children)

4 Imitations

Sounds made by animals: **vov vov** (woof), **miau** (miaou), **bää** (baa)
Sounds made by objects: **pang** (bang), **plask** (splash), **bing-bång** (ding-dong)

5 Greetings, exhortations

(a) Meeting, parting: **Goddag!** (How do you do?), **Välkommen!** (plural – **Välkomna!**) (Welcome), **Adjö!** (Goodbye), **Hej!** (Hallo), **Hejsan!** (Hi there!), **Hej då!** (Be seeing you).

(b) Good wishes, thanks: **Skål!** (Cheers), **Gott nytt år!** (Happy New Year), **Varsågod!** (plural – **Varsågoda!**) (Here you are), **Tack så mycket!** (Thank you), **Ha den ära/n/!** (Many happy returns), **Gratulerar /Grattis!** (Congrat-ulations), **Prosit!** (Bless you).

(c)  Apologies etc.: **Förlåt!** (Sorry), **Ursäkta!** (Excuse/Pardon me), **För all del!** (By all means, Don't mention it), **Hursa?/Vasa?/Förlåt** (Pardon, Could you repeat that?)

6 Expletives (In approximately ascending degree of coarseness): **Sjutton! Kors! Herre Gud! Tusan! Förbaskat! Jesses! Fy fasen! Jäklar! Skit! Helvete! Förbannat! Fy fan! Jävlar! Jävlaranamma!**

# 10 PREPOSITIONS

## 125 PREPOSITIONS – INTRODUCTION

1 Prepositions are indeclinable words or set phrases, generally unstressed in speech except when standing after a verb as a stressed particle (**119, 157**).

2 Swedish prepositions have the following prepositional complements:

(a) a noun:

**Han cyklar till staden.**　　　He's cycling to town.

(b) an object pronoun:

**Vi pratade med honom.**　　　We spoke to him.

Notice that after a preposition the pronoun must, as in English, be in the *object* form.

(c) an infinitive phrase:

**Han gick utan att vänta.**　　　He left without waiting.

(d) a subordinate clause:

**Hon var säker på att hon hade rätt.**
She was sure that she was right.

(e) a prepositional or adverbial phrase:

**Vad gör vi efter idag?**
What are we going to do after today?

**Det håller jag för helt omöjligt.**
I consider that totally impossible.

3 Prepositions may adopt three different positions relative to the complement:

(a) Before the complement (the majority of Swedish prepositions do this):

| | |
|---|---|
| **bakom huset** | behind the house |
| **framför tvn** | in front of the TV |
| **hos Olssons** | at the Olssons' |
| **i augusti** | in August |

(b) After the complement (few prepositions do this; those that do are usually stressed):

| | |
|---|---|
| **året om** | /all/ year round |
| **jorden runt** | round the world |
| **oss emellan** | between you and me |

(c) Bracketing the complement:

| | |
|---|---|
| **för tio år sedan** | ten years ago |
| **sedan ett år tillbaka** | for a year |
| **för din skull** | for your sake |

4 Notice that in Swedish the preposition is correctly placed as the last element in a clause:

(a) in **V**-questions (see **78**):

| | |
|---|---|
| **Vad tänker du på?** | What are you thinking about? |

(b) in relative clauses (see **168.2**):

**Du är den (som) jag drömmer om.**   You are the one of whom I dream.

(c) when the prepositional complement occupies the topic position (**160**):

**Honom kan man inte lita på.**   He's not to be relied on.

(d) in infinitive phrases:

**Du är omöjlig att arbeta med.**   You're impossible to work with.

(e) in exclamations:

**Vilket hus du bor i!**   What a house you live in!

5 Some compound prepositions consist of adverb + preposition (see also **120.5**):

| | |
|---|---|
| **Han kom in i huset.** | He came into the house. |
| **De satt framför brasan.** | They sat in front of the fire. |

## 126   THE MOST COMMON SWEDISH PREPOSITIONS

Here is a list of frequent Swedish prepositions. Examples of common ways in which the ten most frequent prepositions (**av, från, för, i, med, om, på, till, under, vid**) are used are given in paragraphs **127–136**. Otherwise the remaining Swedish prepositions are used in much the same way as their English equivalents.

| | | | |
|---|---|---|---|
| **av** | of, with by | **längs** | along |
| **bakom** | behind | **med** | with, by |
| **bland** | among | **mellan** | between |
| **bredvid** | beside | **mot** | to/wards/, against |
| **efter** | after, for | **om** | /a/round, about, in |
| **enligt** | according to | **på** | on, in, for |
| **framför** | in front of | **sedan** | since |
| **från** | from | **till** | until, to, for |
| **för** | for, by, with, of | **trots** | in spite of |
| **för ... sedan** | ago | **under** | under/neath/, below, |
| **före** | before | | during |
| **genom** | through, by | **ur** | out of |
| **hos** | at (the home of) | **utan** | without |
| **i** | in, on, for | **utanför** | outside |
| **inom** | within | **utom** | except /for/ |
| **inför** | before | **vid** | by, around |
| **kring/omkring** | (a)round | **åt** | to/wards/, for |
| | | **över** | over, above, across |

*Notes:*

1 **efter**

(a) **Efter** corresponds to English 'for' after a number of verbs, to suggest the object of a desire or search:

| | |
|---|---|
| **Jag längtar efter engelsk mat.** | I long for English food. |
| **Vi letar/ringer efter dem.** | We're looking/phoning for them. |

(b) **Stäng dörren efter dig!**          Close the door behind you!

2 **För ... sedan** brackets the complement:

**Detta hände för 10 år sedan.**          This happened ten years ago.

3 **Genom** is used with the infinitive to render English 'by' + 'ing-form' in expressions such as:

**Han vann genom att fuska.**          He won by cheating.

4 Hos corresponds to French 'chez', German 'bei' (= at the place of work/home of):

| | |
|---|---|
| **Vi bor hos Linds.** | We're staying with the Linds. |
| **Han är hos tandläkaren.** | He's at the dentist's. |

Note also:

**Det står hos Freud.**          That's in Freud/'s works/.

5 **Inför** suggests English 'before', often in a figurative sense:

| | |
|---|---|
| **Han stod inför domaren.** | He stood before the judge. |
| **Han ställs inför svårigheter.** | He's faced with difficulties. |
| **Jag var orolig inför resan.** | I was uneasy before (= at the prospect of) the journey. |

6 Åt

(a) renders 'to/wards/' in set expressions of place:

**Åt vilket håll ska jag köra?**　Which direction shall I drive in?
**Kör åt vänster/åt norr.**　Drive to the left/north!

(b) may indicate an indirect object rendered in English by 'for':

**Köp en åt mig också!**　Buy one for me too!

7 Över

(a) corresponds also to English 'past' in clock-time expressions:

**Klockan visar 5 minuter över 2.**　It's five past two.

(b) Note also:

**en karta över Sverige**　a map of Sweden
**en lista över deltagarna**　a list of participants

## 127　AV

**Av** basically suggests origin or source, although **från** is more common with origins that are actual locations. **Av** is also used to indicate the passive agent (see **118, 158, 165**).

| Agent | Material | Cause | Location | Measure | Possession |
|---|---|---|---|---|---|
| *by* | *of* | *from/with* | *off/from* | *of* | *of* |

*BY*
**Huset köptes av en svensk.**　The house was bought by a Swede.
**en roman /skriven/ av Bergman**　A novel /written/ by Bergman

*OF*
**Huset är byggt av tegel.**　The house is built of brick.
**Det står i utkanten av stan.**　It's on the edge of town.
**Kungen av Sverige**　The King of Sweden
**Nio av tio svar var riktiga.**　Nine out of ten answers were correct.
**Det var snällt/duktigt av dig.**　That was kind/clever of you.

*FROM*
**Jag får ont i huvudet av bullret.**　I get a headache from the noise.
**Får du någon glädje av det?**　Do you get pleasure from that?

*WITH*
**Hon grät av rädsla/glädje.**　She cried with fear/with joy.

*OFF*
**Han steg/hoppade av bussen.**　He got/jumped off the bus.

Note also:

| | |
|---|---|
| **på grund av** | because of, due to |
| **med hjälp av** | with the aid of |
| **av misstag** | by mistake |
| **av en händelse** | by accident |

## 128  FRÅN

**Från** (sometimes **ifrån**) is used much the same as English 'from' to suggest origin, a point of departure or vantage.

| Location | Source | Time |
|---|---|---|
| *from* | *from* | *from* |

*FROM*

| | |
|---|---|
| **Det står 220 meter från vägen.** | It's 220 metres from the road. |
| **När flyttade du från Sverige?** | When did you move from Sweden? |
| **Utifrån det vi vet ...** | From what we know ... |

Note also: A number of adverbial expressions of place are formed with post-positioned **ifrån** (see **122.1**):

| | |
|---|---|
| **Var kommer du ifrån?** | Where do you come from? |

## 129  FÖR

**För** corresponds to English 'for' in a wide range of senses, but not generally with time expressions (see **138**):

| Intention/Purpose | Indirect object | Cause |
|---|---|---|
| *for* | *to* | *for* |

*FOR*

| | |
|---|---|
| **ett program för barn** | A programme for children |
| **Jag gör det för dig/för din skull.** | I do it for you/for your sake. |
| **Tack för hjälpen!** | Thanks for your help! |
| **Han är känd/berömd för det.** | He is renowned/famous for that. |
| **Vad gråter du för?** | What are you crying for? |
| **en gång för alla** | once and for all |

*TO*

| | |
|---|---|
| **Förklara det för mig!** | Explain it to me! |
| **Kan jag vara till hjälp för dig?** | Can I be of help to you? |
| **Tala om för oss vad som hände.** | Tell us what happened. |
| **Han berättade historien för mig.** | He told me the story. |

Note also:

| | |
|---|---|
| **Jag är rädd för ormar.** | I'm afraid of snakes. |
| **Han intresserar sig för musik.** | He's interested in music. |
| **Jag har svårt/lätt för språk.** | I find languages hard/easy. |
| **att skriva för hand** | to write by hand |
| **dag för dag** | day by day |
| **för det första/andra osv** | in the first/second place etc. |
| **Vad är det för slags bil?** | What kind of car is it? |

## 130   I

I is the second most frequent word in Swedish, with many idiomatic usages beyond its basic meaning 'in'. With public buildings and places of work or entertainment, English 'in' is often rendered by Swedish **på** (see **133**, **140**). For the uses of **i** with expressions of time, see **138**.

| Location | Material | Time when | Time duration | State | Frequency |
|---|---|---|---|---|---|
| *in/on/at* | *in* | *in* | *for* | *in* | *⊗/per* |

*IN*

| | |
|---|---|
| **Han sitter i rummet.** | He is sitting in the room. |
| **en staty i brons** | a statue in bronze |
| **Han är i god form.** | He's in good shape. |
| **De kommer i april.** | They're coming in April. |

*ON*

| | |
|---|---|
| **Hon sitter i gräset.** | She's sitting on the grass. |

*AT*

| | |
|---|---|
| **Mor är i kyrkan.** | Mother's at church. |

*FOR*

| | |
|---|---|
| **De stannade i fem veckor.** | They stayed for five weeks. |

*PER*

| | |
|---|---|
| **90 kilometer i timmen** | 90 kilometres per hour |
| **en gång i veckan/i månaden** | once a week/a month |

Note also:

| | |
|---|---|
| **Går Eva i skolan/i kyrkan?** | Does Eva go to school/to church? |
| **Klockan är fem minuter i tio.** | It's five minutes to ten. |
| **Jag har ont i magen/huvudet.** | I have a stomach-ache/headache. |
| **Han tvättar sig i ansiktet.** | He washes his face. (See also **43**.) |

## 131    MED

**Med** may be used to render most of the meanings of English 'with'.

| Manner | Possession |
|---|---|
| *by/with/in* | *with* |

*WITH*

| | |
|---|---|
| **Han åkte dit med sin familj.** | He went there with his family. |
| **Han är mannen med sex söner.** | He's the man with six sons. |
| **Hur står det till med dig?** | How are things with you? |
| **Ät inte med fingrarna!** | Don't eat with your fingers! |
| **Det värsta med honom är hans dåliga humör.** | The worst thing with (= about) him is his bad temper. |
| **kaffe med grädde** | coffee with cream |

*BY*

| | |
|---|---|
| **åka med buss/bil/tåg osv** | travel by bus/car/train etc. |
| **Skicka pengarna med posten!** | Send the money by post. |

*IN*

| | |
|---|---|
| **Tala med hög röst!** | Speak in a loud voice! |

Note also:

| | |
|---|---|
| **Får jag prata med honom?** | May I speak to him? |
| **ha dåligt med tid/pengar osv** | to have little time/money etc. |
| **Jag har inte tid med det.** | I've no time for that. |

## 132    OM

**Om** is used in a great many idiomatic senses, perhaps most frequently in certain expressions indicating future time (see **138**).

| Location | Future time when | Subject matter |
|---|---|---|
| *(a)round* | *in* | *on/about* |

*(A)ROUND*

| | |
|---|---|
| **Ta en scarf om halsen.** | Put a scarf round your neck. |

*IN*

| | |
|---|---|
| **De kommer om en vecka.** | They're coming in a week/'s time/. |

*ABOUT/ON*

| | |
|---|---|
| **Vi har pratat om dig.** | We have been talking about you. |
| **en bok om Sverige** | a book about/on Sweden |
| **Det är synd om honom.** | It's a pity about him. |

Note also:

| | |
|---|---|
| **norr om/söder om** | north of/south of |
| **gott om/ont om** | plenty of/little (= a lack of) |
| **tycka synd om** | to feel sorry for someone |
| **tre gånger om dagen/året** | three times a (per) day/year |
| **Vi tycker om dig.** | We like you. |

In certain instances, primarily with parts of the body, **om** is used without an English equivalent (see also **43**):

**Han är smutsig/kall/våt/svettig om händerna.**
His hands are dirty/cold/wet/sweaty.

| | |
|---|---|
| **Jag fryser om tårna.** | My toes are cold. |
| **Du är röd om kinderna.** | Your cheeks are red. |

## 133  PÅ

**På** is used in many idiomatic senses in addition to the basic meaning of 'on /top of/'. **På** is often used to render English 'in' with public buildings and places of work or entertainment (See **140**). For uses of **på** with expressions of time, see **138**.

| Location | Motion | Time when | Time duration | Measure | Possession |
|---|---|---|---|---|---|
| *on/at/in* | *to* | *on* + days | *in, (not) for* | *of* | *of* |
| | | *in* + season | (see **138.4**) | | |
| | | *at* + festival | | | |

*ON*

| | |
|---|---|
| **Det ligger på bordet.** | It's on the table. |
| **Han satte hatten på huvudet.** | He put his hat on his head. |
| **Vi åker dit på söndagarna.** | We go there on Sundays. |

*IN*

| | |
|---|---|
| **Jag arbetar på en bank/ ett hotell.** | I work in a bank/a hotel. |
| **Vi åker dit på vintern.** | We go there in winter. |
| **Han gör allt på väldigt kort tid.** | He does everything in a very short time. |

*AT*

| | |
|---|---|
| **Vi träffades på biblioteket/bion.** | We met at the library/cinema. |
| **Vi åker dit på julen.** | We go there at Christmas. |

*TO*

| | |
|---|---|
| **Vi går på bio/matchen.** | We're going to the cinema/match. |

*OF*

| | |
|---|---|
| **ett barn på fyra år** | a child of four |

| | |
|---|---|
| **titeln på/priset på boken** | the title/price of the book |
| **i början på augusti** | at the beginning of August |

Note also:

| | |
|---|---|
| **Jag tänker ofta på dig.** | I often think of you. |
| **Vi väntar på dig.** | We're waiting for you. |
| **på samma sätt/på detta sätt** | in the same way/in this way |
| **Han är bra/dålig på att simma.** | He is good/bad at swimming. |

## 134   TILL

Basically **till** suggests movement or progression towards some target, but it may also be used to express indirect object relationships.

| Motion | Time when | Indirect object | Possession |
|---|---|---|---|
| *to* | *until* | *to/for* | *of* |

*TO*

| | |
|---|---|
| **Han reser till Amerika.** | He's going to America. |
| **Han kom till makten 1929.** | He came to power in 1929. |
| **ett nio till fem jobb** | a nine-to-five job |
| **Vad sa han till de andra?** | What did he say to the others? |

*UNTIL*

| | |
|---|---|
| **Kan du inte stanna till imorgon?** | Can't you stay until tomorrow? |

*FOR*

| | |
|---|---|
| **Vi åt fisk till lunch.** | We had fish for lunch. |
| **Han köpte en bil till mig.** | He bought a car for me. |
| **Vad använder du det till?** | What do you use that for? |
| **till exempel** | for example |

*OF*

| | |
|---|---|
| **Nils är en gammal vän till mig.** | Nils is an old friend of mine. |

Notice also:

| | |
|---|---|
| **Han är elektriker till yrket.** | He is an electrician by trade. |

Remnants of old genitive case endings are still found in some set phrases after **till**:

| | |
|---|---|
| **Gå till sängs nu, Nils!** | Go to bed now, Nils! See **46.2** |

## 135   UNDER

Basically **under** corresponds to ideas expressed by English 'below', 'under/neath/' etc. However, it is also used to render English 'during'.

| Location<br>*under/below/beneath* | Time duration<br>*during/for* | Measure<br>*under/below* |
|---|---|---|

*UNDER*
**Boken ligger under bordet.**        The book is under the table.
**Bilen körde under bron.**           The car drove under the bridge.
**barn under femton /år/**            children under 15 /years old/
**Är allt under kontroll?**           Is everything under control?

*BELOW*
**vid temperaturer under noll**       at temperatures below zero

*DURING*
**Vad gjorde du under kriget?**       What did you do during the war?
**Vi blev goda vänner under**         We became firm friends during
  **samtalets gång.**                   the course of the conversation.

## 136   VID

**Vid** suggests adjacency or proximity.

| Location<br>*by/at* | Time when<br>*around* |
|---|---|

*BY*
**Vi har en stuga vid kusten.**       We have a cottage by/on the coast.
**Han satt vid fönstret.**            He sat by the window.

*AT*
**Han satt vid bordet.**              He sat at the table.
**Hon studerar vid universitetet.**   She's studying at university.

*AROUND*
**Vi träffas vid tiotiden.**          We'll meet around ten.

Note also:

**vid ankomst/vid avgång**            on arrival/on departure
**vid närmare eftertanke**            on closer consideration
**en man vid namn Jansson**           a man called Jansson
**Han är fortfarande vid liv.**       He's still alive.

# TRANSLATING PREPOSITIONS

## 137   SOME COMMON ENGLISH PREPOSITIONS AND THEIR SWEDISH EQUIVALENTS

Before attempting to render English prepositional phrases into Swedish, consult the table below for help in choosing a suitable Swedish equivalent.

| | Time | Place | Manner | Subject matter | Indirect object | Agent | Measure |
|---|---|---|---|---|---|---|---|
| about | omkring/ vid | omkring | | om | | | omkring |
| above | | över | | | | | över/ framför |
| after | efter | efter/ bakom | efter | | | | |
| against | | mot | mot | | | | |
| at | 138.3 | 140 | | | | | |
| before | före | framför/ före | | | | | |
| below | under | under | | | | | |
| by | före/till | vid/hos | med/ genom | | | av | |
| during | under | | | | | | |
| for | 138.4 | | | | för/att/till | | till/för |
| from | från | från/av | | | | | |
| in | 138.1 | 140 i/på | | | | | |
| into | | in i | | | | | |
| of | | | | 141 | | | 127, 132f, 141 |
| on | 138.2 | 140 | | om | | | |
| over | över | över | | | | | över |
| through | under/ genom | genom | genom | | | | |
| to | till/ i + clock time | 126.6, 130, 133 | | | till/för | | |
| under | | under | under | | | | |
| with | | hos | med | | | | |

## 138   TRANSLATING 'IN, ON, AT' ETC. AS EXPRESSIONS OF TIME

Because of the idiomatic nature of Swedish prepositional expressions of time, it is difficult to formulate rules which are both concise and 100% reliable. For the sake of brevity some variations have been deliberately omitted from what follows. The aim here is to indicate a scheme of basic conventions applicable in the majority of instances.

1 'in' + expressions of time

| In + | Year | Decade/Century | Month | Season |
|---|---|---|---|---|
| past | ⊗år 1949 | på 1800-talet | i januari | i våras/på våren |
| habitual | – | – | i januari | på våren |
| present | – | på 90-talet | i januari | i vår |
| future | ⊗år 2010 | på 2000-talet | i januari | i vår |

*Notes:*

1 The preposition **om** (Eng. 'in') answers the question 'When?' to express future action:

**De reser om en timme/om en vecka/om ett par år.**
They're going in an hour/in a week/in a couple of years.

2 The preposition **på** (Eng. 'in') answers the question 'How long does it/will it take?':

**De reser dit på en timme/på en vecka.**
They can travel there in an hour/in a week.
OR: It will take them an hour/a week to get there.

3 **I våras** etc. and **i vår** etc. both render English 'in spring' etc. but mean 'last/next spring' respectively.

4 For less specific expressions with seasons **på våren** is used for both past and future:

**Detta hände på våren för länge sedan.**
This happened in the spring many years ago.

5 The preposition **på** is usually omitted when the season is followed by a year date:

**Detta hände våren 1986 och kommer att hända igen våren 2062.**
This happened in the spring of 1986 and will happen again in the spring of 2062.

6 Note the idiomatic use of **på** to render 'in/for' as an expression indicating duration in negative sentences (see also 4 'for + duration' below) :

**Jag har inte sett henne på tre år/på länge.**
I haven't seen her for three years/for a long time.

2 'on' + expressions of time

| On + | Weekday | Date |
|---|---|---|
| past | i söndags | den 1 (första) juli |
| habitual | på söndagarna | den 1 (första) juli |
| present | (idag) | den 1 (första) juli |
| future | på söndag | den 1 (första) juli |

*Notes:*

1 **I söndags** etc. and **på söndag** etc. render English 'on Sunday' = last Sunday etc. and 'this/next Sunday' etc. respectively.

2 For less specific expressions of time **på söndag** etc. may be used.

**Detta hände på en söndag för länge sedan.**
This happened on a Sunday/one Sunday a long time ago.

3 For weekday + calendar date expressions Swedish usually has the definite form of the weekday and no preposition:

**Detta hände fredagen den 1 mars och händer igen söndagen den 5 maj.**
This happened on Friday March 1st and will happen again on Sunday May 5th.

4 **I söndags** etc. may be combined with the parts of the day:

**Detta hände i söndags morse.**     This happened on Sunday morning.

3 'at' + expressions of time

| At + | Festival | Clock |
|---|---|---|
| past | **i julas** | **klockan 10 (tio)** |
| habitual | **på jul/på jularna** | **klockan 10 (tio)** |
| present | **i jul** | **klockan 10 (tio)** |
| future | **i jul/ till jul** | **klockan 10 (tio)** |

*Notes:*

1 **I julas** etc. and **i jul** etc. render English 'at Christmas' = 'last Christmas' etc. and 'this / next Christmas' etc. respectively.

2 For less specific expressions of time **på jul** etc. may be used.

**Detta hände på jul för många år sedan.**
This happened at Christmas many years ago.

3 With year-date expressions Swedish usually has the definite form of the festival and no preposition:

**Detta hände julen 1954 och kommer att hända igen julen 1999.**
This happened at Christmas 1954 and will happen again at Christmas 1999.

4 'for' + duration

Swedish **i** + expression of time:

**Han har bott här i tre år.**     He's lived here for three years.

Swedish **under** if English 'for' = 'for the duration of':

**Han bodde här under kriget.**     He lived here for the war.

Swedish **på** renders English 'for/in' in negative clauses:

**Jag har inte bott där på 5 år.**
I haven't lived there for/in five years.

*Note:*

| for a long time | **länge** (no preposition!) |
|---|---|
| not for a long time | **inte ... på länge** |

## 139   PREPOSITIONS IN EXPRESSIONS OF TIME – SUMMARY

| | Past | Habitual | Present | Future |
|---|---|---|---|---|
| **Seasons** | | | | |
| | **förra våren/** | **på våren** | **i vår** | **i vår/ nästa** |
| | **i våras** | | | **vår** |
| | last spring | in/the/spring | this spring | next spring |
| **Festivals** | | | | |
| | **förra julen/** | **på julen** | **i jul** | **i jul/ nästa jul** |
| | **i julas** | **på jularna** | | |
| | last Xmas | at Xmas | this Xmas | next Xmas |
| **Days** | | | | |
| | **igår** | | **i dag** | **i morgon** |
| | yesterday | | today | tomorrow |
| | **i söndags** | **på söndagarna** | | **på söndag** |
| | last Sunday | on Sundays | | next Sunday |
| **Parts of the day** | | | | |
| | **i morse** | **på morgonen** | **nu på** | **imorgon bitti** |
| | | | **morgonen** | |
| | /earlier/this | in the | this | tomorrow |
| | morning | morning/s/ | morning | morning |
| | **i eftermiddags** | **på efter-** | **nu på efter-** | **i eftermiddag** |
| | | **middagen** | **middagen** | |
| | /earlier/this | in the | this | /later/ this |
| | afternoon | afternoon | afternoon | afternoon |
| | **igår kväll** | **på kvällen/** | **ikväll** | **imorgon kväll** |
| | | **kvällarna** | | |
| | last night | in the | this evening | tomorrow |
| | | evening/s/ | | evening |
| | **i natt** | **på natten/** | **i natt** | **i natt** |
| | | **nätterna** | | |
| | last night/ | at night | tonight | /later/ tonight |
| | during the | | | |
| | night | | | |
| **Years, months** | | | | |
| | **i fjol/förra** | | **i år** | **nästa år** |
| | **året** | | | |
| | last year | | this year | next year |
| | **i januari** | **i januari** | **i januari** | **i januari** |
| | last January | in January | this January | next January |

## 140    TRANSLATING 'IN, ON, AT' ETC. AS EXPRESSIONS OF PLACE

Because of the idiomatic usages of **i** and **på**, translation of 'in', 'on', 'at' etc. expressing place relationships is not always straightforward. A rule of thumb (to which there are many exceptions!) is that Swedish usage requires:

| | |
|---|---|
| *på + surface* | *i + volume* |
| **tavlan på väggen** | **möss i väggen** |
| the picture on the wall | mice in the wall |
| **duken på bordet** | **duken i lådan** |
| the cloth on the table | the cloth in the drawer |
| **ett sår på läppen** | **ett sår i munnen** |
| a sore on one's lip | a sore in one's mouth |
| Note: **Han bor på landet** | **Han bor i landet.** |
| He lives in the country/side/ | He lives in the country (i.e. state) |
| | **prata i telefon** |
| | speak on the telephone |
| | **ett program i radio/TV** |
| | a programme on the radio/TV |
| **Han sitter på en stol.** | **Han sitter i en stol.** |
| He's sitting on a (dining) chair. | He's sitting in an armchair. |

*Major exceptions:*

1 **På** = 'in'/'at' with public buildings etc.

**Vi träffades på museet/Domus/sjukhuset/hotellet.**
We met in the museum/in Domus/in the hospital/at the hotel.

2 **På** = 'in'/'at' with place of work or study:

**Hon är på jobbet/på ett möte.**    She's at work/in a meeting.

**Han arbetar på Volvo/på ett varuhus.**
He works at Volvo/in a department store.

3 **På** = 'in'/'at'/'on' with places of entertainment or enjoyment:

**Vi träffades på en dans/på bion/på ett bröllop/på semester.**
We met at a dance/at the cinema/at a wedding/on holiday.

4 **Hos** = 'at' with the names of people or their professions to indicate 'at the place of work/home of':

| Vi var hos Olssons. | We were at the Olssons'/place/. |
| Han är hos frisören. | He's at the hairdresser's. |

5 **Vid** = 'on'/'at'/'by' with many words for things which extend lengthwise:

| Han bor vid kusten. | He lives on the coast. |
| Han stod vid disken/floden. | He stood at the counter/by the river. |

## 141   TRANSLATING 'OF'

The English preposition 'of' may be rendered in a great many ways in Swedish. What follows cannot hope to be complete but will provide hints on how to translate 'of' in the commonest instances:

1 Possessive 'of'

(a) English possessive 'of' is commonly rendered by Swedish s-genitives (cf. **46**):

| the meaning of life | **livets mening** |
| the title of the book | **bokens titel** |

(b) In many cases Swedish prefers a compound noun:

| the tops of the mountains | **fjälltopparna** |
| (cf. the mountain tops) | |
| the leg of the table | **bordsbenet** |
| (cf. the table leg) | |

(c) Double genitives are generally constructed with **till** (cf **134**):

| a friend of yours/the president's | **en vän till dig/presidenten** |

2 'The City of Stockholm' etc.
When English 'of' may be replaced by commas indicating apposition (so-called appositive genitive) it is rendered without a preposition in Swedish:

| the kingdom of Norway | **kungariket Norge** |
| the month of May | **månaden maj** |

*Note:* The city of Stockholm =
  – geographical location                   **staden Stockholm**
  – council, citizens etc.                   **Stockholms stad**
  the battle of Lützen                       **slaget vid Lützen**

3 'A cup of tea' etc.
Expressions with 'of' indicating measure (so-called partitive genitive) are generally rendered without a preposition in Swedish:

| a cup of tea | **en kopp te** |
| a pair of shoes | **ett par skor** |

| | |
|---|---|
| 12 kilos of peas | **12 kilo ärter** |
| a large number of Swedes | **ett stort antal svenskar** |

*Notes:*

| | | |
|---|---|---|
| 1 | Half of/part of the book | **hälften av/en del av boken** |
| 2 | Swedish usually has **på** when English 'of' is followed by a number: | |

| | |
|---|---|
| a boy of 5 | **en pojke på 5 år** |
| a wage of 50 kronor | **en lön på 50 kronor** |

## 4 Dates

Swedish usually has no preposition for 'of' used in dates:

| | |
|---|---|
| the first of January | **den 1 (första) januari** |
| in May of 1956 | **i maj 1956** |

## 5 'A heart of stone' etc.

'Of' indicating material is rendered by **av** in Swedish (cf. **127**):

| | |
|---|---|
| a heart of stone | **ett hjärta av sten** |
| a statue of gold | **en staty av guld** |

## 6 'The king of Sweden' etc.

'Of' indicating origin may generally be rendered by Swedish **av** or **från** (The sense of geographical origin is much stronger with **från**):

| | |
|---|---|
| the king of Sweden | **kungen av Sverige** |
| there was a young man of Nantucket | **det var en ung man från Nantucket** |

## 7 'North of' etc.

'Of' with compass points and directions left/right = **om** in Swedish:

| | |
|---|---|
| north of Malmö | **norr om Malmö** |
| left of the church | **till vänster om kyrkan** |

| | |
|---|---|
| *Note:* the north of England | **norra England** |

# 11  CONJUNCTIONS

## 142  COORDINATING CONJUNCTIONS

These join clauses or elements of the same kind and are always found between the words or groups of words that they link (see **149**). They do *not* affect the word order within the groups of words that they link.

Coordination (linking) of:

| | |
|---|---|
| *Hans* och *Greta* **lyssnar på jazz.** | two subjects |
| **De** *sitter* och *lyssnar.* | two verbs |
| *Jag tycker om Olle* **och** *han älskar mig.* | two main clauses (straight word order) |
| *Popmusik älskar jag,* **och** *det gör hon också.* | two main clauses (inverted word order) |
| **Jag hoppas** *att han vinner* och *att han har rekordtid.* | two subordinate clauses |

*Coordinating conjunctions* include:

| | | |
|---|---|---|
| *och/samt* | **Möblerna och tavlorna såldes.** | and |
| *eller* | **Pengar eller livet!** | or |
| *men* | **Han är intelligent men ful.** See **145.6**. | but |
| *utan* | **Han var inte full utan bara trött.** See **145.6**. | but |
| *fast* | **Mor var sjuk, fast det kunde jag ju inte veta.** | but, /al/though |
| *för* | **Han kom inte för han var sjuk.** | as, because |
| *så* | **Det är sent, så vi går nu.** | so |
| *som* | **Då som nu var det stor arbetslöshet här.** | as |

*Note:* **och** links elements of equal weight, whereas **samt** links elements of unequal weight:

**Kansliet samt biblioteket hålls stängda under sommaren.** (**Kansliet** is more important.)
The offices and library are closed during the summer.

## 143  SUBORDINATING CONJUNCTIONS

These link main clauses to subordinate clauses, and always introduce the subordinate clause wherever it is positioned in the sentence. Some subordinating conjunctions therefore begin the sentence:

Cf.   **Jag sover** *när* **jag är trött.**   I sleep when I'm tired.
      MC          sub conj + SC

**När jag är trött sover jag.**   When I'm tired I sleep.
sub conj + SC   MC

Some subordinating conjunctions never introduce the sentence, however:

**Hon kom hit**   *för att* **hon ville lära sig svenska.**
                  sub conj + SC
She came here     (in order) to learn Swedish.

Subordinating conjunctions and other words (see **144**) which introduce subordinate clauses do affect the word order and occupy the first position in the subordinate clause (see **169**). There are two main types of subordinating conjunction:

1 *General subordinators* introduce indirect speech (**att**) and indirect yes/no questions (**om**), but impart no meaning to the clause, unlike other subordinating conjunctions in 2 below:

       *att*   **Han sa** *att* **han arbetade hårt.**        that
cf.            **Jag arbetar hårt.**

       *om*    **Jag undrar,** *om* **han arbetar så mycket.**   whether, if
cf.            **Arbetar han så mycket?**

2 *Other subordinating conjunctions* introduce different kinds of adverbial clause (cf. **155, 168**):

(a) Time:

**När/Då/Sedan han hade parkerat bilen, gick han in.**   when, after
**Medan gräset gror, dör kon.**                          while
**Innan vi gick hem tackade vi värdinnan.**              before

(b) Cause:

**Vi vann** *därför att* **vi var bäst.**                 because
**Eftersom/Sedan de var sämre, förlorade de.**           since, as,
                                                         because

(c) Condition:

**Om/Ifall du är snäll ska du få glass.**                if

(d) Concession:

**Han är glad** *fast/än/* **han inte är kry.**           although

(e) Intention:

**Vi måste friställa folk** *för att* **vi ska rädda firman.**   in order that

| | |
|---|---|
| **Han skrev upp det** *så* **/att/ han skulle minnas det.** | so that |
| **Se upp** *så* **/att/ du inte blir överkörd!** | so that |

(f) Result:

| | |
|---|---|
| **Han sprang** *så* **fort** *att* **han blev andfådd.** | so/... that/ |

(g) Comparison:

| | |
|---|---|
| **Han är** *lika* **stor** *som* **hans bror.** | as ... as ... |
| **Du är inte** *så* **gammal** *som* **jag.** | as ... as ... |
| **Hon var äldre** *än* **jag väntat mig.** | than |
| *Ju* **äldre jag blir** *desto* **tröttare blir jag.** | the ... the ... |

## 144  OTHER SUBORDINATORS

These are words which are not conjunctions, but nevertheless introduce subordinate clauses.

1 *Interrogative pronouns* (v-words) and *adverbs* (cf. **78**).
These words introduce indirect v-questions (cf. **147.2**, **148**):

| | | |
|---|---|---|
| | **Jag undrade** *vart* **han hade tagit vägen.** | where |
| cf. | **Vart har han tagit vägen?** | |
| | **Jag undrar** *vem som* **kysser henne nu.** | who |
| | **Jag vet inte** *vilken* **du menar.** | which |

2 *Relative pronouns* and *adverbs* (cf. **77**)
These words introduce relative clauses (cf. **168.2**), which usually form attributes to subjects, objects or complements:

| | |
|---|---|
| **Brevet** *som* **jag skickade var maskinskrivet.** | which, that |
| The letter /that/ I sent was typewritten. | |

| | |
|---|---|
| **En man** *vars* **namn jag har glömt kom fram till mig.** | whose |
| A man whose name I have forgotten came up to me. | |

| | |
|---|---|
| **Han hittade en skog** *där* **det fanns lingon.** | where |
| He found a forest where there were lingonberries. | |

| | |
|---|---|
| **Gustav II Adolf blev med tiden tämligen fet,** *vilket* | |
| **alltid nämns i skolböckerna.** | which |
| Gustavus Adolphus in time became rather fat, which is always mentioned in the textbooks. | |

## 145  SOME PROBLEM CONJUNCTIONS

1 'After' = both preposition and conjunction in English. **Efter** is only a preposition and cannot alone introduce a clause.

The house burned down shortly after they left.
**Huset brann ner kort** *efter* **/det/ att de åkte.**

2 'As' = 'for' = **för (ty)**

He disappeared as he was afraid.    **Han försvann för han var rädd.**

**Ty** is used only in formal contexts.

= 'while' = **medan**

As he was speaking he went red.    *Medan* **han talade rodnade han.**

= 'because' = **eftersom/då**

As he isn't coming we will begin.
**Eftersom han inte kommer börjar vi.**

= 'like' = **/lik/som**

Now as before it is very difficult.    **Nu** *liksom* **förr är det mycket svårt.**

3 'As . . . as . . . '

– when a comparison is made in a positive clause = **lika . . . som**

He is as gifted as his sister.    **Han är** *lika* **begåvad** *som* **sin syster.**

– when a comparison is made in a negative clause = **så . . . som**

He is not as gifted as his sister.
**Han är inte** *så* **begåvad** *som* **sin syster.**

4 'Before' – as a conjunction after a positive main clause = **innan**

We visited him before we came here.
**Vi hälsade på honom** *innan* **vi kom hit.**

– as a conjunction after a negative main clause = **förrän**

It was not long before he arrived.
**Det dröjde inte länge** *förrän* **han kom.**

– as an adverb = 'earlier', 'previously' = **förr/förut/tidigare**

I have never been to Dalarna before.
**Jag har aldrig varit i Dalarna** *förr/förut/tidigare.*

– as a preposition = **före/innan**

We met Jan before Easter.    **Vi träffade Jan** *före/innan* **påsk.**

5 'Both' – as a conjunction – 'both X and Y' = **både . . . och . . .**

Both Erik and Eva were language students.
*Både* **Erik** *och* **Eva var språkstuderande.**

– as an indefinite pronoun – 'both Xs' = **båda**

Both students studied languages.    ***Båda* studenter studerade språk.**

6 'But'

– as a conjunction after a positive clause or a negative clause not directly contradicting the first clause (i.e. but *in spite of that*) = **men**

The essay is long but does not say very much.
**Uppsatsen är lång *men* den säger inte mycket.**

The essay is not long but is very boring.
**Uppsatsen är inte lång *men* den är mycket tråkig.**

– as a conjunction after a negative main clause, the second clause directly contradicting the first (i.e. but *on the contrary*) = **utan**

The essay isn't long but is actually quite short.
**Uppsatsen är inte lång *utan* egentligen ganska kort.**

Notice also: **inte bara . . . utan också . . .**

**Hon var *inte bara* vacker *utan också* intelligent.**
She was not only beautiful but also intelligent.

– as a preposition = **utom**

All students but one have passed.
**Alla studenter *utom* en har blivit godkända.**

7 'That' – as a subordinating conjunction = **att**

They said /that/ they were pleased.  **De sa /*att*/ de var nöjda.**

– as a relative pronoun (= 'which', 'whom') = **som**

He bought the house /that/ we liked.
**Han köpte huset /*som*/ vi tyckte om.**

– in cleft sentences (cf. **167**) = **som**

It was my idea that won the prize.  **Det var min idé *som* vann priset.**

– in the expression 'now that' = **nu då/när**

Now that she has arrived we can begin.
***Nu då* hon har kommit kan vi börja.**

# 12 WORD ORDER AND SENTENCE STRUCTURE

## 146 WORD CLASSES AND SENTENCE ELEMENTS

Hitherto in this book we have examined word classes (or parts of speech), i.e. words grouped according to their form or meaning, e.g. nouns, verbs. In this section of the book we examine sentence elements, i.e. the function of words and groups of words in the sentence.

| | **Vi** | **har** | **inte** | **köpt** | **tidningen** | **ikväll** |
|---|---|---|---|---|---|---|
| | (We | have | not | bought | the paper | tonight) |
| *Word class* | *Pronoun* | *Verb* | *Adverb* | *Verb* | *Noun* | *Adverb* |
| *Sentence Element* | *Subject* | *Finite verb* | *Clausal adverbial* | *Non-finite verb* | *Object* | *Other adverbial* |

A sentence element is any word or group of words in Swedish which can be moved to the beginning of a sentence (main clause statement):

***Ikväll* har vi inte köpt tidningen.**
Tonight we haven't bought the paper.

***Tidningen* har vi inte köpt ikväll.**
(Literally: The paper we haven't bought tonight.)

## 147 SENTENCE TYPES

Most sentences possess both a subject (see **151**) and a finite verb (see **152**).

1 In describing clauses we often use the terms FV1-clause, FV2-clause.

   In FV1-clauses the finite verb comes first in the sentence.
   In FV2-clauses the finite verb comes second, after some other element.

2 The five sentence types in Swedish are shown in the table below.

   S = subject
   straight (word order) = subject – finite verb
   inverted (word order) = finite verb – subject

| Position: 1 | 2 | 3 | 4–7 | Word order: |
|---|---|---|---|---|
| *STATEMENT* | | | | |
| *Subject* | *Finite verb* | – | *etc.* | |
| **Han** | **kommer** | – | **hem idag.** | *FV-2, straight* |
| | | | | |
| *Non-subject* | *Finite verb* | *Subject etc.* | | |
| **Idag** | **kommer** | **han** | **hem.** | *FV-2, inverted* |
| *YES/NO QUESTIONS* | | | | |
| | *Finite verb* | *Subject* | *etc.* | |
| | **Kommer** | **han** | **hem idag?** | *FV-1, inverted* |
| | **Ska** | **han** | **inte komma hem idag?** | *FV-1, inverted* |
| *V-QUESTION* | | | | |
| *V-word* | *Finite verb* | *Subject* | *etc.* | |
| **Varför** | **kommer** | **han** | **hem idag?** | *FV-2, inverted* |
| **Vem** S | **kommer** | – | **hem idag?** | *FV-2, straight* |
| **Vad** S | **händer** | – | **därborta?** | *FV-2, straight* |
| *COMMAND* | | | | |
| | *Finite verb* | *Subject* | *etc.* | |
| | **Kom** | – | **hem nu!** | *FV-1, no subject* |
| *WISH* | | | | |
| | *Finite verb* | *Subject* | *etc.* | |
| | **Må** (Subjunctive) | **det** | **gå dig väl!** | *FV-1, inverted* |
| | **Leve** | **brudparet!** | – | *FV-1, inverted* |
| *Subject* | *Finite verb* | – | *etc.* | |
| **Det** | **vore** | – | **roligt att träffas!** | *FV-2, straight* |

*Translations:* He's coming home today. Today he's coming home. Is he coming home today? Won't he come home today? Why is he coming home today? Who is coming home today? What's happening over there? Come home now! May it go well for you! Long live the bride and groom! It would be fun to meet.

*Notes:*

1 *V-questions* begin with an interrogative pronoun or v-word (see **78**).

2 *Yes/no questions* are so called because the answer to them is often 'yes' or 'no'.

3 Notice the difference between v-questions (FV2) and yes/no questions (FV1).

## 148   MAIN CLAUSE STRUCTURE

Many main clause sentences possess other elements not mentioned in **147** above. These are included in the scheme below, which may be used to analyse most main clause sentences in Swedish.

| 1 | 2 | 3 | 4 | 5 | 6 | 7 |
|---|---|---|---|---|---|---|
| Topic | Finite verb | Subject | Clausal adverbial | Non-finite verb | Object/ Complement | Other adverbial |

**STATEMENT**

| | | | | | | |
|---|---|---|---|---|---|---|
| Han (S) | kommer | – | – | – | – | hem idag. |
| Imorse | hade | han | ännu inte | packat | väskan. | |
| Väskan | hade | han | ännu inte | packat | – | i morse. |
| Sedan | blev | de | tyvärr | – | arga. | |

**YES/NO QUESTION**

| | | | | | | |
|---|---|---|---|---|---|---|
| | Kommer | de | aldrig | – | – | till Malmö? |
| | Brukar | de | aldrig | komma | – | till Malmö? |

**V-QUESTION**

| | | | | | | |
|---|---|---|---|---|---|---|
| Vem (S) | kommer | – | – | – | – | hit ikväll? |
| Vem (O) | gav | du | – | – | pengarna till? | |
| När | tänker | de | – | åka | – | till Norge? |

**COMMAND**

| | | | | | | |
|---|---|---|---|---|---|---|
| | Ring | – | alltid | – | – | före tolv! |

**WISH**

| | | | | | | |
|---|---|---|---|---|---|---|
| | Må | du | aldrig | få ångra | dig! | |
| | Leve | kungen! | | | | |
| Det (S) | vore | – | inte | – | så dumt! | |

Key: (S) = subject, (O) = object

*Translations:* He's coming home today. This morning he still hadn't packed the case. (Lit: The case he still hadn't packed this morning.) Then, alas, they got angry. Do they never come to Malmö? Don't they ever come to Malmö? Who's coming here tonight? Who did you give the money to? When are they thinking of going to Norway? Always ring before twelve! May you never regret it! Long live the king! That wouldn't be such a bad idea!

Notice that:

1 Main clause sentences always have a finite verb and usually a subject.
2 All positions except those occupied by the finite verb may be left vacant.
3 The subject usually occupies positions 1 or 3 (see **151**).
4 The topic position is always occupied in statements and v-questions, but is vacant in yes/no questions.
5 Only one sentence element at a time may occupy the topic position (see **160**).
6 There may be more than one finite verb, clausal adverbial, non-finite verb, object, complement or several other adverbials.
7 **V**-words may be subject or object in **v**-questions.

## 149   LINK POSITION

The link position (L) is an additional position necessary before the topic in order to accommodate conjunctions:

| | L | T | FV | S | CA | NFV | O/C | OA |
|---|---|---|---|---|---|---|---|---|
| Han kommer, | men | han | tänker | – | inte | stanna | – | länge. |
| Kommer du, | eller | – | stannar | du | – | – | – | hemma? |

*Translations:* He is coming but he's not thinking of staying long. Are you coming or are you staying at home?

## 150  EXTRA POSITIONS

The extra positions ($X^1$, $X^2$) are additional positions necessary both before the topic position and after the OA position to accommodate elements of various kinds outside the clause. These elements often duplicate elements within the clause proper.

| $X^1$ | T | FV | S | CA | NFV | O/C | OA | $X^2$ |
|---|---|---|---|---|---|---|---|---|
| 1 Olle, | han | är | – | ju | – | sjuk | idag, | han. |
| 2 Paris, | det | är | – | väl | – | en vacker stad. | | |
| 3 | Inte | gör | vi | – | – | det, | – | inte! |
| 4 I Lund, | där | vill | jag | – | bo. | | | |
| 5 När vi kom fram, så | | kokade | vi | – | – | kaffe. | | |
| 6 | Det | är | – | inte | – | sant | – | att tiden läker alla sår. |
| See also **151, 166.** | | | | | | | | |
| 7 | Det | är | – | – | – | roligt | – | att spela tennis. |

*Translations:* 1 Olle, he's ill today of course, he is. 2 Now Paris, that's a beautiful city. 3 We're not doing that, we're not. 4 In Lund, that's where I want to live. 5 When we got there we made coffee. 6 It isn't true that time heals all wounds. 7 It is fun playing tennis.

If there is also a link position, the order is:

| L | $X^1$ | T etc. |
|---|---|---|
| men | Olle, | han är rolig ... |
| but | Olle, | he's funny |

# MAIN CLAUSE POSITIONS (SENTENCE ELEMENTS)

## 151  SUBJECT AND FORMAL SUBJECT

The subject (S) may be:

– a noun phrase: **Snön ligger djupt.**  The snow lies deep.
**Annika åker skidor.**  Annika goes skiing.

| | | |
|---|---|---|
| – a pronoun: | *Han* **äter middag.** | He is eating dinner. |
| – an adjective: | *Rött* **är väl vackert.** | Red is beautiful, isn't it? |
| – a verb: | *Att ljuga* **är fult.** | Lying is bad. |
| – a subordinate clause: | *Att vi förlorade matchen* **är begripligt.** | That we lost the match is understandable. |

The formal subject (FS) **det** must be inserted when there is a postponed or real subject (RS):

*Det* (FS) **sitter en** *polis* (S) **i vardagsrummet.**
There's a policeman sitting in the living room.
(Cf. **En polis sitter i vardagsrummet.**)

## 152    FINITE VERB

The finite verb (FV) is the verb which carries the tense, i.e. which indicates present or past time. The finite forms are, therefore, the present, past, imperative and subjunctive forms.

| | |
|---|---|
| **Han** *springer* **fort.** | He is *running* fast. |
| **Han** *sprang* **fort.** | He *ran* fast. |
| *Spring* **fortare!** | *Run* faster! |

In two-verb constructions the finite verb is often a modal or modal equivalent verb:

**De** *kan* **springa fort.**          They *can* run fast.

## 153    NON-FINITE VERB

The non-finite verb (NFV) usually occurs only together with a finite verb (**152**). Non-finite forms include the infinitive, supine, present participle and past participle.

| | |
|---|---|
| **De kan** *springa* **fort.** | They can run fast. |
| **Vi har** *sprungit* **hela vägen.** | We have run the whole way. |
| **De kom** *springande* **nerför gatan.** | They came running down the street. |
| **Hunden är** *bortsprungen* **nu.** | The dog has run off now. |

## 154    CLAUSAL ADVERBIAL

1 The clausal adverbial (CA) modifies the sense of the clause as a whole. It is often a simple adverb:

| *FV* | *CA* | *etc.* | |
|------|------|--------|---|
| **Vi åker** | *inte* | **till Sverige på sommaren.** | = not |
|  | *alltid* |  | = always |
|  | *aldrig* |  | = never |
|  | *ofta* |  | = often |
|  | *sällan* |  | = seldom |
|  | *faktiskt* |  | = actually |
|  | *ju* |  | = of course |

Cf. Word order in the English main clause:

| | *CA* | *FV* | |
|------|-------|------|---|
| We | *never* | go | to Sweden in the summer. |

2 Clausal adverbials are also called 'mobile qualifiers' as they adopt different positions in the main clause compared with the subordinate clause (see **148, 159, 164, 169, 170.2**).

3 Notice the relative order when there are several clausal adverbials:

(a) Short modal adverbs:                      **ju, nog, väl, då**
(b) Short pronominal and conjunctional adverbs:  **alltså, därför, ändå**
(c) Longer modal adverbs:                    **verkligen, egentligen, faktiskt**
(d) Negations:                                 **inte, aldrig**

**De har *ju*** (1) ***därför*** (2) ***faktiskt*** (3) ***aldrig*** (4) **rest utomlands.**

## 155   OTHER ADVERBIALS

Other adverbials (OA) comprise expressions of manner, place, time, cause, condition etc. They are sometimes called *MPT-adverbials* for this reason, and often consist of a preposition + noun construction or of a subordinate clause:

| | |
|---|---|
| **Vi kommer *med tåg.*** <br>       OA-manner | We're coming by train. |
| **Vi kommer *till Stockholm.*** <br>       OA-place | We're coming to Stockholm. |
| **Vi kommer *på torsdag.*** <br>       OA-time | We're coming on Thursday. |
| **Vi kommer *om vi har tid.*** <br>       OA-condition | We will come if we have time. |
| **Vi kommer *när vi är lediga.*** <br>       OA-time | We'll come when we are free. |

Notice that the relative order of OAs is usually (but not always):

**Vi kommer** *med tåg* (Manner) *till Stockholm* (Place) *på torsdag* (Time) *om vi har tid* (Condition).

If the adverbial of manner is long, however, the order may be P T M:

**Han reser till Frankrike på sommaren med egen bil.**
He travels by car to France in the summer.

Some simple adverbs are also OAs:

**Vi kom dit/hem/ut/bort/ner.**       We got there/home/out/down.

OAs usually come at the end of sentences but often begin main clauses. See **160**.


## 156   OBJECTS AND COMPLEMENTS

*Transitive* verbs (**115**) take a direct object:       **Nils äter kakan.**
*Intransitive* verbs (**115**) take no object:       **Nils sitter i soffan**.

The direct object (DO) – which goes in the Object (O) position – may comprise:

| | | |
|---|---|---|
| a noun phrase: | **Någon har stulit *hans bil*.** | Someone has stolen his car. |
| a pronoun: | **Anna kysste *honom*.** | Anna kissed him. |
| a subordinate clause: | **Jag vet *att han är där*.** | I know that he is there. |

*Ditransitive* verbs possess both a direct and an indirect object (see **115**).

The indirect object (IO) is usually a person for whose sake an action is undertaken:

**Jag gav *studenten min bok*.**       **Jag gav *min bok till studenten*.**
    IO       DO              DO     IO
I gave the student my book.       I gave my book to the student.

Notice that the order of the objects is usually as in English, i.e:

– a prepositionless object precedes an object with a preposition:

**Han lånade** *boken*       *till Nils.*
            –prep     +prep
He lent     the book    to Nils.

– if neither object has a preposition the indirect object precedes the direct object:

| Han lånade | *Nils* | *boken.* |
|------------|--------|----------|
|            | IO     | DO       |
| He lent    | Nils   | the book. |

The predicative complement (C) occupies the same position as the object (O), following the object if there is one. It is found in sentences with *copular* verbs such as: **vara, bli, heta, kallas, verka, tyckas, se ... ut, utse ... till, göra ... till**. The complement agrees with the subject or object.

*Subject complements*

**Olle och Mari är *studenter.***     Olle and Mari are students.
**De blir säkert *nervösa.***     They will surely get nervous.

*Object complements*

**Det gjorde honom *besviken.***     They made him disappointed.
**De kallade Sture för *Stumpen.***     They called Sture 'Stumpen'.

## 157   VERB PARTICLE

See compound verbs, **119**. The verb particle (Part) occupies a position between the Non-finite verb and the Object/Complement:

| 1 | 2 | 3 | 4 | 5 | 5a | 6 | 7 |
|---|---|---|---|---|----|---|---|
| T | FV | S | CA | NFV | Part | O/C | OA |
| Jag | tycker | – | inte | – | om | honom. | |
| | Har | du | aldrig | tyckt | om | henne? | |
| Du | kommer | – | nog | att tycka | om | henne. | |

*Translations:* I don't like him. Have you never liked her? You will probably like her.

## 158   PASSIVE AGENT

See passive, **118, 165**. The passive agent (Agent) occupies a position between the Object/Complement and the Other adverbial:

| 1 | 2 | 3 | 4 | 5 | 6 | 6a | 7 |
|---|---|---|---|---|---|----|---|
| T | FV | S | CA | NFV | O/C | Agent | OA |
| Han | blev | – | inte | omkörd | – | *av bussen.* | |
| Han | beviljades | | – | – | avsked | *av styrelsen* | igår. |

*Translations:* He was not overtaken by the bus. He was allowed to resign by the board yesterday.

## 159   MAIN CLAUSE STRUCTURE – EXTENDED POSITIONAL SCHEME WITH EXAMPLES

| | | 1 | 2 | 3 | 4 | 5 | 5a | 6 | 6a | 7 | |
| L | X¹ | T | FV | (S) | CA | NFV | Part | O/C | Agent | OA | X² |
|---|---|---|---|---|---|---|---|---|---|---|---|
| 1 | | Han | hade | – | inte | packat | – | väskan | – | imorse. | |
| 2 | | Imorse | hade | han | inte | packat | – | väskan. | | | |
| 3 | | Vi | ger | – | – | – | – | Olle gåvan | – | ikväll. | |
| 4 | | Sedan | blev | de | tyvärr | – | – | arga. | | | |
| 5 | | Det | har | – | redan | kommit | – | två poliser. | | | |
| 6 | och – | det | är | – | ju | – | – | roligt | – | – | att spela tennis. |
| 7 | | Sten | brukade | – | – | kyssa | – | oss, | – | – | Maja och mig. |
| 8 | men Nils, | han | är | – | inte | – | – | dum, | – | – | han. |
| 9 | | De | ringde | – | – | – | upp | oss | – | hemma. | |
| 10 | | Vi | blev | – | – | upp-ringda | – | – | av Olssons | hemma. | |
| 11 | | Far | dödades | – | – | – | – | – | – | – | under kriget. |
| 12 | | De | gifte | sig | aldrig. | | | | | | |
| 13 | | Vi | känner | honom | inte. | | | | | | |

*Translations:*  1 He hadn't packed the case this morning. 2 This morning he hadn't packed the case. 3 We will give Olle the gift tonight. 4 Then they unfortunately got angry. 5 Two policemen have already arrived. 6 and it is of course fun to play tennis. 7 Sten used to kiss us, Maja and me.  8 but Nils, he's not stupid, he isn't.  9 They rang us up at home. 10 We were rung up by the Olssons at home. 11 Father was killed during the war. 12 They never married. 13 We don't know him.

| KEY to table | | For details see paragraph: |
|---|---|---|
| L(ink) = conjunction | | **149** |
| X¹ = extra position- | duplicate elements in the sentence | **150** |
| T(opic) | any sentence element | **160** |
| F(inite) V(erb) | verb carrying the tense | **152** |
| S(ubject) | includes reflexive pronoun, unstressed object | **151** |
| C(lausal) A(dverbial) | | **154** |
| N(on-) F(inite) V(erb) | infinitive, supine or participle | **153** |
| (Verb) Part(icle) | only with separable compound verbs | **157** |

# MOVING ELEMENTS WITHIN THE MAIN CLAUSE

## 160  TOPICALIZATION

1 The subject most frequently occupies the topic position, but it may be replaced by moving to the front almost any other sentence element. When the subject is not the topic it follows the finite verb.

| | T | FV | S | CA | NFV | O | OA |
|---|---|---|---|---|---|---|---|
| Base sentence: | Han | tänker | – | inte | sälja | bilen | i år. |
| New topic 1 (*OA* to topic): | | | | | | | |
| | I år | tänker | han | inte | sälja | bilen. | ← |
| New topic 2 (*O* to topic): | | | | | | | |
| | Bilen | tänker | han | inte | sälja | ← | i år. |
| New topic 3 (*CA* to topic): | | | | | | | |
| | Inte | tänker | han | ← | sälja | bilen | i år. |
| New topic 4 (*Verb phrase* to topic): | | | | | | | |
| | Sälja bilen tänker | han | inte | /göra/ | ← | i år. | |

Notice other possible topics:
*Direct speech* to topic:

| | Tusan! | sa | han. |
|---|---|---|---|

*Complement* to topic:

| | Vacker | var | han | inte. |
|---|---|---|---|---|

*Translations:* He's not thinking of selling the car this year. This year he's not thinking of selling the car. (Lit.: The car he is not thinking of selling this year.) (Surely) he's not thinking of selling the car this year! Selling the car this year /is something/ he's not thinking of doing. 'Blast!' he said. Beautiful he was not.

Topicalization of other adverbials (especially time, place) is by far the most frequent type:

**Vi åkte till Lund i våras.**　　　> *I våras* **åkte vi till Lund.**
　　　　　　　　　　　　　　　> *Till Lund* **åkte vi i våras.**

The OA, topicalized or not, often consists of a subordinate clause:

**Vi åkte till Lund när vi kom hem.**　> *När vi kom hem* **åkte vi till Lund.**

*Translations:* We went to Lund last spring. Last spring we went to Lund. To Lund we went last spring. We went to Lund when we got home. When we got home we went to Lund.

### 2 Natural topics

Most natural topics are unstressed and represent familiar information or are used to link sentences together:

*Vi* **behövde en semester, så** *i somras* **reste vi till Värmland.** *Där* **träffade vi några gamla vänner.** *De* **har en stor villa.** *Den* **har tio rum.** *Vi* **bodde där en hel vecka.** *Sedan* **måste vi tyvärr resa hem igen.**

*Translation:* We needed a holiday, so last summer we went to Värmland. There we met some old friends. They have a big house. It has ten rooms. We lived there for a whole week. Then alas we had to come home again.

### 3 Emphatic topics

These are rarer and often represent new information. The following emphatic topics are either stylistically marked or used for contrast:

*Förskräckligt* **är det.** *En tidning* **köpte vi också.** *Det* **kan jag aldrig tro på.** *I fjol* **dog han (inte i år).** *Springa efter flickor* **kan han, men** *studera* **vill han inte.**

*Translations:* (Lit.: Terrible it is.) (Lit.: A newspaper we bought too.) That I can never believe. Last year he died (not this year). (Lit.: Run after girls he can, but study he will not).

## 161　WEIGHT PRINCIPLE

The weight principle is revealed in different structures in **162–66** below. It can be formulated as follows: Unstressed familiar information (a short element) tends to be placed to the left in the sentence, while heavy new information (a long element) tends to be placed to the right in the sentence. Thus the balance in most sentences is 'right-heavy'.

1 The principle means that elements losing their stress may move leftwards (+/– indicates +stress/ –stress):

| T | FV | S | CA | | NFV | O/C | OA |
|---|----|---|----|--|-----|-----|-----|
| | | O– ⟵ | | | | O+ | |

**Han  träffade  henne  aldrig.**
He never met her.

| | | | OA– ⟵ | | | OA+ | see **162**f |
|--|--|--|------|--|--|-----|--------------|

**Vi  kunde  –  trots halkan  köra  –  fort.**
We could, despite the slippery conditions, drive fast.

2 Occasionally, as in the case of **inte**, this leftward movement is not accommodated within the positional scheme:

| T | FV | S | CA | NFV | O/C | OA |
|---|----|---|----|-----|-----|-----|
| | | ⟵ | inte | see **164** | | |

**Dricker inte  Olle  –  –  vin?**
Doesn't Olle drink wine?

3 Some elements that are stressed, such as subjects introducing new information, may be postponed (moved rightwards):

| T | FV | S | CA | NFV | O/C | OA | $X^2$ |
|---|----|---|----|-----|-----|-----|----|
| S(NP)+ ⟶ | | | | | S(NP)+ | | |

**Det  har  –  inte  kommit  några brev  idag.**
No letters have come today.

S(IP/subcl)+ ⟶ S(IP/subcl)+
**Det  är  –  –  –  tråkigt  –  att få vänta
på brev.**

It's annoying having to wait for letters.

(NP = indefinite noun phrase, IP = infinitive phrase, subcl = subordinate clause) see **166**.

**Det** (place holder subject) replaces the subject in this case.

4 In passive transformation both leftward and rightward movements occur simultaneously:

| T | FV | S | CA | NFV | O/C | agent | OA |
|---|----|---|----|-----|-----|-------|-----|
| A– | | | | | B+ | | |

**En flicka  körde  –  –  –  lastbilen.**
A girl drove the truck.

B– ⟵ ⟶ (A+)   see **165**
**Lastbilen  kördes  –  –  –  –  av en flicka.**
The truck was driven by a girl.

## 162  ADVERBIAL SHIFT

The OA may occupy the OA or T positions, but may also be moved to the CA position in order to leave an element in the final stressed position:

cf. **Han utnämndes till generalsekreterare i FN *1953*** (OA).
He was appointed Secretary General of the United Nations in 1953.

**Han utnämndes *1953*** (OA) **till generalsekreterare i FN.**
He was in 1953 appointed Secretary General of the United Nations.

Moving the OA leftwards may make the expression more formal:

cf. **Han har stannat hemma *under de senaste dagarna*** (OA).
He has stayed home over the past few days.

**Han har *under de senaste dagarna*** (OA) **stannat hemma.**
He has over the past few days stayed home.

cf. **Jag brukar tillbringa semestern i Spanien *varje år*** (OA).
I usually spend the holidays in Spain every year.

**Jag brukar *varje år*** (OA) **tillbringa semestern i Spanien.**
I usually every year spend the holidays in Spain.

## 163   UNSTRESSED OBJECTS

Unstressed object pronouns and reflexive pronouns often move leftwards into the subject position. This occurs only with a simple verb (present, past).

| | T | FV | S | CA | NFV | O/C | OA |
|---|---|---|---|---|---|---|---|
| | | | O –stress | | | O +stress | |
| cf. | Jag · | känner | – | inte | – | honom. | |
| | Jag | känner | honom | inte. | | | |
| | Han | fick | – | inte | – | det. | |
| | Han | fick | det | inte. | | | |
| | Olle | tvättar | sig | inte. | | | |
| (cf. | Olle | har | – | inte | tvättat | sig | idag.) |

*Translations:* I don't know *him.* I don't know him. He didn't get that. He didn't get it. Olle doesn't wash. Olle hasn't washed today.

## 164   POSITION OF **INTE**

The position of **inte** (and **icke, ej, aldrig** etc.) varies. In the main clause **inte** comes immediately *after* the finite verb or subject (see **148, 154**):

| | |
|---|---|
| **Peter kommer inte idag.** | Peter isn't coming today. |
| **Idag kommer Peter inte.** | Today Peter isn't coming. |
| **Idag har Peter inte kommit.** | Today Peter hasn't come. |

In the subordinate clause **inte** comes immediately *before* the finite verb (see **169**):

**Olle sa, att Peter inte kommer idag.**
      S    I    V                   SIV = subject-**inte**-verb
Olle said that Peter isn't coming today.

One exception has been discussed in **163**, where the unstressed object intrudes between the verb and **inte**. Another exception is found in cases like the following:

> **Idag kommer inte 'Peter /men Olle kommer./**
cf. **Idag kommer Peter 'inte /men han kommer imorgon./**

Here **inte** precedes the subject in a main clause so that **Peter** remains in the stress position at the end of the sentence.

Other cases in which **inte** is moved from its usual position result from a desire to restrict its effect from negating the entire clause to negating only a word or group of words:

| | | |
|---|---|---|
| **Alla pojkar ljuger inte.** | = | either: Some boys do not lie. |
| | | or:    No boys lie. |
| **Inte alla pojkar ljuger.** | = | Not all boys lie, /but some do/. |

## 165  PASSIVE TRANSFORMATION

By transforming the active verb into a passive form, elements may be moved radically within the clause:

Active verb     *Eleverna* (S) **tyckte mycket om** *henne* (O).
                      The pupils liked her a lot.

Passive verb    *Hon* (S) **var mycket omtyckt** *av eleverna* (Agent)
                    **/men inte av kollegerna/.**
                    She was much liked by the pupils /but not by her colleagues/.

Passive transformation can be used in either main or subordinate clauses (cf. topicalization, **160**). For the position of elements in the passive sentence, see **159**, examples 10, 11.

## 166  EXISTENTIAL SENTENCE

If we do not wish to introduce a subject containing new, heavy information too soon, we can postpone the subject (i.e. move it rightwards in the sentence), but must then fill the topic position in a statement with a formal subject (place holder subject):

| | | |
|---|---|---|
| *En kines* **sitter i köket.** > | *Det* | **sitter**   *en kines* **i köket.** |
| Subject | Formal | Real |
| | subject | subject |

A Chinaman is sitting in the kitchen.

There's a Chinaman sitting in the kitchen.

***Att sluta röka* är svårt. >**
Subject
Stopping smoking is difficult.

***Det* är svårt *att sluta röka.***
FS            RS
It's difficult to stop smoking.

*Type 1*: When the real subject is an indefinite noun phrase (like **en kines**) then it occupies the O/C position.

| T | FV | S | CA | NFV | O/C | OA | X² |
|---|----|---|----|-----|-----|----|----|
| *Det* | **finns** | – | – | – | ***ingen ketchup*** | **hemma.** | |
| *Det* | **sitter** | – | **ofta** | – | ***en kines*** | **i köket.** | |
| | **Sitter** | **det** | **ofta** | – | ***en kines*** | **i köket?** | |

*Translations:* There's no ketchup in the house. There's often a Chinaman sitting in the kitchen. Is there often a Chinaman sitting in the kitchen?

The verb in Swedish existential sentences is always intransitive, and usually expresses:

| Existence: | **finnas** |
|---|---|
| Non-existence: | **fattas, saknas** |
| Location: | **vara, sitta, stå, ligga** |
| Motion: | **komma, gå** |

In English the only corresponding constructions are: 'there is/are -ing'.

*Type 2*: When the real subject is an infinitive phrase (like **att sluta röka**) then it occupies the X² position (see **150, 151**):

| T | FV | S | CA | NFV | O/C | OA | X² |
|---|----|---|----|-----|-----|----|----|
| *Det* | **är** | – | – | – | **troligt** | – | ***att han vinner.*** |
| *Det* | **har** | – | **alltid** | **varit** | **en gåta för mig** | – | ***varför han fick nobelpriset.*** |

*Translations:* It is probable that he will win. It's always been a mystery to me why he got the Nobel Prize.

Note that in this case **det** = 'it'.

## 167   CLEFT SENTENCE

In order to emphasize an element together with the action of the verb, that element (W) may be extracted from the sentence and inserted into the construction:

**Det är/var (W) som** ...

The remainder of the original sentence is downgraded and relegated to the **som**-clause added onto the end:

Cf. **Anders skickade mig en bok förra veckan.**
Anders sent me a book last week.

> **Det var** *en bok* **(W) som Anders skickade mig förra veckan /inte en skiva/**
> **Det var** *Anders* **(W) som skickade mig en bok förra veckan /inte Göran/**
> **Det var** *förra veckan* **(W) som Anders skickade mig en bok /inte den här veckan/**

*Translations:* It was a book that Anders ... It was Anders who ... It was last week that ...

The cleft sentence is also very common in questions:

**Var det** *oppositionsledaren* **(W) som kritiserade regeringen?**
Was it the Leader of the Opposition who criticised the government?
(cf. **Kritiserade oppositionsledaren regeringen?**)

**Är det** *jag* **(W) som måste bestämma?**
Is it me who must decide?

**Är det** *öl* **(W) som han dricker?**
Is it beer he's drinking?

## SUBORDINATE CLAUSES

**168**    SUBORDINATE CLAUSE AS AN ELEMENT IN THE MAIN CLAUSE SENTENCE

1 Subordinate clauses usually constitute the subject, object or other adverbial in a main clause sentence. As such they may occupy several different positions. In looking at the main clause in this way we can talk of first stage analysis (cf. **169**):

| T | FV | S | CA | NFV | O/C | OA | $X^2$ |
|---|----|---|----|----|-----|----|----|
| Subject clause: | | | | | | | |
| *Att du är frisk* | gläder – | | – | – | mig. | | |
| Det | gläder – | | – | – | mig | – | *att du är frisk.* |
| | | | | | | | |
| Object clause: | | | | | | | |
| Han | sa | | – | inte – | | – | igår | *att han skulle bort.* |
| *Att han skulle bort* | sa | han | inte – | | – | igår. | |

Adverbial clause:

| | | | | | |
|---|---|---|---|---|---|
| **Vi** | **åker** | – | – | – | – | *när han kommer.* |

*När han kommer* **åker vi.**

*Translations:* That you are better pleases me. I am pleased that you are better. He didn't say yesterday that he was going away. (Lit.: That he was going away he didn't say yesterday.) We'll leave when he comes. When he comes we'll leave.

Adverbial clauses also begin with: **därför att, eftersom, fast(än), innan, medan, om, sedan, trots att.**

Notice that:

1 Subject and object clauses occupy the T or $X^2$ positions.
2 Most adverbial clauses (time, condition, cause) occupy the T, CA or OA positions.
3 Some adverbial clauses (result) may only occupy the OA position:

| *T* | *FV* | *S* | *CA* | *NFV* | *O/C* | *OA* |
|---|---|---|---|---|---|---|
| **Man** | **måste** | – | – | **stödja** | **honom** | *för att han inte ska falla.* |
| **Jag** | **var** | – | – | – | **så arg** | *att jag genast gick därifrån.* |

*Translations:* One has to support him so that he doesn't fall. I was so angry that I left immediately.

2 A relative clause usually functions as an attribute to a noun (subject, object) and begins with the indeclinable **som (där, dit)**:

**Han tittade på flickorna** (O) *som satt på bänken.*
He looked at the girls who were sitting on the bench.

**Filmen** (S) *som vi gick på* **var fantastisk.**
The film that we went to was fantastic.

3 An independent clause is a subordinate clause which stands alone as a sentence and does not form part of a larger main clause sentence. It is usually an exclamation or wish:

| *Conj.* | *S* | *CA* | *FV* | *NFV* | *O/C* | *OA* |
|---|---|---|---|---|---|---|
| **Om** | **du** | **bara** | **visste** | – | **allt!** | |
| **Att** | **ni** | **inte** | **blir** | – | **trötta!** | |

*Translations:* If you only knew everything! (Lit.: That you don't get tired!)

## 169  SUBORDINATE CLAUSE STRUCTURE

Subordinate clauses (which may be elements in main clause sentences) also possess an internal structure of their own. In looking at this we may talk of second stage analysis (cf. **168**):

| | *1* | *2* | *3* | *4* | *5* | *6* | *7* |
|---|---|---|---|---|---|---|---|
| *Matrix* | *Conj.* | *S* | *CA* | *FV* | *NFV* | *O/C* | *OA* |
| Vi åker | när | han | kommer. | | | | |
| Vi frågade | om | de | inte | hade | packat | väskan. | |
| | Eftersom | de | inte | /hade/ | sagt | ett ord, – | visste vi inget. |
| Vi tyckte, | /att/ | det | inte | var | – | roligt | längre. |
| Om vi är tysta, | och om | vi | inte | busar, – | – | – | får vi se på TV. |

*Translations:* We'll leave when he arrives. We asked whether they hadn't packed the case. As they hadn't said a word we knew nothing. We thought (that) it wasn't funny any longer. If we are quiet and if we're not naughty, we can watch TV.

Notice the following characteristics of the subordinate clause:

1 There is *no* topic in the subordinate clause; the order is always: conjunction – subject – CA – finite verb, i.e.

– the clause always begins with a subordinating conjunction or other subordinator (see **143f**).

– the clausal adverbial comes before the finite verb. (Remember S-I-V: Subject **– Inte** –Verb, **164**)

– the word order is straight (S-FV).

2 The subject position is always occupied.

3 The conjunction **att** may sometimes be omitted.

4 The auxiliary **har/hade** may be omitted when there is a supine (in the NFV position). This omission of **har** is common in written Swedish, unusual in normal spoken Swedish.

5 Notice also that the adverbial splits the infinitive in Swedish:

**Fredrik lovade /att/ *inte* (CA) säga något.**
Fredrik promised not to say anything.

**Jag hoppas /att/ *snart* (CA) få träffa dig igen.**
I hope to meet you again soon.

**Jag hoppas att *i min nuvarande ställning* (OA) fortsätta att tjäna mitt land.**
I hope in my present position to continue to serve my country.

**170  THREE TYPES OF SUBORDINATE CLAUSE WITH MAIN CLAUSE STRUCTURE**

These are all exceptions, in different ways, to **169** above, in that the subordinate clause forms part of a main clause sentence (cf. **168**) but has a word order that is similar to that of the main clause (see **148**).

1 **Att**-clauses with a 'topic':
When a non-subject comes immediately after the conjunction **att**, the finite verb and subject are inverted:

|  | Conj. | 'Topic' | FV | S |
|---|---|---|---|---|
| **Fredrik sa,** | **att** | **igår** | **tänkte** | **han åka till stan.** |

Fredrik said that yesterday he was thinking of going to town.

2 **Att**-clauses with FV-CA order:
In some cases the clausal adverbial adopts the same position as in the main clause, i.e. *after* the finite verb, rather than its usual subordinate clause position *before* the finite verb:

|  | Conj. | S | FV | CA |
|---|---|---|---|---|
| **Fredrik sa,** | **att** | **han** | **tänkte** | **inte åka idag.** |

Fredrik said that he was not thinking of leaving today.

This is only found in spoken Swedish.

| Write: | Conj. | S | CA | FV |
|---|---|---|---|---|
| **Fredrik sa,** | **att** | **han** | **inte** | **tänkte åka idag.** |

An explanation for this order is that the **att**-clause is regarded as a statement in direct speech, i.e. as a main clause, cf.:

**Fredrik sa: 'Jag tänker inte åka idag'.**
Fredrik said 'I am not thinking of going to town'.

The conjunction **att** then functions almost as a colon.

3 Conditional clauses with yes/no question order:
Conditional clauses are usually introduced by **om** or **ifall**:

**Om du inte skriver till mor, blir hon ledsen.**
If you don't write to Mum, she will be upset.

But conditional clauses are also found which possess no subordinating conjunction, and rely on inverted word order (FV–S) to indicate condition:

**Skriver du inte till mor, blir hon ledsen.**
cf. **Skriver du inte till mor?** (Yes/no question)

Clauses of this type also occur in English:

Had I known when you were arriving, I would have waited.

cf. **Hade jag vetat när du skulle komma, skulle jag ha väntat.**

Were you to agree to this, it would be disastrous.

cf. **Skulle du gå med på detta, vore det katastrofalt.**

# DIFFERENCES BETWEEN SWEDISH AND ENGLISH WORD ORDER

## 171   MAJOR WORD ORDER AND SENTENCE STRUCTURE PROBLEMS – SUMMARY

A number of aspects of word order are similar in Swedish and English. This summary concentrates only on the differences.

Key:  S   = subject FV = finite verb CA = clausal adverbial
   T   = sentence element (non-subject) which may come first in the sentence
   W   = word(s) moved for emphasis or presented as a new subject

1 Main clause – inversion (**147**ff, **159**, **160**)

| Swedish: | English: |
|---|---|
| S – FV – T | S – FV – T |
| **Vi åker hem nu.** | We're going home now. |

In Swedish non-subjects often come first in the main clause, and this causes inversion of subject and finite verb.

| T – FV – S | T – S – FV |
|---|---|
| **Nu åker vi hem.** | Now we're going home. |

In English the order is usually subject – verb. (cf. however: Up went the lift.)

2 Main clause – adverb(ial)s (i.e. **inte**, **aldrig**) (**147**ff, **154**, **164**)

| S – FV – CA | S – CA – FV |
|---|---|
| **De leker aldrig.** | They never play. |

In main clauses in Swedish the clausal adverbial (adverb) usually comes immediately *after* the finite verb. In English it usually comes immediately *before* the finite verb.

3 Subordinate clause – adverb(ial)s (i.e. **inte**, **aldrig**) (**164**, **169**)

| S – CA – FV | S – FV – CA |
|---|---|
| **De sae, att de inte hade skrivit.** | They said that they had not written. |
| **De vet att jag aldrig dricker.** | They know I never drink. |

In subordinate clauses in Swedish the clausal adverbial (adverb) always comes immediately *before* the finite verb.

Remember: S-I-V : Subject – **Inte** – Verb. In English the position varies.

4 Adverbs split the infinitive (**169**)

**att** – CA – NFV(inf)
**Vi bad honom att genast sluta röka.**
to – NFV(inf) – CA
We asked him to stop smoking immediately.

5 Emphasizing part of a clause (**167**)
A word or words to be emphasized (W) may be extracted from a clause and placed in this special construction. The rest of the sentence is downgraded to a subordinate clause after **som**. W can represent most elements in a Swedish clause.

| | |
|---|---|
| Base clause | **Anders skickade mig en bok förra veckan.** |
| | Anders sent me a book last week. |
| **Det är/var (W) som . . .** | **Det var *en bok* som Anders skickade mig förra veckan.** |
| **Vem/Vad är det som . . .?** | **Vem var det som skickade mig en bok . . .?** |
| | **Vad var det som Anders skickade mig . . .?** |
| **Var det (W) som . . .?** | **Var det *en bok* som Anders skickade mig . . .?** |
| | **Var det *Anders* som skickade mig en bok . . .?** |
| | **Var det *förra veckan* som Anders skickade mig en bok?** |

6 Presenting a new subject (**166**)

| | |
|---|---|
| S – FV | S – FV |
| **En kines sitter i köket.** | A Chinaman is sitting in the kitchen. |
| **Det** – FV – S | There is – S – FV-ing |
| **Det sitter en kines i köket.** | There is a Chinaman sitting in the kitchen. |

Questions:

| | |
|---|---|
| FV – **det** – S | Is there – S – V-ing? |
| **Sitter det ofta en kines i köket?** | Is there often a Chinaman sitting . . .? |

7 Objects etc. with and without stress (**163**)

S – FV – CA – O                     S – FV – CA – O
**Jag känner inte *honom*.**        I don't know *him*.

S – V – O – CA
**Jag känner honom inte.**

When objects lose their stress in Swedish they move left in the sentence. In English voice stress is used.

8 Verb particles (**157**)

S – FV – Part – O                   S – FV – O – Part
**Jag ringde upp honom igår.**      I rang him up yesterday.
**Vi kastade bort dem.**            We threw them away.

In Swedish the particle precedes the object pronoun. In English the particle always follows the object pronoun.

# 13 WORD FORMATION

The lexicon of Swedish is constantly being altered by four main processes:

| | | | |
|---|---|---|---|
| 1 Borrowing: | French 'pièce' | > Swedish **pjäs** | play |
| 2 Compounding: | **ett *hus*** + **ett *tak*** | > **ett hustak** | house roof |
| 3 Affixation: | ***o-*** + ***lycklig*** | > **olycklig** | unhappy |
| 4 Abbreviation: | ***fotografi*** | > **foto** | photo |

Borrowing from other languages involves the eventual assimilation of a loanword into the Swedish system of orthography, pronunciation and inflexion.

## 172   COMPOUNDING

1 The first element of a compound may be a noun, adjective, verb, pronoun, numeral, adverb, preposition or word group, while the second element is usually a noun, adjective or verb:

| | | | |
|---|---|---|---|
| Noun + noun: | **bilresa** (car journey) | Verb + noun: | **skrivbord** (writing desk) |
| Noun + adjective: | **hjärtlös** (heartless) | Verb + adjective: | **sittriktig** (ergonomic) |
| Noun + verb: | **soltorka** (sun dry) | Verb + verb: | **frystorka** (freeze dry) |

For separable and inseparable compound verbs (particle verbs) see **119**.

2 Compound nouns may be formed by four main methods:

(a) Noun + Noun

**en bil** + **ett däck**            > **ett bildäck**    (car tyre)

(b) Noun (minus **-a/-e**) + Noun

**en flicka** + **en skola**            > **en flickskola** (girls' school)
**en pojke** + **ett namn**            > **ett pojknamn** (boys' name)
**en lärare** + **ett yrke**            > **(ett) läraryrke** (teaching profession)

(c) Noun + **s** + Noun

**en parkering** + **ett hus**            > **ett parkeringshus** (multi-storey car park)

(d) (Noun + old case ending in **-u/-o/-e/-a**) + Noun

| | |
|---|---|
| **en vecka** + **ett slut** | > **ett veckoslut** (weekend) |
| **en vara** + **ett hus** | > **ett varuhus** (department store) |

New compounds formed by this last method are very rare. Notice that the second element in compounds determines the gender and inflexion of the compound.

Whether or not **-s-** is used as a link between nouns depends to some extent on the form of the elements (first element = FE). Generally speaking the following have **s**-link:

– Nouns whose FE ends in **-/n/ing**, **-ling**, **-an**, **-nad**, **-/i/tet**, **-/a/tion**, **-het**:

**vandringsled**, **älsklingsrätt**, **självkostnadspris**, **stationsinspektör**

– Nouns whose FE is itself a compound:

cf. **fot** + **boll**        >    **fotboll**
    **fotboll** + **s** + **lag**   >    **fotbollslag**    (football team)

Others: **skolboksförlag**, **ordbildningslära**, **daghemsföreståndare**, **bilbärgningskår**, **järnvägsövergång**

### 173   AFFIXATION

Affixation is carried out by adding a *prefix* or *suffix* to a *stem*. Whilst prefixes do not alter the word class or inflexion of the stem, suffixes are often employed for this very purpose:

| | | | |
|---|---|---|---|
| cf. | **o-** | + | **vän** | > **ovän** |
| | negative prefix | | noun stem | noun |
| | | | (friend) | (enemy) |
| | **vänlig** | + | **-het** | > **vänlighet** |
| | adjective stem | | noun suffix | noun |
| | (friendly) | | | (friendliness) |
| | **färg** | | + **-a** | > **färga** |
| | noun stem | | verb suffix | verb |
| | colour | | | to colour |

Generally speaking prefixes and suffixes are much vaguer and simpler in meaning than the stems they modify.

1 Prefixes: What follows is a list of some frequent examples only.

|  | Prefix | Meaning | Example |
|---|---|---|---|
| (a) Negative and pejorative | o- | not, opposite of, bad, wrongly | olycklig |
|  | in-/im-/il- | – " – | intolerant |
|  | miss- | – " – | misslyckas |
|  | van- | – " – | vantrivas |
| (b) Attitude | sam- | together with | samarbete |
|  | ko- | – " – | koordinera |
|  | mot- | against | motståndare |
| (c) Location and direction | före- | before | företrädare |
|  | efter- | after | efterskrift |
|  | ex- | from | exportera |
|  | an- | towards | ankomma |
|  | und- | away from | undkomma |
|  | re- | again | reorganisera |
|  | gen | again | gengångare |
| (d) Conversion: + verb suffix > verb | an- + -a | (transitivising) | anropa |
|  | för- + -a | make into | förnya |
|  | be- + -a | – " – | befria |

2 Suffixes: What follows is a list of some frequent examples only.

|  | Suffix | Example |
|---|---|---|
| (a) Nouns denoting people | -are | läsare |
|  | -ande | studerande |
|  | -ende | gående |
|  | -ant | emigrant |
|  | -ent | konsument |
|  | -ör | frisör |
|  | -ing | värmlänning |
|  | -ist | cyklist |
| feminines | -inna | värdinna |
|  | -/er/ska | sjuksköterska |
|  | -essa | prinsessa |
|  | -ös | dansös |
|  | -ris | servitris |
| (b) Nouns denoting activity | -/n/ing | skrivning |
|  | -ande | skrivande |
|  | -an | början |
|  | -else | jämförelse |
|  | -nad | saknad |
|  | -sion | recension |
|  | -tion | realisation |
| (c) Nouns denoting status | -het | brottslighet |
|  | -lek | storlek |
|  | -dom | sjukdom |
|  | -skap | vänskap |
|  | -nad | tystnad |

| | Suffix | | Example |
|---|---|---|---|
| | **-ska** | | **ondska** |
| | **-an** | | **önskan** |
| | **-else** | | **frestelse** |
| (d) Conversion: | **-bar** | possible to | **körbar** |
| verb > adj. | **-lig** | possible to | **rörlig** |
| | **-abel** | possible to | **diskutabel** |
| | **-aktig** | tendency | **slösaktig** |
| | **-sam** | tendency | **arbetsam** |
| | **-ig** | tendency | **slarvig** |
| (e) Conversion: | **-enlig** | according to | **lagenlig** |
| noun > adj. | **-mässig** | corresponding to | **planmässig** |
| | **-vänlig** | 'friendly' | **miljövänlig** |
| | **-aktig** | characteristic of | **svinaktig** |
| | **-artad** | – " – | **granitartad** |
| | **-/i/sk** | belonging to | **brittisk** |
| | **-ant** | – " – | **elegant** |
| | **-ent** | – " – | **intelligent** |
| (f) Conversion: | **-a** | | **färga, burka, cykla** |
| noun, adj | **-era** | | **paketera, adressera,** |
| > verb | | | **decentralisera** |
| | **-na** | become + adj | **svartna, mörkna** |
| | **-ja** | make + adj. | **glädja** |
| | (+ *mutation*) | (transitivizing) | See also **116**. |

3 Productive and non-productive affixes:
Productive affixes are those still being used to form derivatives whose meaning can easily be predicted from the form:

**-bar** = possible to, therefore: **tänkbar** = possible to think, **användbar** = possible to use etc.

Non-productive affixes are those no longer used to form derivatives:

   **-lek: kärlek, storlek** etc.

Non-productive affixes may have been borrowed with many loanwords but have never been used to form any indigenous derivatives, e.g.: Latin **kon-: konflikt, konsonant**.

## 174  ABBREVIATION

1 Abbreviation involves the loss of a morpheme or part of a morpheme:

| | Whole morpheme lost: | Part morpheme lost: |
|---|---|---|
| (a) Initial reduction | **/bi/cykel** | **/automo/bil** |
| (b) Final reduction | **bio/graf/** | **lok/omotiv/** |
| | **livs/medelsaffär/** | **el/ektricitet/** |

|  | foto/grafi/ | kolla/tionera/ |
|---|---|---|
| (c) Medial reduction | te/kopps/fat | mo/torho/tell |
|  | Tele/graf/verket | mo/torveloci/ped |

2 Final reduction + **-is, -a(n)** in colloquial Swedish:

| kond(itori) | + **is** > **kondis** | mor | + **a** > **morsa** |
|---|---|---|---|
| dag(hem) | + **is** > **dagis** | syster | + **a** > **syrra** |
| grat(ulerar) | + **is** > **grattis** | Margareta | + **a** > **Maggan** |
| god(saker) | + **is** > **godis** | Elisabeth | + **a** > **Bettan** |

3 Hypocorism:
Pet names for boys are often formed by shortening the vowel and adding
**-e**:

| **Karl** > **Kalle** | **Nils** > **Nisse** | **Jan** > **Janne** |
|---|---|---|
| **Lars** > **Lasse** | **Olof** > **Olle** | **Sigurd** > **Sigge** |

4 Acronyms:
When the reduction leaves only an initial letter for each element an
acronym results:

(a) Alphabetisms: **bh** (=**bysthållare**); **TV**; **VM** (= **världsmästarskap**)

(b) Respelling of alphabetisms: **behå**, **teve**

(c) Acronyms pronounced as words: **SAAB, ASEA, NATO, EPA, SAS**

(d) Hybrid forms: **p-plats** (**parkeringsplats**); **T-bana** (**tunnelbana**)

## 175   LIST OF COMMON ABBREVIATIONS

These abbreviations are often found without full stops.

| **AB** | **Aktiebolag** | Co. Ltd, PLC |
|---|---|---|
| **ang.** | **angående** | re |
| **anm.** | **anmärkning** | note |
| **ansl.** | **anslutning** | tel. extension |
| **bil.** | **bilaga** | enclosure |
| **bl.a.** | **bland annat** | inter alia |
| **ca, c., c:a** | **cirka** | approximately |
| **do, d:o** | **dito** | ditto |
| **dvs, d.v.s.** | **det vill säga** | i.e. |
| **d.y.** | **den yngre** | the younger |
| **dyl.** | **dylikt** | similar |
| **dåv.** | **dåvarande** | the then |
| **d.ä.** | **den äldre** | the elder |
| **e.d., el.dyl.** | **eller dylikt** | or similar |
| **eg.** | **egentligen** | really |
| **e.Kr.** | **efter Kristus** | A.D. |

| el, e., l. | eller | or |
| el | elektrisk | electrical |
| em, e.m. | eftermiddag | p.m. |
| enl. | enligt | according to |
| e.o. | extraordinarie | extra-ordinary |
| ev. | eventuellt | possibly |
| ex. | exempel | example |
| | exemplar | copy, copies |
| f. | förre | former |
| | följande | following |
| f.d. | före detta | ex- |
| f.Kr. | före Kristus | B.C. |
| fm, f.m. | förmiddag | a.m. |
| f.n. | för närvarande | at present |
| forts. | fortsättning | continued |
| frk | fröken | Miss |
| fr.o.m. | från och med | with effect from |
| f.ö. | för övrigt | otherwise |
| följ. | följande | following |
| föreg. | föregående | previous |
| förf. | författare | author |
| förk. | förkortning | abbreviation |
| ggr | gånger | times |
| g.m. | gift med | married to |
| hr | herr | Mr |
| häft. | häftad | paperback |
| i allm. | i allmänhet | generally |
| inb. | inbunden | hard cover |
| inkl. | inklusive | including |
| inv. | invånare | inhabitant(s) |
| i st.f. | i stället för | instead of |
| jfr. | jämför | cf., compare |
| jvstn | järnvägsstation | railway station |
| kap. | kapitel | chapter |
| kl. | klockan | o'clock, at (a time) |
| | klass | class |
| kr. | kronor | kronor |
| l. | eller | or |
| m.a.o. | med andra ord | in other words |
| m.fl. | med flera | etc. |
| m.m. | med mera | etc. |
| motsv. | motsvarande | corresponding to |
| m.ö.h. | meter över havet | metres above sea level |
| möjl. | möjligen | possibly |

| | | |
|---|---|---|
| NB | nedre botten | lower ground floor |
| nr | nummer | No. |
| nuv. | nuvarande | present |
| o. | och | and |
| o.a. | och annat | etc. |
| Obs! | observera | NB, notice |
| o.d., o.dyl. | och dylikt | and the like |
| omkr. | omkring | approx. |
| osv, o.s.v. | och så vidare | etc. |
| p.g.a. | på grund av | because |
| PM | promemoria | memorandum |
| r. | rad | line |
| red. | redaktör | editor |
| s. | sida | page |
| | sekund | second |
| s | singular/is/ | singular |
| | substantiv | noun |
| | subjekt | subject |
| | söder | south |
| | socialdemokrat | Social Democrat |
| sa., s:a | summa | total |
| s.a.s. | så att säga | so to speak |
| sg. | singular/is/ | singular |
| s.o.h. | söndagar och helgdagar | Sundays and bank holidays |
| s.k. | så kallad | so-called |
| sms. | sammansättning | compound |
| st. | styck/en/ | number; each |
| S:t, S:ta | sankt, sankta | male/saint, female/saint |
| t. | till | to |
| t. | timme | hour |
| tel., tfn | telefon | telephone |
| t.ex., t ex | till exempel | e.g. |
| tf. | tillförordnad | acting |
| t.h. | till höger | to the right |
| t.o.m., t o m | till och med | even, up to and including |
| tr. | trappa (-or) | floor(s) |
| t.v. | till vänster | to the left |
| | tills vidare | for now |
| ung. | ungefär | approx. |
| uppl. | upplaga | edition |
| utg. | utgåva | edition |
| | utgivare | publisher |
| vanl. | vanligen | usually |
| vard. | vardagar | weekdays |

| v. | vecka | week |
|---|---|---|
|  | vers | verse |
|  | vänster | left |
|  | väg | road |
|  | västra | west(ern) |
| VD | verkställande direktör | managing director |
| v.g.v. | var god vänd! | PTO |
| åld. | ålderdomligt | archaic |
| äv. | även | also |
| ö. | östra | eastern |
|  | över | over |
| övers. | översättare | translator |

# 14  ORTHOGRAPHY

**176**  SMALL OR CAPITAL LETTER?

1 Capital letters are used in Swedish in the same way as in English in the following cases:

(a) At the beginning of a sentence.

(b) After a colon in direct speech:  **Herren sade: "Varde ljus."**

(c) In proper names:  **Ingvar Andersson, Volvo, Kungsgatan, Malmö, Danmark, "Fadren" av August Strindberg.**

(d) In order to show respect:  **Gud, Herren, Hans Majestät Konungen**

2 Small letters are used in Swedish in many cases where English has a capital:

(a) In the names of weekdays, months, seasons and festivals:

| | |
|---|---|
| **måndagen den 6 juni** | Monday the 6th of June |
| **jul, påsk, pingst, midsommar** | Christmas, Easter, Whitsun, Midsummer |

(b) In nouns and adjectives denoting nationality, language, religion, political affiliation and those deriving from a place name:

**Han är engelsman men han talar svenska.**
He is an Englishman, but he speaks Swedish.

| | |
|---|---|
| **Karl läser en dansk roman.** | Karl's reading a Danish novel. |
| **Sven är socialdemokrat.** | Sven is a Social Democrat. |
| **Lars är stockholmare.** | Lars is a Stockholmer. |

(c) In titles with names:

**Jag har träffat herr Lind, fru Lind, doktor Olsson och ingenjör Ek.**
I've met Mr Lind, Mrs Lind, Doctor Olsson and Mr Ek, the engineer.

3 Swedish has a capital only in the first word in names consisting of two
or more words if none of the subsequent words is a proper noun:

|      |                     |                           |
|------|---------------------|---------------------------|
|      | **Den helige ande** | the Holy Spirit           |
| but: | **Svarte Rudolf**   | Black Rudolf              |
|      | **Peter den store** | Peter the Great           |
|      | **Svenska akademien** | the Swedish Academy     |
|      | **Förenta staterna** | the United States        |
| but: | **Republiken Sydafrika** | the Republic of South Africa |

This applies also to book titles:

|                          |                         |
|--------------------------|-------------------------|
| **Röda rummet**          | The Red Room            |
| **Gamla testamentet**    | the Old Testament       |
| **En midsommarnattsdröm** | A Midsummer Night's Dream |

*Exceptions*:

|                          |                    |
|--------------------------|--------------------|
| **Kungliga Biblioteket** | the Royal Library  |
| **Sveriges Radio**       | Swedish Radio      |

– street names with two or more words:

**Södra Vägen, Östra Hamngatan**

4 Swedish compound nouns have a capital letter if the second element is
a proper noun, even if the first is not:

|       |                    |                    |
|-------|--------------------|--------------------|
|       | **Sydamerika**     | South America      |
| cf.:  | **södra England**  | Southern England   |
|       | **Nordsverige**    | Northern Sweden    |
| cf.:  | **norra Sverige**  | Northern Sweden    |
|       | **Mellaneuropa**   | Central Europe     |
|       | **Storstockholm**  | Greater Stockholm  |
|       | **Semestersverige** | Holiday Sweden    |

5 Swedish sometimes has capital letters in correspondence for **Ni**, **Er** and
occasionally for **Du**, **Dig**, **Din**, though these are falling out of use.

6 In Swedish a new line of poetry or song does not automatically begin
with a capital letter. In most instances capitals are used in poetry and song
the same way as in text.

## 177    SPELLING OF WORDS ENDING IN -M, -N

1 Final **-m** is not doubled even after a short vowel:

**dum, hem, rum, program**

*Exceptions*: **damm, lamm**

2 Final **-n** is not doubled in many words even after a short vowel:

**man, an, den, din, en, han, hon, vän, in, igen, kan, men, min, mun, män, än, sin, sen (sedan)**

*Exceptions*: **grann, sann, tunn, fann** (**<finna**), **hann** (**<hinna**), **känn** (**<känna**)

3 Between vowels **-m, -n** are always doubled after a short vowel:

| | |
|---|---|
| hem – hemmet | rum – rummet |
| man – mannen | vän – vännen |
| dum – dumma | allmän – allmänna |
| in – inne | fram – framme |

4 A word containing **-mm-** or **-nn-** usually drops one **-m** or **-n** when a consonant is added in an inflected form, e.g. an adjective in the neuter form or a verb adding a weak past tense ending. This always happens if **-d** or **-t** is added:

| | |
|---|---|
| ett nummer – numret | tunn – tunt |
| glömma – glömt | en sommar – somrar |
| gammal – gamla | känna – känt |

*Exceptions*:

(a) Before the **s**-genitive:     **ett lamms svans**

(b) Before the **s**-passive:     **det känns varmt**

(c) Before a suffix:     **kännbar, tunnhet**

(d) In compounds:     **tunnbröd, dammkorn**

# 15   PUNCTUATION

In many cases English and Swedish punctuation is similar. Only the main points and major differences are listed in the paragraphs below.

## 178   THE COMMA

1 The comma is generally used:

(a) Between main clauses in the same sentence, if it is necessary for clarification:

**Landslaget vann matchen, och alla gick hem glada.**
The national team won the match, and everyone went home happy.

(b) Around any words that are parenthesized or in apposition:

**Många små fabriker, såsom Åkerströms, har stängt.**
Many small factories, such as Åkerströms, have closed.

**Bo Hansson, Malmö FF, var landslagets bästa spelare.**
Bo Hansson, Malmö FF, was the best player in the national team.

(c) To mark off exclamations:

| | |
|---|---|
| **Janne, kan du komma ett tag?** | Janne, can you come here a moment? |
| **Ja, det kan jag!** | Yes, I can! |

(d) In decimals:

| | |
|---|---|
| **5,5 procent** | 5.5 % |

Note, however:

| | |
|---|---|
| **3 000 (tretusen)** | 3,000 (three thousand) |

2 The comma is *not* generally used:

(a) Before **att** clauses, unless both clauses are long:

| | |
|---|---|
| **Han sa att han var sjuk.** | He said that he was ill. |

(b) Before subordinate clauses where the subordinator is omitted:

| | |
|---|---|
| **Han sa han skulle komma.** | He said /that/ he would come. |
| **Bussen han skulle åka med kom aldrig.** | The bus /that/ he was going to come on never arrived. |

(c)  Around adverbs:

**Detta är emellertid osäkert.**   This is, however, uncertain.

(d)  After introductory or closing phrases in letters:

**Bäste herr Jansson!**          Dear Mr Jansson,
**Med vänlig hälsning**          With kind regards,


## 179   THE FULL STOP

The full stop ends a sentence which comprises a statement. It is often omitted in common abbreviations:

**mm, t ex, t o m** See also **175**.


## 180   THE EXCLAMATION MARK

This is used more widely in Swedish than in English. It is found after all exclamations, greetings, commands, imperatives and warnings:

**Mina damer och herrar!**       Ladies and gentlemen.
**Vad vackert det var här!**     How beautiful it is here!
**Lycka till!**                  Good luck!
**OBS!**                         N.B.


## 181   THE APOSTROPHE

1  The apostrophe is *not* used before or after the genitive **-s**, unlike English:

**pojkens far**                  the boy's father
**pojkarnas far**                the boys' father

2  The apostrophe is used, however, on occasion to indicate the genitive of nouns ending in **-s, -z, -x**:

**Anders'/Anders kamrater**      Anders' friends
**Marx'/Marx skrifter**          Marx's writings

3  The apostrophe is used to show the omission of letters:

**'dag ropa' han.**              G'day, he shouted.

Notice that there is no apostrophe in the following short forms:

**dan (dagen), stan (staden), sa (sade), ska (skall), nån (någon)**

## 182    DIRECT SPEECH CONVENTIONS

The most common Swedish convention for indicating direct speech in
printed Swedish is the use of a dash (**pratminus**) before each speaker's
comments. If the words indicating direct speech immediately precede the
direct speech, a colon is used instead of the English comma:

**Polisen frågade**: – **Vad heter du?**
– **Martin, kom svaret.**
– **Och var bor du?**
**Martin viskade**: – **Stockholm. Eller rättare sagt, Bromma.**

Also used in printing is:              **»Vad heter du?»**
Also used in manuscript is:            **"Vad heter du?"**

## 183    THE HYPHEN

The hyphen is used:

(a) In some compound nouns:            **Karl-Erik, Peterson-Berger**

(b) In cases where the first of two elements has a common second element:

**sön- och helgdagar**          =    **söndagar och helgdagar**
**bok- och pappershandel**      =    **bokhandel och pappershandel**

(c) In compounds with **icke-** :

**icke-rökare, icke-socialist**

(d) In compounds where the first element is an acronym. See also **174.4**:

**LO-kongressen, T-banan**

(e) In compounds where the first element is a number. For compounding
see **172**:

**en 50-öring, 1980-talet**

# 16 WRITTEN AND SPOKEN SWEDISH

This section deals briefly with some constructions and word choices generally found only in written or only in spoken Swedish. For a general account of pronunciation, see paragraphs **1–20**; for pronunciation of some difficult words, see **14**, **15**; for some syntax differences between spoken and written Swedish, see **170.2**.

## 184 WORDS FREQUENTLY OMITTED IN SPOKEN SWEDISH

1 Subordinating conjunction **att** after verbs of saying, thinking, perceiving:

**Hon sa hon hade läst brevet.**   She said she'd read this letter.

2 Relative pronoun **som** as object or after a preposition:

**Mannen jag pratade med heter** The man I spoke to is called
**Jansson.**                       Jansson.

cf. **Mannen** (subject) **som kom** The man who came is called
**heter Johansson.**                Johansson.

3 Verbs of motion after a modal auxiliary:

**Jag måste till Lund idag.**   I have to go to Lund today.
**De ville hem.**               They wanted to go home.
**Vi ska bort.**                We are going away.

4 The pronoun **jag** when in an initial unstressed position:

**Hade tänkt vi skulle på bio.**
Thought we might go to the cinema.

## 185 WORDS AND CONSTRUCTIONS FREQUENTLY INSERTED IN SPOKEN SWEDISH

The following usages are more common in spoken than in written Swedish:

1 Formal subject (see **151**, **166**):

**Det satt två gubbar på en bänk.** There were two old men sitting
                                    on a bench.

(cf. **Två gubbar satt ...**)      Two old men were sitting ...

2 Cleft sentence (see **167**):

**Det var han som tog pengarna.** It was him who took the money.
(cf. **Han tog pengarna.**)        He took the money.

3 Duplication (see **150**):

**Han som står därborta, honom känner jag.**
Him standing over there, I know him.

**Jag har inte varit där, inte.**
I haven't been there, I haven't.

4 Supplementary **du** in commands:

**Kom hit, du!**                Come here! See **114**.

5 Supplementary **så**:

(a) After an adverbial as topic:

**Förr i tiden, så hade man inte TV.**   In the old days we didn't have TV.

(b) After a subordinate clause as topic, introduced by **när**, **om**, **sedan**:

**När han kommer, så kan vi börja.**
When he arrives, (then) we can start.

6 The particles **ju**, **nog**, **väl**, **nämligen**.
These adverbs are used in speech to alter the sense of a statement subtly
by indicating the speaker's/listener's (likely) reaction to it. See **123.7**.

## 186   WORDS USUALLY FOUND ONLY IN WRITTEN SWEDISH

Some words and constructions found in written Swedish may sound stilted
in informal written or in spoken Swedish. In the notes below somewhat
less formal alternatives are suggested:

| *Written/formal:* | *Spoken/less formal:* |
| --- | --- |
| 1 Demonstratives **denne, denna, detta, dessa** | **den, det, de** or: **den här, det här, de här** etc. |
| **Han älskar denna flicka.** <br> He loves that girl. | **Han älskar den flickan.** <br> He loves that girl. |
| 2 Possessive **dess** | End article or repetition of noun in s-genitive: |
| **Jag tycker om stugan. Dess läge är så vackert.** <br> I like the cottage. Its location is so beautiful. | **Jag tycker om stugan. Stugans läge/ Läget är så vackert.** <br> I like the cottage. The /cottage's/ location is so beautiful. |

*Written/formal:*

*Spoken/less formal:*

3  Relative **vars**
   **De vars namn börjar på S**
   Those whose names begin
   with S

**som ... som ...**
**De som har namn som börjar på S**
Those who have names beginning
with S

4  Conjunction **då**
   **Då han fick se mig blev han arg.**
   When he saw me he got angry.

**när**
**När han fick se mig blev han arg.**
When he saw me he got angry.

5  Conjunction **samt**
   **Mannen och hustrun samt
   barnen**
   The man and his wife and
   children

**och**
**Mannen, hustrun och barnen**

The man and his wife and
children

6  Conjunction **såväl ... som**
   **Såväl lärda som olärda lyssnade
   på honom med behållning.**
   Both educated and uneducated
   benefited from listening to him.

**både ... och**
**Både lärda och olärda lyssnade på
honom med behållning.**
Both educated and uneducated
benefited from listening to him.

7  Conjunction **så att**
   **Han åt så att han blev sjuk.**
   He ate so that he was sick.

**så**
**Han åt så han blev sjuk.**
He ate so that he was sick.

8  Conjunction **därför att**
   **Jag säger det inte därför att
   jag vill klandra.**
   I do not say this because I wish
   to criticize.

**för att**
**Jag säger det inte för att jag vill
klandra.**
I do not say this because I wish to
criticize.

9  Conjunction **ty**
   **Vägen var våt ty det hade
   just regnat.**
   The road was wet as it had
   recently been raining.

**för**
**Vägen var våt för det hade just
regnat**
The road was wet as it had
recently been raining.

10  Conjunction **emedan**
    **Försöket misslyckades emedan
    det var illa förberett.**
    The attempt failed since it
    was badly prepared.

**eftersom, för att**
**Försöket misslyckades eftersom det
var illa förberett.**
The attempt failed since it was
badly prepared.

11  Adverb **även**
    **Anders reste sig, och det
    gjorde även Bertil.**
    Anders got up, as did Bertil.

**också/med**
**Anders reste sig och det gjorde
också Bertil/det gjorde Bertil med.**
Anders got up, as did Bertil.

| *Written/formal:* | *Spoken/less formal:* |
|---|---|
| 12 Conjunction **såsom** | **som, liksom** |
| **De gjorde såsom de hade blivit befallda.** | **De gjorde som de hade blivit befallda.** |
| They did as they had been told. | They did as they had been told. |

# LINGUISTIC TERMS

This list comprises only those terms that may not be familiar to a student of language or those that are not already explained in the text. In some cases these are not directly transferable to English grammar.

ABSTRACT NOUNS refer to unobservable notions, e.g., **svårighet**, **musik**, **påstående**, difficulty, music, assertion.

ADJECTIVE PHRASE consists of an adjective or a participle with optional words which modify or limit its meaning, e.g. **Han är /*ganska*/ dum**, He is /rather/ silly.

ADVERB PHRASE consists of an adverb with optional words which modify or limit its meaning, e.g. **Han körde /*ganska*/ fort**, He drove /quite/ fast.

ADVERBIAL (see CLAUSAL ADVERBIAL, OTHER ADVERBIALS)

AFFIX is a prefix added to the beginning or suffix added to the end of a word, e.g. **olycklig**, unhappy; **god*het***, goodness.

AGENT is the person or thing carrying out the action in a passive construction, e.g. **Bilen kördes *av inspektören***, The car was driven by the inspector.

AGREEMENT is a way of showing that two grammatical units have a certain feature in common, e.g. **min*a* hund*ar***, my dogs; **slott*et* är stor*t***, the castle is big.

APPOSITION is where two noun phrases describe the same phenomenon, e.g. **Olle, *min bror*, är sjuk**, Olle, my brother, is ill.

ASSIMILATION is the process whereby a sound changes to become more like or identical with another sound, e.g. pronunciation of **min bror** as [mimbrɷːr]. The two sounds may merge completely, as in the case of **-d** in the past tense of the verb **använda** + **-*de*** > **använde**.

ATTRACTION is a grammatical error often caused by the speaker's losing sight of the true agreement and becoming distracted by another word, e.g. ***Typiskt* för detta barn är en viss blyghet**, Typical of this child is a certain shyness. This should read **Typisk** to agree with (**en**) **blyghet**.

ATTRIBUTIVE is used to describe adjectives that precede the noun and modify it, e.g. **ett *stort* hus**, a big house.

CLAUSE is a syntactic unit that usually consists of at least a finite verb and a subject (though the subject may be understood, as in most imperative clauses, e.g. **Skjut inte budbäraren!,** Don't shoot the messenger!). There are two major types of clause: main clauses (MC) and subordinate clauses (SC), e.g. **Middagen stod på bordet** (MC), **när**

**jag kom hem** (SC), The dinner was on the table when I got home. (Cf. SENTENCE.)

CLAUSAL ADVERBIAL denotes an adverb modifying the sense of the clause as a whole, e.g. **Han är *inte* dum**, He's not stupid; **De är *aldrig* lata**, They are never lazy.

COLLECTIVE NOUNS are nouns whose singular form denotes a group, e.g. **familj**, family; **boskap**, cattle.

COMMON NOUNS are all nouns that are not PROPER NOUNS, e.g. **en hund**, a dog, **två katter**, two cats.

COMPLEMENTS express a meaning that adds to (or complements) that of the subject or object. They can be either an ADJECTIVE PHRASE or a NOUN PHRASE, e.g. **Olle och Sven är *intelligenta*. De är *studenter*.** Olle and Sven are intelligent. They are students.

COMPLEX VERB has two or more parts: **Jag *har ätit* sniglar**, I have eaten snails.

COMPOUND VERB is a verb consisting of a STEM and a prefixed PARTICLE, which may be inseparable or separable from the stem, e.g. **betala**, pay, but **köra *om/om*köra**, overtake.

CONGRUENCE (= AGREEMENT)

CONJUGATION denotes the way a verb is inflected, its pattern of endings, and also the different groups of verbs with the same endings, e.g. past tenses in: Conj. I **kalla-de**, Conj. IIb. **köp-te**, Conj. III **bo-dde**.

COPULAR verbs (or copulas) link the noun or adjective complement to the subject, e.g. **Eva *blev* läkare**, Eva became a doctor; **Sven *blev* besviken**, Sven was disappointed.

COPULATIVE means 'linking' (see COPULAR).

CORRELATIVE is the word or phrase that a pronoun replaces or refers to, e.g. **Filmen** is replaced by **som** in **Filmen som vi såg var urfånig**, The film we saw was really silly.

COUNT NOUN is a noun that describes an individual countable entity and therefore usually possesses a plural form, e.g. **bok – böcker**, book-s; **ägg-ägg**, egg-s; **pojke-pojkar**, boy-s.

DECLENSION denotes the different ways of INFLECTING the noun in the plural, e.g. **flick*or*, pojk*ar*, park*er*, äppl*en*, män,** girls, boys, parks, apples, men. It is also used to describe adjective + noun constructions such as the indefinite declension of the adjective, e.g. **en sådan liten bil**, a little car like that, or the definite declension of the adjective, e.g. **den lilla bilen**, the little car.

DEFINITE refers to a previously mentioned entity, cf. *Tjuven* **har stulit klockan**, The thief has stolen the clock. The indefinite refers to a new entity, e.g. *En tjuv* **har stulit klockan**, A thief has stolen the clock.

DERIVATIVE refers to a word derived from a *stem*, usually by the addition of an affix; e.g. **angå**, concern; **begå**, commit and **föregå**, precede are all derivatives of the verb **gå**, go.

DIRECT OBJECT refers to a person or thing directly affected by the action of a (transitive) verb, e.g. **Pojken slog** *bollen/sin syster*, The boy hit the ball/his sister.

DUPLICATION involves the repetition of a subject, object or adverbial, usually in a pronoun or adverb form, e.g. *Olle*, **han är inte dum**, *han*, Olle, he isn't stupid, he isn't.

DURATIVE VERB (or verb of duration) denotes a continued action (e.g. **sova**, sleep), a constant change (e.g. **växa**, grow) or an intermittent action (e.g. **droppa**, drip).

ELLIPSIS involves the omission of a word or word group in the sentence, e.g. **Jag ville röka men jag fick inte** /*röka*/, I wanted to smoke but I was not allowed to /smoke/.

END WEIGHT is the principle that long, heavy expressions come at the end of the sentence, e.g. **Han åkte sedan** *med en gammal lastbil utan strålkastare*, He then travelled in an old truck without lights.

FIGURATIVE SENSE is a sense other than the literal, e.g. **Det kostar skjortan!** It costs an arm and a leg (literally: It costs your shirt).

FINITE VERB is a verb showing by its form tense, mood or voice (active/passive) (cf. NON-FINITE VERB).

FORMAL SUBJECT is **det** in cases when the REAL SUBJECT is postponed, e.g. *Det* (FS) **sitter en gubbe** (RS) **därborta**, There's an old man sitting over there.

FRONTING is moving an element to the beginning of the sentence, cf. **Vi älskar rödvin**, We love red wine and **Rödvin älskar vi**, Red wine we love.

GENDER can be by sex: **karlen – han**, the chap – he, **tjejen – hon**, the lass – she, or grammatical gender: **ett hus, ett barn, en matta,** a house, a child, a carpet.

GRAMMATICAL SUBJECT (= FORMAL SUBJECT)

HOMONYM is a word that is identical in spelling to another word, e.g. **komma** = either 'to come' or 'comma'.

IDIOM(ATIC) indicates a usage that is not readily explicable from grammar.

IMPERATIVE is the mood of the verb expressing command or warning or direction, e.g. **Kom!**, Come on!; **Rör om!**, Stir.

IMPERSONAL constructions do not involve a person but usually the impersonal pronoun **det**, e.g. **Det snöar**, It's snowing.

IMPLIED SUBJECT is actually an object which functions as subject in a non-finite clause, e.g. **Vi bad** *honom* **skriva en rad**, We asked him to drop us a line.

INDECLINABLE describes a word that does not INFLECT, e.g. the adjectives **bra**, good; **utrikes**, foreign; **öde**, deserted, which take no endings for neuter or plural.

INDEFINITE (cf. DEFINITE)

INDIRECT OBJECT is usually a person or animal benefiting from an action: e.g. **Vi gav *honom* pengarna**, We gave him the money.

INFINITIVE PHRASE is a phrase consisting of an infinitive accompanied by optional words which modify it, e.g. **att skriva brev**, to write a letter.

INFLECT means to change form by modifying an ending, e.g. the verb **skriva** (write) inflects **skriv, skriva, skriver, skrev, skrivit, skriven**, etc.

INFLEXIBLE (= INDECLINABLE)

INFLEXION (see INFLECT)

INTERROGATIVE means question, e.g. an interrogative pronoun asks a question: *Vem var det?*, Who was that?; *Varför kom du hit?*, Why did you come here?

INVERTED word order denotes verb – subject order, e.g. **Idag åker vi**, Today we leave.

MATRIX is that part of a main clause sentence remaining when the subordinate clause is removed, e.g. *Eva lovade* **att hon skulle skriva till oss**, Eva promised that she would write to us.

MORPHEME is the smallest part of a word expressing some meaning: in the word **bilarna**, the cars, there are three morphemes: **bil**, 'car', **ar**, plural morpheme, **na**, definite morpheme.

MUTATED VOWEL is one that changes in different forms of the word, e.g. o > ö in **son – söner**, son – sons; **stor – större**. big – bigger.

NOMINAL means a word or phrase acting as a noun, e.g. *Simning* **är roligt**, Swimming is fun; *Att simma* **är roligt**, To swim is fun.

NON-COUNT NOUN is one, often denoting an abstract or substance, that does not usually take a plural, e.g. **mjöl**, flour; **bensin**, petrol; **luft**, air; **vatten**, water; **glädje**, joy.

NON-FINITE VERB forms are those forms not showing tense or mood, namely infinitive, supine and participles.

NOUN PHRASE is a noun often accompanied by one or more words before or after the noun which modify it, e.g. **en vacker dikt som jag lärde mig**, a beautiful poem that I learned.

NUMBER is a collective term for singular and plural usually marked by an ending, e.g. **två penn*or***, two pens.

OTHER ADVERBIALS (or content adverbials or sentence adverbials) are usually an adverb, noun phrase or subordinate clause denoting manner, place, time or condition. e.g. **Han åker *med tåg*** (Manner) *till Stockholm* (Place) *i morgon* (Time) *om han har tid* (Condition). He will travel by train to Stockholm tomorrow if he has time.

PARENTHETICAL means bracketing, e.g. the prepositional expression *för* **10 dagar** *sedan*, ten days ago.

PART OF SPEECH means word class, e.g. noun, adjective, verb, conjunction, etc.

PARTICLE is a stressed adverb or preposition appearing together with a verb to form a single unit of meaning, a particle verb, e.g. *om* in

**köra om**, overtake; *ned* in **skriva ned**, write down.

PARTITIVE indicates that a part is implied, e.g. *en del av* **pengarna**, some of the money; *en flaska* **vin**, a bottle of wine; *ett kilo* **potatis**, a kilo of potatoes.

PEJORATIVE means deprecating as in e.g. **din dumma åsna**, you stupid ass.

PERIPHRASTIC means paraphrasing.

POSTPOSITIONED means coming after something.

PREDICATE forms the only compulsory part of the clause other than the SUBJECT. The predicate is the verb plus any object, complement or adverbial: **Han** *spelar* **/***piano dagligen***/**, He plays /the piano every day/.

PREDICATIVE(LY) indicates that an element is found after the verb.

PREDICATIVE COMPLEMENT is a word or word group (often a NOUN PHRASE or ADJECTIVE PHRASE) which complements, i.e. fills out, the subject, e.g. **Hon är** *hans lärare* **och hon säger att han är** *lat*, She is his teacher and she says that he is lazy.

PREPOSITIONAL PHRASE consists of a preposition plus a prepositional complement (usually a NOUN PHRASE or INFINITIVE PHRASE), e.g. **flickan** *med det långa håret,* the girl with the long hair; **flickan gick** *utan att säga adjö*, the girl left without saying goodbye.

PRE-POSITIONED means coming in front of something.

PRODUCTIVE implies that a word class or method of word formation is still being used to produce new words, e.g. the suffix **-vänlig** in **sittvänlig**, comfortable to sit in.

PROPER NOUNS are names of specific people, places, occasions or events, books, etc. e.g. **Olle, Stockholm, Krig och fred**.

RAISING is the practice of moving an element from a subordinate clause to the front of the main clause (see FRONTING), e.g. *Det sa* **Pelle att vi inte skulle göra** *that*, Pelle said that we should not do *that*.

REAL SUBJECT is the postponed subject, e.g. **Det är roligt** *att dricka vin*, It's nice to drink wine. (See FORMAL SUBJECT).

RECIPROCAL or RECIPROCATING indicates a mutual activity in either the pronoun, e.g. **De älskar varandra**, They love one another, or in the verb, e.g. **De kysstes länge**, They kissed for a long time.

REFLEXIVE applies to both pronouns and verbs. Reflexive pronouns refer to the subject in the same clause. They have a separate form in the 3rd person, e.g. **Han har rakat** *sig*, He has shaved (himself). Reflexive verbs incorporate such a pronoun: **De har** *lärt sig* **svenska**, They have learned Swedish.

SEMANTIC denotes the meaning of words.

SENTENCE is a syntactic unit that contains a complete meaning and consists of one or more clauses (cf. CLAUSE). Thus the following three examples are all sentences: **Titta där!**, Look there!; **Hon tar bussen, när det regnar**, She takes the bus when it rains; **Om du tror, att jag kan**

**komma ihåg, vad han sa, när vi besökte honom förra veckan, har du fel**, If you think that I can remember what he said when we visited him last week, you're wrong.

SIMPLE VERB is one that only consists of one word, e.g. **hjälp!**, help!; **(han)** *sover*, (he) sleeps; **(han)** *gick*, (he) went.

STATEMENT is a declarative sentence or clause ending with a full stop.

STEM is the part of the verb common to all of its forms and onto which the inflexional endings are added, e.g. *dansa, dansar, dansade, dansat*.

SUBJECT indicates the theme or topic of the clause: *Tåget* **kom för sent**, The train was late; *Jag* **tycker om sill**, I like herring; *Vad* **gjorde du?**, What did you do?; *Det hon sa* **var rolig**, What she said was funny.

SYLLABLE consists of a vowel plus one or more consonants, e.g. **ö, dö, rör, röst, in-du-stri-ar-be-ta-re**.

TAG QUESTION in English consists of verb + subject (+ negative) at the end of a statement to invite a response from the listener: He likes salmon, *doesn't he?* In Swedish **va?** or **eller hur?** usually suffice: **Han gillar lax,** *eller hur?*

TERMINATIVE VERBS denote an action or process implying a state of change or leading to a change or cessation, e.g. **somna**, fall asleep; **låsa**, lock.

TOPIC is the position at the beginning of all main clause *statements* and v-questions. It is usually occupied by the subject, e.g. *Vi/Studenterna* **tycker om öl**, We/The students like beer. But in Swedish, non-subjects, especially ADVERBIAL expressions of time or place, often occupy the topic position, e.g. *I morgon* **spelar jag fotboll**, Tomorrow I'm playing football.

VERB PHRASE consists of a FINITE VERB alone or several finite and NON-FINITE VERBS in a chain, e.g. **Han** *reser*, He is travelling; **Han** *måste kunna springa*, He must be able to run.

VOICED indicates a consonant produced with vibration of the larynx, e.g. b, d, g, v, m, n, r, l

VOICELESS indicates a consonant produced without vibrating the larynx, e.g. p, t, k, f, s, z.

# SHORT BIBLIOGRAPHY

Åkermalm, Åke, *Modern svenska*, Gleerups, Lund, 3 ed., 1979.

Andersson, Erik, *Grammatik från grunden*, Hallgren & Fallgren, Uppsala, 2 ed., 1994.

Elert, Claes Christian, *Ljud och ord i svenskan 2*, Almqvist and Wiksell, Stockholm, 1981.

Holm, Lars and Larsson, Kent, *Svenska meningar*, Studentlitteratur, Lund, 1980.

Holmes, Philip and Hinchliffe, Ian, *Swedish: A Comprehensive Grammar*, Routledge, London, 1994.

Holmes, Philip and Hinchliffe, Ian, *Swedish Word Formation. Introduction and Exercises*, Hull, 1995.

Jörgensen, Nils and Svensson, Jan, *Nusvensk grammatik*, Liber, Malmö, 1986.

Kjellin, Olle, *Svensk prosodi i praktiken*, Studieförlaget, Uppsala, 1978.

Lindberg, Ebba, *Beskrivande svensk grammatik*, AWE Gebers, Stockholm, 2 ed., 1980.

Montan, Per and Rosenqvist, Håkan, *Prepositionsboken*, Skriptor, Stockholm, 1982.

*Nationalencyklopediens ordbok*, 3 vols, Höganäs, 1995.

*Svensk ordbok*, Esselte Studium, Stockholm, 1986.

*Svenska akademiens ordlista över svenska språket*, Norstedts, Stockholm, 11 ed., 1986.

*Svenska skrivregler*, Svenska språknämnden, 2 ed, 2001.

Thorell, Olof, *Att bilda ord*, Skriptor, Stockholm, 1984.

Thorell, Olof, *Svensk grammatik*, Esselte Studium, Stockholm, 2 ed., 1977.

Ulf Teleman, Steffan Hellberg and Erik Andersson, *Svenska Akademiens grammatik*, 4 vols, Stockholm, 1999.

Wellander, Erik, *Riktig svenska*, Norstedts, Stockholm, 3 ed., 1973.

Wessén, Elias, *Vårt svenska språk*, Almqvist and Wiksell, Uppsala, 3 ed., 1970.

Wijk-Andersson, Elsie, *Ny grammatik. Det svenska språkets struktur*, Studieförlaget, Uppsala, 1981.

# INDEX

Numbers refer to *paragraphs* and *sub-paragraphs*. Words in ordinary type are linguistic terms. Words in bold are Swedish. Words in italics are English.